CATEGORIAL FEATURES

Proposing a novel theory of parts of speech, this book discusses categorization from a methodological and theoretical point of view. It draws on discoveries and insights from a number of approaches – typology, cognitive grammar, notional approaches and generative grammar – and presents a generative, feature-based theory.

Building on up-to-date research and the latest findings and ideas in categorization and word-building, Panagiotidis combines the primacy of categorial features with a syntactic categorization approach, addressing the fundamental, but often overlooked, questions in grammatical theory.

Designed for graduate students and researchers studying grammar and syntax, this book is richly illustrated with examples from a variety of languages and explains elements and phenomena central to the nature of human language.

PHOEVOS PANAGIOTIDIS is Associate Professor of Linguistics in the Department of English Studies at the University of Cyprus.

T0370777

In this series

CAMBRIDGE STUDIES IN LINGUISTICS

General Editors: P. AUSTIN, J. BRESNAN, B. COMRIE,
S. CRAIN, W. DRESSLER, C. J. EWEN, R. LASS, D. LIGHTFOOT,
K. RICE, I. ROBERTS, S. ROMAINE, N. V. SMITH

CATEGORIAL FEATURES
A Generative Theory of Word Class Categories

CATEGORIAL FEATURES

A GENERATIVE THEORY OF WORD CLASS CATEGORIES

PHOEVOS PANAGIOTIDIS

University of Cyprus

CAMBRIDGE
UNIVERSITY PRESS

Shaftesbury Road, Cambridge CB2 8EA, United Kingdom

One Liberty Plaza, 20th Floor, New York, NY 10006, USA

477 Williamstown Road, Port Melbourne, VIC 3207, Australia

314–321, 3rd Floor, Plot 3, Splendor Forum, Jasola District Centre, New Delhi – 110025, India

103 Penang Road, #05–06/07, Visioncrest Commercial, Singapore 238467

Cambridge University Press is part of Cambridge University Press & Assessment, a department of the University of Cambridge.

We share the University's mission to contribute to society through the pursuit of education, learning and research at the highest international levels of excellence.

www.cambridge.org
Information on this title: www.cambridge.org/9781009342438

© Phoevos Panagiotidis 2015

First published 2015
First paperback edition 2022

A catalogue record for this publication is available from the British Library

Library of Congress Cataloging-in-Publication data
Panagiotidis, Phoevos.
Categorial features : a generative theory of word class categories / Phoevos Panagiotidis.
    pages cm – (Cambridge studies in linguistics ; 145)
ISBN 978-1-107-03811-0 (Hardback)
1. Grammar, Comparative and general–Grammaticalization.   2. Categorial grammar.
3. Language, Universal.   I. Title.
P299.G73P36 2014
415–dc23   2014020939

ISBN   978-1-107-03811-0   Hardback
ISBN   978-1-009-34243-8   Paperback

Contents

Preface

The project resulting in this monograph began in 1999, when I realized that I had to answer the question of why pronouns cannot *possibly* be 'intransitive determiners', why it is impossible for Determiner Phrases (DPs) consisting of a 'dangling D head' (a turn of phrase my then PhD supervisor, Roger Hawkins, used) – that is, made of a Determiner without a nominal complement – to exist. The first answer I came up with was Categorial Deficiency, extensively argued for in Chapter 5. Back then, however, Categorial Deficiency of functional heads was just an idea, which was expounded in my (2000) paper. The case for it was limited to arguments from biuniqueness and the hope was that it would eventually capture Head Movement. The paper was delivered at the April 2000 Spring Meeting of LAGB, in the front yard of UCL, in the open: the fire alarm, this almost indispensable element of British identity and social life, went off seconds after the talk started. It did not look good. However, Categorial Deficiency did find its way into my thesis and the (2002) book version thereof.

There were more serious problems, though: I quickly realized that 'uninterpretable [N]' and 'uninterpretable [V]' mean *nothing* if we have no inkling of the actual interpretation of 'interpretable [N]' and 'interpretable [V]'. This inevitably brought me to the question of the nature of categorial features and what it means to be a noun, a verb and an adjective. Surprisingly, this was an issue very few people found of any interest, so for a couple of years or so I thought I should forget about the whole thing. This outlook changed dramatically in 2003, when Mark Baker's book was published: a generative theory of lexical categories with precise predictions about the function and interpretation of categorial features. On the one hand, I was elated: it was about time; on the other, I was disappointed: what else was there to say on lexical categories and categorial features?

Quite a lot, as it turned out. Soon after my (2005) paper *against* syntactic categorization, I had extensive discussions with Alan Bale and, later, Heidi Harley. These were the impetus of my conversion to a syntactic decomposition approach. At around the same time, Kleanthes Grohmann and I thought it would be a good idea to see if his Prolific Domains could be shown to be co-extensive to the categorially uniform subtrees making up mixed projections (Bresnan 1997).

It is easy to figure out that I have incurred enormous intellectual debts to a number of people; this is to be expected when working on a project stretching for well over a decade. Before naming names, however, I have to gratefully acknowledge that parts of this project were generously funded by Cyprus College (now European University Cyprus) through three successive faculty research grants, between 2003 and 2006.

Moving on to people now: Paolo Acquaviva, whom I met in 2009 at the Roots workshop in Stuttgart, made me regain faith in my project and provided me with priceless insight on where we could go after we finished with categories and how roots really mattered. I owe to David Adger some pertinent and sharp questions on Extended Projections, feature (un)interpretability and mixed projections. Relentless and detailed commentary and criticism by Elena Anagnostopoulou go a long way, and they proved valuable in my sharpening the tools and rethinking all sorts of 'facts'. Thanks to Karlos Arregi I had to seriously consider adpositions and roots inside them. Mark Baker, talking to me in Utrecht in 2001 about the book he was preparing, and discussing nouns and verbs in later correspondence, has been an inspiration and an indispensable source of encouragement. Thank you, Hagit Borer, for asking all those tough questions on idiomaticity. I am truly indebted to Annabel Cormack, who significantly deepened (or tried to deepen) my understanding of the foundational issues behind lexical categories and their interpretation. Discussing roots and categorizers with David Embick in Philadelphia in 2010 served as a one-to-one masterclass for me. Kleanthes Grohmann – enough said: a valuable interlocutor, a source of critical remarks, a true collega. Heidi Harley, well, what can I say: patience and more patience and eagerness to discuss pretty much everything, even when I would approach it from an outlandish (I cannot really write 'absurd', can I?) angle, even when I would be annoyingly ignorant about things; and encouragement; and feedback. Most of what I know about Russian adjectives I owe to Svetlana Karpava and her translations. Richie Kayne has been supportive and the most wonderful person to discuss all those 'ideas' of mine with throughout the years. Richard Larson, thank you for inviting me to Stony Brook and for all the stimulating discussions that followed. Winnie Lechner helped me immensely in investigating the basic questions behind categorization and category and his contribution to my thinking about mixed projections was momentous and far-ranging. Alec

Marantz took the time and the effort when I needed his sobering feedback most, when I was trying to answer too many questions on idiomaticity and root interpretation. Discussions with Sandeep Prasada, and his kindly sharing his unpublished work on sortality with me, provided a much-needed push and the opportunity to step back and reconsider nominality. Gratitude also goes to Marc Richards, the man with the phases and with even more patience. Luigi Rizzi has been a constant source of support and insight, through both gentle nudges and detailed discussions. David Willis' comments on categorial Agree and its relation to movement gave me the impetus to make the related discussion in Chapter 5 bolder and, I hope, more coherent.

I also wish to thank the following for comments and discussion, although I am sure I must have left too many people out: Mark Aronoff, Adriana Belletti, Theresa Biberauer, Lisa Cheng, Harald Clahsen, Marijke De Belder, Carlos de Cuba, Marcel den Dikken, Jan Don, Edit Doron, Joe Emonds, Claudia Felser, Anastasia Giannakidou, Liliane Haegeman, Roger Hawkins, Norbert Hornstein, Gholamhosein Karimi-Doostan, Peter Kosta, Olga Kvasova, Lisa Levinson, Pino Longobardi, Jean Lowenstamm, Rita Manzini, Ora Matushansky, Jason Merchant, Dimitris Michelioudakis, Ad Neeleman, Rolf Noyer, David Pesetsky, Andrew Radford, Ian Roberts, Peter Svenonius, George Tsoulas, Peyman Vahdati, Hans van de Koot, Henk van Riemsdijk.

I also wish to thank for their comments and feedback the audiences in Cyprus (on various occasions), Utrecht, Pisa, Potsdam, Jerusalem, Patras, Paris, Athens and Salonica (again, on various occasions), Cambridge (twice, the second time when I was kindly invited by Theresa Biberauer to teach a mini course on categories), Chicago, Stony Brook, NYU and CUNY, Florence, Siena, Essex, Amsterdam, Leiden, York, Trondheim, Lisbon and London.

Needless to say, this book would have never been completed without Joanna's constant patience and support.

My sincere gratitude goes out to the reviewers and referees who have looked at pieces of this work: from the editor and the referees at *Language* who compiled the long and extensive rejection report, a piece of writing that perhaps influenced the course of this research project as significantly as key bibliography on the topic, to anonymous referees in other journals, and to the reviewers of Cambridge University Press. Last but not least, I wish to express my gratitude to the Editorial Board of the Cambridge Studies in Linguistics for their trust, encouragement and comments.

Finally, I wish to dedicate this book with sincere and most profound gratitude to my teacher, mentor and friend Neil V. Smith.

1   *Theories of grammatical category*

1.1   Introduction

In this first chapter, we will review some preliminaries of our discussion on parts of speech and on the word classes they define. As in the rest of this monograph, our focus will be on lexical categories, more specifically nouns and verbs. Then I will present a number of approaches in different theoretical frameworks and from a variety of viewpoints. At the same time we will discuss the generalizations that shed light on the nature of parts of speech, as well as some necessary conceptual commitments that need to inform our building a feature-based theory of lexical categories.

First of all, in Section 1.2 the distinction between 'word class' and 'syntactic category' is drawn. The criteria used pre-theoretically, or otherwise, to distinguish between lexical categories are examined: notional, morphological and syntactic; a brief review of prototype-based approaches is also included. Section 1.3 looks at formal approaches and at theories positing that nouns and verbs are specified in the lexicon as such, that categorial specification is learned as a feature of words belonging to lexical categories. Section 1.4 introduces the formal analyses according to which categorization is a syntactic process operating on category-less root material: nouns and verbs are 'made' in the syntax according to this view. Section 1.5 takes a look at two notional approaches to lexical word classes and raises the question of how their insights and generalizations could be incorporated into a generative approach. Section 1.6 briefly presents such an approach, the one to be discussed and argued for in this book, an account that places at centre stage the claim that categorial features are interpretable features.

1.2   Preliminaries to a theory: approaching the part-of-speech problem

As aptly put in the opening pages of Baker (2003), the obvious and fundamental question of how we define parts of speech – nouns, verbs and adjectives – remains largely unresolved. Moreover, it is a question that is rarely addressed in a thorough or satisfactory manner, although there is a lot of stimulating work on the matter and although there is no shortage of both typological and theoretical approaches to lexical categories. In this book I am going to argue that we can successfully define nouns and verbs (I will put aside adjectives for reasons to be discussed and clarified in Chapter 2) if we shift away from viewing them as broad taxonomic categories. More specifically, I am going to make a case for word class categories as encoding what I call *interpretive perspective*: nouns and verbs represent different viewpoints on concepts; they are not boxes of some kind into which different concepts fall in order to get sorted. I am furthermore arguing that nouns and verbs are ultimately reflexes of two distinctive features, [N] and [V], the LF-interpretable features that actually encode these different interpretive perspectives.

The theory advanced here gives priority to grammatical *features*, to categorial features more precisely. As mentioned, it will be argued that two unary categorial features exist, [N] and [V], and that the distinct behaviour of nouns and verbs, of functional elements and of categorially mixed projections result from the syntactic operations these features participate in and from their interpretation at the interface between the Faculty of Language in the Narrow sense (FLN) and the Conceptual–Intentional systems. The feature-driven character of this account is in part the result of a commitment to fleshing out better the role of features in grammar. Generally speaking, I am convinced that our understanding of the human Language Faculty will advance further only if we pay as much attention to features as we (rightly and expectedly) do to structural relations. True, grammatical features, conceived as instructions to the interfaces after Chomsky (1995), will ultimately have to be motivated externally – namely, by properties of the interfaces. However, we know very little about these interfaces and much less about the Conceptual–Intentional systems that language interfaces with. So, we cannot be confident about what aspects of the Conceptual–Intentional systems might motivate a particular feature or its specific values, or even its general behaviour. To wit, consider the relatively straightforward case of Number: we can hardly know how many number features are motivated by the Conceptual–Intentional systems to form part of the Universal Grammar (UG) repertory of features – that is, without looking at language first. More broadly speaking, it is almost a truism that most of the things we know about the interface between language and the Conceptual–Intentional systems, we do via our studying *language*, not via studying the Conceptual–Intentional systems themselves.

However, having thus mused, this monograph, a restrictive theory of categorial features, sets itself somewhat humbler aims. In a nutshell, I believe that a conception of categorial features as setting interpretive perspectives, a view that can be traced back at least to Baker (2003), combined with a *syntactic decomposition* approach to categories, as in Marantz (1997, 2000) and elsewhere, can achieve a very broad empirical coverage. This is more so when such a theory incorporates valuable insights into parts of speech from the functionalist-typological literature and from cognitive linguistics. The theory here captures not only the basic semantics of nouns and verbs, but also their position in syntactic structures, the nature of functional categories and the existence and behaviour of mixed projections. It also makes concrete predictions as to how labels are decided after Merge applies – that is, which of the merged items projects, the workings of recategorization and conversion, and the properties of mixed projections.

1.2.1   On syntactic categories and word classes: some clarifications

Rauh (2010) is a meticulous and very detailed survey of approaches to syntactic categories from a number of theoretical viewpoints. In addition to the sheer amount of information contained in her book and the wealth of valuable insights for anyone interested in categories and linguistic theory in general, Rauh (2010, 209–14, 325–39, 389–400) makes an important terminological distinction between parts of speech (or what we could call 'word categories') and syntactic categories.[1] Roughly speaking, syntactic categories are supposed to define the *distribution* of their members in a syntactic derivation. On the other hand, parts of speech correspond to the quasi-intuitively identified classes into which words fall. In this sense, members of a part-of-speech category/word class may belong to different syntactic categories; consequently, syntactic categories are significantly finer-grained than parts of speech. As this is a study of a theory of word class categories, I think it is necessary to elaborate by supplying two examples illustrating the difference between parts of speech and syntactic categories.

Since the late 1980s Tense has been identified in theoretical linguistics as a part of speech, more specifically a *functional category*. However, finite Tense has a very different syntactic behaviour, and distribution, to those of *to*, the infinitival/defective Tense head. Hence, infinitival/defective *to* can take PRO subjects, cannot assign nominative Case to subjects, and so on. Thus, although

---

[1] A distinction already made in Anderson (1997, 12).

both future *will* and infinitival *to* belong to the same part of speech, the category Tense, they belong to different *syntactic* categories, if syntactic categories are to be defined on the grounds of distribution and distinct syntactic behaviour.

Of course, one may (not without basis) object to applying distinctions such as 'part of speech' versus 'syntactic category' to functional elements. However, similar considerations apply to nouns – for example, proper nouns as opposed to common ones, as discussed already in Chomsky (1965). Proper and common nouns belong to the same part of speech, the same word class; however, their syntactic behaviour (e.g., towards modification by adjectives, relative clauses and so on) and their distribution (e.g., whether they may merge with quantifiers and determiners . . .) are distinct, making them two separate syntactic categories. This state is, perhaps, even more vividly illustrated by the difference between count and mass nouns: although they belong to the same word class, Noun, they display distinct syntactic behaviours (e.g., when pluralized) and differences in distribution (e.g., regarding their compatibility with numerals), as a result of marking distinct formal features.[2]

The stand I am going to take here is pretty straightforward: any formal feature may (and in fact does) define a syntactic category, if syntactic categories are to be defined on the grounds of syntactic behaviour and if syntactic behaviour is the result of interactions and relations (exclusively *Agree* relations, according to a probable hypothesis) among formal features. At the same time, only *categorial* features define word classes – that is, parts of speech. This will turn out to hold not only for lexical categories like noun and verb, as expected, but for functional categories as well.

Henceforth, when using the term 'category' or 'categories', I will refer to word class(es) and part(s) of speech, unless otherwise specified.

1.2.2   Parts of speech: the naïve notional approach
Most of us are already familiar with the *notional* criteria used in some school grammars in order to define parts of speech. Although these are typically relatively unsophisticated, notional criteria are not without interest. Furthermore, there are cognitive approaches that do employ notional criteria with interesting results, Langacker (1987) and Anderson (1997) being the most prominent among them. Indeed, contemporary notional approaches can turn out to be germane to the project laid out here, as they foreground salient

---

[2] An anonymous reviewer's comments are gratefully acknowledged here.

criteria of semantic interpretation in their attempt to define parts of speech; such criteria are central to any approach seeking to define parts of speech in terms of their interpretive properties as classes.

Let us now rehearse some more familiar and mainly pre-theoretical notional criteria employed to define nouns and verbs and to distinguish between them. So, typically, notional criteria distinguish between nouns and verbs as follows:

(1)

NOUN	VERB
'object' concept	action concept
'place' concept	'state' concept
abstract concept	

Counterarguments are not hard to come up with and criticism of something like (1) is too easy, the stuff of 'Introduction to Linguistics' courses. Let us, however, first of all observe that the state of affairs in (1) reflects both a notional and (crucially) a *taxonomic* approach to categories. This notional and taxonomic definition of categories – that is, deciding if a word goes into the 'noun' box or the 'verb' box on the basis of its meaning – is indeed deeply flawed and possibly totally misguided. Consequently, yes, there are nouns and verbs that do not fall under either of the above types: there are nouns that denote 'action' concepts, such as *handshake, race, construction* and so on. And we can, of course, also say that some verbs 'denote abstract concepts', such as *exist, emanate* or *consist (of)*.

Still, as already mentioned, we need to make a crucial point before disparaging notional approaches: the table in (1) employs notional criteria to create a rigid taxonomy; it therefore creates two boxes, one for a 'Noun' and one for a 'Verb', and it sorts concepts according to notional criteria. Which of the two decisions, using notional criteria to sort concepts or creating a rigid taxonomy, is the problem with the classification above? The answer is not always clear. Research work and textbooks alike seem to suggest that the problem lies with employing notional criteria: they generally tacitly put up with the rigid taxonomic approach. An example of this is Robins (1964, 228 et seq.) who advises against using 'extra-linguistic' criteria, like meaning, in our assigning words to word classes. However, the notional criteria are anything but useless: Langacker (1987) and Anderson (1997), for instance, return to them to build a theory of parts of speech – we will look at them in more detail in Section 1.5.

Equally importantly, when considering notional conceptions of categories, we need to bring up the observation in Baker (2003, 293–4) that concepts of particular types get canonically mapped onto nouns or verbs cross-linguistically; see also Acquaviva (2009a) on nominal concepts. Two representatives of types of concepts that canonically get mapped onto a category are object concepts, which are mapped onto 'prototypical' nouns (e.g., *rock* or *tree*), and dynamic event concepts, which are mapped onto 'prototypical' verbs (e.g., *buy, hit, walk, fall*), an observation made in Stowell (1981, 26–7). Contrary to actual or possible claims that have been made in relation to the so-called 'Nootka debate', no natural language expresses the concept of rock, for instance, by using a simplex verb. Put otherwise, not all nouns denote objects but object concepts are encoded as nouns (David Pesetsky, personal communication, September 2005). So, maybe it is necessary to either sharpen the notional criteria for category membership or recast them in a different theoretical environment, instead of summarily discarding them.

1.2.3   Parts of speech: morphological criteria

Pedagogical grammars informed by 100 years of structural linguistics typically propose that the noun–verb difference is primarily a morphological one, a difference internal to the linguistic system itself. In a sense, this is the exact opposite of notional approaches and of all attempts to link category membership to ontological or, even, modest semantic criteria. This is a point of view that many formal linguists share (cf. Robins 1964, 228 et seq.), at least in practice if not in principle. However, this approach to parts of speech goes much further back, to *Tēkhnē Grammatikē* by Dionysius Thrax and to *De Lingua Latina*, by Marcus Terentius Varro, who was Dionysius' contemporary. In both works, 'division into parts of speech is first and foremost based on morphological properties ... the parts of speech introduced ... are primarily defended on the basis of inflectional properties' (Rauh 2010, 17–20). A contemporary implementation of these old ideas is illustrated in the table in (2), where the distinction between noun and verb is made on the basis of inflectional properties.

(2)

NOUN	VERB
number	tense
case	aspect
gender	agreement[3]

Of course, here too, some semantic interpretation is involved, albeit indirectly: for instance, the correlation of nouns with number, on the one hand, and of verbs with tense, on the other, does not appear to be accidental – or, at least, it

---

[3] Agreement with arguments, subjects most typically.

should not be accidental, if important generalizations are not to be missed. Both number morphology and tense morphology, characteristic of nouns and verbs respectively, have specific and important *semantic* content: they are unlike declension or conjugation class morphology, which are arbitrary, Morphology-internal and completely irrelevant to meaning.[4] We have also to set grammatical case aside, which appears to be the result of processes between grammar-internal features, and agreement with arguments, which is a property of the Tense head or of a related functional element. Having done thus, the interesting task underlying a (simplified) picture like the one in (2) is to understand *why* the remaining generalizations hold:

a. Nouns exclusively pair up with Number, a category about individuation and quantity.
b. Verbs exclusively pair up with Tense, a category about anchoring events in time.[5]

I think that the above generalizations are strongly indicative of deeper relationships between the lexical categories of noun and verb and the functional categories of Number and Tense respectively, relationships that go beyond Morphology. Moreover, I will argue that these are relationships (noun–Number and verb–Tense) which actually *reveal* the true nature of the semantic interpretation of lexical categories.

1.2.4   Parts of speech: syntactic criteria
As implied above, an assumption tacitly ('in practice if not in principle') underlying a lot of work involving some treatment of categories is that the noun–verb difference is one concerning purely the linguistic system itself. One way to express this intuition is by claiming that the noun–verb difference is exclusively and narrowly *syntactic*, in a fashion similar to the difference between nominative Case and accusative Case. For instance, we could claim that the fundamental difference between nouns and verbs is that nouns project no argument structure, whereas verbs do (Grimshaw 1990). Given the complications that such an approach would incur with respect to process nominals, one could alternatively appeal to a similar, or even related, intuition and

---

[4] Gender systems typically fall somewhere in between (Corbett 1991).

[5] Nordlinger and Sadler (2004) and Lecarme (2004) argue that nominals (certainly encased inside a functional shell) can be marked for independent tense – that is, bear a time specification independent from that of the main event (and its verb). However, Tonhauser (2005, 2007) convincingly argues against the existence of nominal Tense, taking it to be nominal Aspect instead.

rephrase the noun–verb distinction along the terms of whether the expression of their argument structures is obligatory or not:[6]

(3)

	NOUN	VERB
Obligatory expression of argument structure?	no	yes

Of course, there are serious complications regarding a generalization like the one in (3), and we will review some of these complications in Chapter 6 when we investigate mixed projections and nominalizations more closely. However, (3) has the look of a nice concrete difference, readily expressible and sufficiently fundamental. Having said that, in relatively recent approaches to argument structure, beginning with Hale and Keyser (1993, 2002), through Kratzer (1996) and all the way to Ramchand (2008), Pylkkänen (2008) and elsewhere, argument structure has no longer been viewed as the direct unmediated projection of lexical properties of the verb, as the result of the celebrated Projection Principle. On the contrary, the growing trend is to have arguments hosted by functional categories: for instance, Agents, as in *Carla built a shed*, are by now commonly understood as the specifiers of a Voice category (Kratzer 1996). In other words, argument structure is currently understood as functional structure that *somehow* reflects or translates lexical properties of the verb.

The above and other complications notwithstanding, the obligatory expression of argument structure is something that characterizes the projections *containing a verb*, unlike those that contain a noun. Having said that, it would be desirable if this difference could in turn be somehow derived, instead of standing as an irreducible axiom. One motivation for this is that the (non-) obligatory expression of argument structure also plays a very significant role in our discussion of adjectives and, even more so, of adpositions: adjectives seem to possess some kind of argument structure, especially when used predicatively, whereas adpositions seem to *be* pure argument structures of some sort – matters we will come back to in Chapter 2.

1.2.5   An interesting correlation

Setting up a broad framework of assumptions in which a theory of categorial features will be developed, I have reaffirmed the understanding that, in its

---

[6] Fu, Roeper and Borer (2001) influentially explain away such 'complications' by claiming that process nominals contain verb phrases (VPs). Certainly, the expression of argument structure in nominals can be a more intricate affair than Indo-European facts suggest: Stiebels (1999) discusses Nahuatl, a language where all sorts of derived nominals, not just those with an event reading, express their argument structure via affixes common with their base verbs.

naïve version, the notional–taxonomic definition of parts of speech is fallacious, with an emphasis on the problematic character of parts of speech as *taxonomies*. At the same time, it has also been suggested, albeit in a tentative fashion, that we would nevertheless have to vigorously seek criteria of a conceptual/semantic nature in our endeavour to capture the noun–verb distinction, as opposed to purely morphological or syntactic – that is, grammar-internal – ones. This desideratum makes a lot of sense, at least intuitively speaking, given that the distinction between noun and verb seems to matter for interpretive reasons. It also appears that the noun–verb distinction would reflect some sort of conceptually significant difference regarding the very elements in the clause that are nouns or verbs – something that can hardly be claimed about, say, the difference between Nominative and Accusative. I think that we must regard the noun–verb distinction as one reflecting conceptually significant differences, if important generalizations are not to be missed: recall that the vast majority of words for physical objects are nouns cross-linguistically; object concepts (*tree, rock, stick* etc.) are mapped onto nouns. Of course, not all nouns denote concepts of physical objects. Baker (2003, 290–5) discusses this generalization in an insightful way, crucially adding that the nouns *rock* and *theory* cannot belong together in any conceptual taxonomic category, despite their both being nouns, following here the discussion in Newmeyer (1998, chap. 4). However, what Baker does not mention is this: the fact that *rock* and *theory* are both nouns is an argument against the taxonomic aspect of the naïve notional approach, not against using notional–semantic criteria to define categories – compare Acquaviva (2009a), to which we will return in Chapter 4.

So, there appears to exist a correlation, after all, between object concepts and nouns, as well as dynamic action concepts (*hit, run, jump, eat* etc.) and verbs. How can such a correlation be captured?

1.2.6   Prototype theory

In the functional–typological methodological tradition, categories are viewed as *prototypes*. In work by Givón (1984, chap. 3) and Croft (1991) categories are conceived as prototypes occupying fuzzy areas along a continuum of temporal stability, after Ross (1973). In this line of research, lexical categories like nouns, adjectives and verbs are understood to differ with respect to their *protypical time stability*. Hence, prototypical nouns are the most time-stable, whereas prototypical verbs are the least time-stable; prototypical adjectives lie somewhere in between. Put slightly differently: nouns are the most time-stable category, verbs the least time-stable one, with adjectives in between. Baker

(2003, secs. 1.1–1.3) elaborates on the issues with this approach and with the prototypical approach in general, principally along the lines of prototypes *predicting* very little. Thus, a verb like *persist* encodes time-stability by definition, whereas a noun like *tachyon* has time-instability encoded in its meaning. Of course, the existence of nouns like *tachyon*, which express non-time-stable concepts does not contradict protypicality: *tachyon* would qualify as a non-protypical noun. Similar facts hold for non-prototypical verbs expressing more or less time-stable concepts. This is precisely the problem of what prototype-based theories of word classes actually *predict*. Consider, for instance, the mid-section of the time stability continuum, where non-prototypical relatively time-stable 'verbal' concepts, non-prototypical relatively non-time-stable 'nominal' concepts and 'adjectival' ones (between nouns and verbs, by definition) co-exist: the question is what conceptual mechanism decides which category concepts populating that middle area are assigned to? Is category-assignment performed at random? This is a matter that Rauh (2010, 313–21) also raises, although departing from a slightly different set of theoretical concerns; she goes on to argue for discrete boundaries between categories.

A more interesting issue is one mentioned above: prototypical (like *rock*) and less prototypical (like *theory*) nouns and prototypical (like *buy*) and less prototypical (like *instantiate*) verbs all behave in the same fashion as far as *grammar itself* is concerned (Newmeyer 1998, chap. 4). Clearly, to the extent that prototypicality matters for the mechanism of the Language Faculty per se, and to the extent that prototypicality is reflected on the *grammatical* behaviour of nouns, verbs and adjectives, prototype effects spring from factors external to the syntax.[7]

The limited role of prototypicality as far as the grammar-internal behaviour of more prototypical or less prototypical members of a category is concerned is acknowledged in Croft (1991, 2001), who argues that prototypicality correlates with two kinds of markedness patterns across languages. First, prototypicality correlates with *structural* markedness, in that items deviating from the semantic prototype (e.g., referential expressions that denote events, like *handshake* or *wedding*, or object-denoting words used as predicates, like *ice* in *The water became ice*) tend to occur with additional morphemes. Interestingly, this is a generalization about the functional layer *around* an event-denoting noun or an object-denoting predicate, not about the lexical elements themselves.

---

[7] I am grateful to a reviewer for this discussion.

A second markedness pattern that prototypicality correlates with, again according to Croft (1991, 2001), is *behavioural* markedness: namely, that items deviating from the semantic prototype tend to have a more limited distribution than prototypical items. Again, distribution is a question of the functional layer within which a lexical category is embedded. In this respect, distribution is a matter of syntactic category, as opposed to a matter of word class/part of speech. This distinction is also rehearsed in detail and with reference to both empirical evidence and conceptual arguments, in Newmeyer (1998, chap. 4) and Rauh (2010, 325–39). Concluding this very brief overview, Croft's theory of course allows for the possibility that prototypical and non-prototypical items behave in exactly the same way (like *stone* and *theory* in English); moreover, his theory makes the weak prediction that the non-prototypical members of a category will not be less marked than the prototypical ones.

Despite the criticism above, work on defining categories along the lines of prototypes brings an extremely important insight to the discussion of categories: namely, the relevance of *time stability* in defining parts of speech as well as what their interpretation would be. The significance of this contribution will be revisited in Chapter 4, when the interpretation of verbs will be addressed.

1.2.7   Summarizing: necessary ingredients of a theory of category

The table in (4) outlines some empirical differences between nouns and verbs:

(4)

NOUNS	VERBS
number	tense (aspect)
Case-marked	Case-assigning
gender	agreement with arguments
argument structure covert	argument structure overt
determiners	particles

The task at hand, the one that the theory of categorial features to be presented here will take up, is to explain these differences in a principled manner. We have already discussed the shortcomings of prototype-based analyses: they neither predict the identical grammatical behaviour of prototypical nouns like *stone* to that of non-prototypical ones like *theory*, nor do they *explain* the differences between nouns and verbs. Still, most generative theories of category are not faring any better (Baker 2003, chap. 1): they are also descriptive part-of-speech systems that make no predictions about either the *syntactic* behaviour or the *semantic* interpretation of an element *x* belonging to a category N or V. In other words, they set up categorial feature systems which (occasionally) cross-classify, but generative theories of category do not tell us what these categories do and in what way they are different from each other. As Baker (2003, chap. 1) correctly acknowledges, a theory of category must be explanatory or, at least, predictive.

In the rest of this chapter, I will present some generative theories of word classes, along with Langacker's (1987) and Anderson's (1997) versions of a notional part-of-speech theory.

1.3   Categories in the lexicon

In order to make solid the desideratum expressed by Baker (2003) for an explanatory theory of category, let us consider the system in Chomsky's (1970) *Remarks on Nominalization*, also known as the 'Amherst system' (Rauh 2010, 94), so-called because it was revised to include prepositions in a series of lectures by Chomsky in Amherst, Massachusetts. The reason for doing so is twofold. First, this system is still quite popular and (at least) influential. By 'popular', I mean that, in its near-original version, it is still tacitly presupposed in a substantial body of work touching upon the question of parts of speech and grammatical categories. Moreover, it has given rise to some theories of category vying for explanatory adequacy, such as the ones in Stowell (1981), Déchaine (1993) and van Riemsdijk (1998a). Second, the Amherst system is – crucially – *feature based*: it therefore avails itself of a theoretical and methodological machinery which, potentially, makes it suitable for capturing important generalizations and for making predictions of an explanatory nature – again, like its version in Stowell (1981). Furthermore, its being expressed in terms of features makes it compatible with both lexicalist and non-lexicalist (including weak lexicalist) views on grammatical structure. In these respects, it informs the theory presented in this monograph in a significant and substantial way.

Having said that, the Chomskian categorial feature system has the major handicap of making no predictions, as it is purely taxonomic. It is summarized in tabulated form in (5):

(5)

	N	V
Noun	+	−
Verb	−	+
Adjective	+	+
Preposition	−	−

So, let us comment on the system represented in (5): we have the cross-categorization of four categories by means of two binary features. Hence, instead of three (or four) *primitive* lexical categories, we have two primitive binary features: [N] and [V] with their (expected) ± values. The attributes [N] and [V] are not identified with any sort of interpretation, at least not in the original Amherst system and not in any clear-cut way, and the ± values apparently mark the positive versus negative value of such an attribute, whatever it may represent. The picture, however, certainly looks elegant, as now it is possible to *cross-categorize* lexical categories. Having said that, this cross-categorizing cannot become truly significant, or even useful, until we resolve the question of what these features, and their values, stand for. To make this clearer, it is very difficult to get the batteries of properties characteristic of nouns and verbs in (4) to result from the system in (5). Following Baker (2003), I agree that this is the main problem with the Amherst feature system: it is a purely taxonomic system that does not predict much. Should we take up a more clement attitude to it, the Amherst system establishes cross-categorizations at an abstract level: nouns share a [+N] feature with adjectives, verbs a [+V], again with adjectives, and the two appear to be completely dissociated. Although these are hardly trivial predictions, they are clearly not robust enough to capture the picture in (4) or, even, part thereof. One reason for this problem is exactly that we do not know what the attributes [N] and [V] stand for. All we have at this point is nouns and adjectives forming a natural class, both being [+N], and verbs and adjectives forming a natural class because of their [+V] value; finally, prepositions also belong to a natural class with nouns (both categories being [−V]) and verbs, too (due to a common [−N] value) – but not with adjectives (cf. Stowell 1981, 21–2).

Departing from the natural classes defined by the Amherst system of categorial features [±N] and [±V], Stowell sets out in the first chapter of his (1981) thesis to show that these are classes to which syntactic and morphological rules actually refer. These classes are given in (6).

(6)   *Natural classes according to the Amherst system*

[+N]	nouns, adjectives
[−N]	verbs, prepositions
[+V]	verbs, adjectives
[−V]	prepositions, nouns

Simultaneously, he argues that syntactic rules do not refer to 'unnatural' classes like {noun, verb} or {adjective, preposition}. He goes on to spell out some of the rules that refer to the natural classes above:

- the [+N] categories, nouns and adjectives, project phrases where *of*-insertion applies in English, as in *destruction of the city* and *fearful of ghosts*;
- the [−N] categories, verbs and prepositions, are the Case-assigning ones: only they can take 'bare NP objects' (Stowell 1981, 23);
- the [+V] categories, verbs and adjectives (and participles), can be prefixed with *un*– in English (a word formation rule); in German they can function as prenominal modifiers, as in the examples in (7):

(7)   [+V] *prenominal modifiers in German*
a. der [seinen Freundin überdrüssige] Student
   the   his   girlfriend   weary   student
   'The student weary of his girlfriend.'

b. die [mit   ewigen   Snee   bedeckten] Berge
   the   with   eternal   snow   covered   mountains
   'The mountains covered with eternal snow.'

- Finally, XPs headed by the [−V] categories, nouns and prepositions, can be clefted.

A second argument for the syntactic and morphological significance of the classes defined by the categorial features [±N] and [±V] is that in many languages these classes collapse together into a single category – for example, nouns and adjectives, or verbs and adjectives. This is arguably not possible between nouns and verbs, or adjectives and prepositions.

Generally speaking, Stowell (1981) attempts to show that classes not defined by the two categorial features [±N] and [±V] do not form natural classes to which syntactic or morphological rules are sensitive. Hence, Stowell's attempt to make categorial features relevant for syntax genuinely informs the account developed here as a desideratum. Déchaine (1993) is another important analysis in this line of thinking.

Déchaine (1993, 25–36) begins with a review and criticism of previous accounts of categorial features. She then introduces her own system of categorial features, one that aspires to capture the natural classes that categories form and to which grammatical rules refer (as in Stowell), the lexical–functional distinction and biuniqueness between functional elements and some lexical categories.[8] She therefore proposes, for the first time to the best of my knowledge, three privative/unary/monovalent categorial features: [Functional],

---

[8] The lexical–functional distinction and biuniqueness are examined in Chapter 5 of this book.

[Nominal] and [Referential]. The cross-classification of these features yields the following category system (Déchaine 1993, 38):

(8)   *The Déchaine (1993) categorial system*
      [Nominal]   *Adjective*
      [Nominal] [Referential]   *Noun*
      [Referential]   *Verb*
      –   *Preposition*
      [Functional] [Nominal]   *Kase*
      [Functional] [Nominal] [Referential]   *Determiner*
      [Functional] [Referential]   *Tense*
      [Functional]   *Comp*

Some comments are in order: the primacy of [Nominal], as opposed to a purported feature [Verbal], is argued for on the basis that some processes select only for nouns (and adjectives) and on the basis of reinterpreting acquisition facts. Prepositions are labelled (via the absence of *any* categorial feature specification) as a sort of 'elsewhere' lexical category that no derivational process can target (we return to this in Chapter 2, Section 2.9). The general idea is that derivational affixes attach to and derive only categories that are specified as [Nominal] or [Referential], which is to say that these two are the features defining lexical categories. The noun–Determiner connection, Extended Projections (Grimshaw 1991), the (non-)identity between adjectives and adverbs, the modifying role or non-referential categories are all examined in turn as evidence for (8). A nice summary of the system and its rationale, and also of the desire to establish categorial features on the basis of fundamental conceptual categories, is given in Déchaine (1993, 71): '[Nominal] is to be preferred over [Verbal] as the basic feature which distinguishes categories; [Referential] provides a means of characterizing the notion of core extended projection;[9] and [Functional] provides a principled distinction between open-class and closed-class items.' A final innovation in Déchaine's system is, to my mind, her manifest effort to reconceptualize categorial features as semantically significant; this becomes almost evident from the passage above and by the way she names her features, especially the abstract, but crucial to her system, [Referential] feature.

    Moving on, the above three generative systems of categorial features and – to a significant extent – Baker (2003) unambiguously incorporate the thesis that lexical items come from the *lexicon* specified for category, by virtue of features like [N] and [V]. So, *dog* is a noun and *write* is a verb because we have

---

[9] That is, the projection of V and that of N.

memorized them as such and because they are part of the lexicon – the lexicon containing everything in language that must be memorized: 'a list of exceptions, whatever does not follow from general principles' (Chomsky 1995, 234). In other words, lexical elements come from the lexicon labelled for a category: noun, verb and so on. The lexicon contains entries like *dog* [+N, −V] and *do* [−N, +V]. Of course, this is roughly the way most traditional grammars view the matter, as well.

Baker (2003) explicitly announces that he aims to give *content* to the features [N] and [V], rather than view them as convenient labels that create taxonomies. He revises the system in (5) by positing two privative features, like Déchaine (1993), instead of the received binary ones. Importantly, these are expressly hypothesized to be *LF-interpretable* features as well as to trigger particular syntactic behaviours. The table in (9) summarizes this:

(9)

	Semantic interpretation	*Syntactic behaviour*
[N]	sortality	referential index
[V]	predication	specifier

Sortality is what makes nouns nominal. Baker (2003, 290) essentially treats a *sortal concept* as one that canonically complies with the principle of identity: a sortal concept is such that it can be said about it that it is the same as or different from X.[10] Furthermore, sortality is understood as the very property that enables nouns to bear referential indices. At the same time, [V], which makes verbs, is taken to encode predication. Baker also argues that verbs are the only lexical categories that can stand as predicates *without* the mediation of a functional category *Pred*. The predicative nature of verbs is correlated with them arguably being the only lexical category that projects a specifier.

Baker's (2003) system yields the following lexical categories:

(10)   Nouns   [N]   → sortal concepts, referential indices in syntax
         Verbs   [V]   → predicates, with (subject) specifiers in syntax
         Adjectives −   → 'other' concepts, pure properties

Baker's account makes a wide-ranging set of predictions about verbal and other predicates in co-ordination, the behaviour of causatives, and the noun–individuation relation (namely, the elective affinities between nouns, Number

---

[10] We will return to a more detailed discussion of sortality in Chapter 4.

and quantifiers). His account, which forms the basis from which our theory of categorial features departs, is revised in Chapter 4, extended in Chapters 5 and 6 and further pored over in the Appendix.

1.4   Deconstructing categories

1.4.1   Distributed Morphology

An alternative and very dynamic approach to word classes and the nature of parts of speech emerged in the 1990s within the framework of Distributed Morphology. The basic idea is non-lexicalist: the syntactic deconstruction of words. Therefore, categories like nouns and verbs are products of syntactic operations and do not come marked on lexical items. Nouns and verbs are not pre-packaged as such in the lexicon, they are 'made' so in the course of the syntactic derivation. The empirical consequences of syntactic categorization have been explored in detail in a significant body of work, including – but not restricted to – Harley and Noyer (1998), Embick (2000), Alexiadou (2001), Folli, Harley and Karimi (2003), Arad (2003, 2005), Folli and Harley (2005), Harley (2005a, 2005b, 2007, 2009, 2012a), Marantz (2005, 2006), Basilico (2008), Embick and Marantz (2008), Lowenstamm (2008), Acquaviva (2009b), Volpe (2009), Acquaviva and Panagiotidis (2012) and, in a slightly different framework but in considerable detail, Borer (2005, 2009) and De Belder (2011). I will not attempt to summarize the diverse and insightful findings of this line of research and inquiry; I will only present the way it works and return to it in Chapter 3.

So, suppose that lexical elements (*roots*) do not come pre-packaged with categorial features from the lexicon. In other words, and very roughly speaking, the lexicon (or its equivalent) contains entries like *dog* and *do* without them bearing any categorial features. Words of the 'lexical categories' N, V and A are created in the syntax via the combination of at least a *categorizing* head and a root: roots themselves are category-less or 'acategorial'. Thus, 'noun', 'verb' and 'adjective' are not categories specified on lexical items in a pre-syntactic lexicon: *categorization is a syntactic process*.

More precisely, according to the syntactic decomposition of categories, acategorial roots are inserted in syntax. Dedicated syntactic heads, *categorizers* – a nominalizer (n), a verbalizer (v) and an adjectivizer (a) – make them nouns, verbs or adjectives. Of course, the projections of n and v (and a) may contain more than just themselves and a root:

(11)

See Marantz (2000) – also Halle and Marantz (1993) – for the background regarding the categorial decomposition in Distributed Morphology. We will return to this framework, in which the theory presented here is couched, in Chapter 3.

1.4.2   Radical categorylessness

A radical way to do syntactic decomposition is to posit not only that lexical elements (*roots*) do not come pre-packaged with categorial features from the lexicon but also that there are *no* dedicated categorizers in Syntax, either. This is what is argued for in Borer (2003, 2009), De Belder (2011), and also Alexiadou (2001): that the functional environment dominating a root actually defines the category of the structure containing the root. An obvious conceptual consequence of such an approach is that it is not Comp and Tense that 'go with' a verb, let alone that are *selected* by a verb, or vice versa. Instead, Comp and Tense *make* a root a verb. Similarly, Det and Num do not 'go with' a noun: Det and Num *make* a root a noun. This is illustrated in the simplified trees below:

(12)

Expanding upon the rationale of this approach, we can say that the noun–verb distinction is *purely* configurational. Nouns and verbs are essentially *structures* containing a root and being characterized *purely and exclusively* by the functional environment around the said root. So, what matters is the syntactic positioning of the root. To illustrate, if a root (say SLEEP) is inserted within a functional complex like the following, then it becomes a verb:

(13)

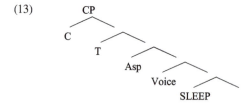

Similarly, if the selfsame root SLEEP is inserted within a functional complex like the following, then it becomes a noun:

(14)
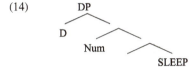

As part of a programme of radical constructionalism, where any root can be slotted into any functional superstructure, as happens above, syntactic categorization without categorizers also informs Borer (2005) but is significantly revised in Borer (2009). The radical categorylessness approach will become especially cogent for the discussion in Chapter 6, when mixed projections are examined.

1.5 The notional approach revisited: Langacker (1987) and Anderson (1997)

Cognitive Grammar (Langacker 1987) is a non-formal theory of grammar. It argues that grammar is 'inherently meaningful' and that language constitutes 'an integral facet of cognition' (Langacker 1987, 590). There is no syntactic mechanism independent of semantics, and there are no levels of representation, at least not in the way these are understood in modular approaches to the Language Faculty. To wit, Cognitive Grammar does use diagrams to represent grammatical meanings and structures, but differences in grammatical behaviour are directly attributed to conceptual/semantic differences.[11] Thus, it is no wonder that Langacker's approach to categories is a notional one. However, and remembering the distinction I drew between notional and taxonomic treatments of category, Cognitive Grammar does not treat categories as big boxes in which concepts (or rather, the words expressing them) are sorted according to ontological criteria. Instead, different categories in Cognitive Grammar are understood as different *conceptualizations*. That is an extremely important point in understanding the semantics of categories like noun and verb by themselves: shifting away from naïve ontological taxonomies, Langacker (1987) understands categories as a *particular way* in which concepts are 'seen'. Rauh (2010, 238) provides an example of how 'noun' is understood; Langacker (1987) describes nouns as nominal predications that designate a THING.

---

[11] I gratefully acknowledge comments by an anonymous reviewer on Cognitive Grammar.

However, THING does not stand for a physical object (this would bring us back to naïve ontologically informed taxonomies of school grammars) but, rather, as a 'region in some domain' (Langacker 1987, 189). Immediately it becomes evident, at least intuitively, how *rock*, *theory* and *wedding* can all be nouns: they define *areas* in different conceptual domains. Of course, a lot depends on what these conceptual domains are and, most crucially, how exactly they are mapped on words – see Acquaviva (2009a) for criticism and Acquaviva and Panagiotidis (2012) for discussion. However, understanding categories as conceptualizations instead of ontologies constitutes a major step in understanding what they mean and how they work.

As far as the other 'basic' categories are concerned, adjectives and adverbs conceptualize ATEMPORAL RELATIONS (Langacker 1987, 248), whereas verbs are understood as conceptualizing PROCESSES. Regarding the generalization in Section 2.5 – namely, that the majority of words meaning physical objects are nouns cross-linguistically – Langacker (2000, 10) captures it by appealing to the prototypicality of THING when it comes to object concepts and to the protypicality of PROCESS when it comes to 'an asymmetrical energetic interaction involving an agent and a patient'. The details are very interesting and certainly intricate; however, they are not readily translatable to a formal framework like the one employed here.

Turning now to Anderson (1997), the picture is similar to that presented by Langacker's approach, with three important differences: Anderson's framework is a formal one and expresses generalizations by encoding them as *features*. He understands categories as 'grammaticalisations of cognitive – or notional – constructs' (Anderson 1997, 1), thus making his theory more compatible with the underpinnings of a generative theory: he essentially claims that categories are ways in which *grammar*, which forms a separate module from general cognition, translates or imports ('grammaticalizes') concepts. Third, he formalizes the different categories, the different grammaticalizations of concepts, using two features and a relation of preponderance between them: a feature P, standing for predicativity or, rather, *predicability*, and a feature N, standing for the ability to function as an argument. The resulting categories for English are the following:

(15)   {P}   auxiliary
        {P;N}   verb
        {P:N}   adjective
        {N;P}   noun
        {N}   name
        { }   functor

Explicating, auxiliaries {P} are only usable as predicates, names {N} only as arguments, and functors { } as neither. Adjectives {P:N} are the result of a balanced relationship between predicability and the ability to function as arguments, whereas in verbs {P;N} predicability takes preponderance over possible argumenthood and vice versa in nouns {N;P}. To my mind it is precisely this 'preponderance' factor that makes the relation between two features very hard to formalize any further. Moreover, in Anderson's system there is again a conflation between the category by itself, say 'verb', and the functional layer around it. For instance, saying that verbs by themselves may function as arguments is misleading, as verbs can only function as arguments when they are embedded within a nominalizing functional shell, in which case they form part of a mixed projection, such as gerunds, nominalized infinitives and the like.

1.6   The present approach: LF-interpretable categorial features make categorizers

The theory to be presented in this monograph is one of categorial features. In this it is in the spirit first of all of the original Amherst system and of its refinements, developments and reconceptions – namely, Stowell (1981), Déchaine (1993) and Baker (2003). It is inevitably also in the spirit of the way Head-Driven Phrase Structure Grammar (HPSG) and Lexical Function Grammar (LFG) treat grammatical category: as a feature or as the result of feature combinations; see Rauh (2010, chap. 6) for a survey of how category is treated in these frameworks in terms of features. Finally, it displays affinities with Anderson (1997), in that it seeks to capture parts of speech as the phenotypes of different categorial features. Moreover, as in Baker's and Anderson's systems, I will seriously explore the idea that categorial features encode conceptual (if not notional) content – namely, that they encode differ-ent conceptualizations: what I will call different *interpretive perspectives* on concepts. In this, we will follow the lead of Langacker (1987) and seek to understand categorial features as setting up different perspectives on concepts. In specifying the interpretive perspectives which [N] and [V] encode, we will capitalize both on insights in Baker (2003) as well as those regarding time stability in the functional–typological literature. Finally, once we take categor-ial features to encode conceptual content (technically speaking: to be LF-interpretable), then we will be able both to explore their participation in syntactic relations, most notably Agree, and to establish them as the very features that make categorizers, *n* and *v*, necessary in frameworks like

Distributed Morphology, which do categorization syntactically. In other words, we will weave together a seemingly disparate number of yarns in order to hopefully produce a coherent theory of lexical, functional and mixed categories.

As is already evident, the role of categorial features in defining grammatical category is taken very seriously in this monograph, especially in the light of its theoretical and methodological commitment to syntactic decomposition and to viewing categorization as a syntactic process. I understand categorial features as LF-interpretable and as no different from other syntactic features: in other words, I take [N] and [V] to be instructions to an interface, viz. the interface between the Faculty of Language in the Narrow sense (FLN) and the Conceptual–Intentional systems (which I will still informally call 'LF'). At the same time, contra Panagiotidis (2005), I delegate all true categorial distinctions to categorizers. I consider them to be true syntactic heads, and I will go as far as claiming that the nominalizer *n* and the verbalizer *v* are the only *lexical* heads in Syntax, serving as the elements that enable roots to structurally combine with bundles (or, perhaps, batteries) of FLN-intrinsic features, selected from a pool made available by UG.

The resulting theory proposes that each categorizer is the locus of a categorial feature. Categorial features introduce fundamental interpretive perspectives in which the categorizers' complements are to be interpreted. These fundamental perspectives are *necessary* when the categorizers' complements consist of roots and/or root projections: this subsumes Embick and Marantz's (2008, 6) *Categorization Assumption*.

The theory also predicts the existence of uninterpretable categorial features; these are taken to flag bundles/batteries of features (i.e., *functional heads*) that must have lexical material in their complement. This thesis provides a simple solution to how we can state the relationship between functional projections and the lexical material they dominate. Under the straightforward assumption that uninterpretable categorial features act as Probes for Agree relations, the theory can also capture the biunique relationship between particular functional and lexical elements – for example, the biunique relation between Number and nouns. Appealing to Agree relations between uninterpretable and interpretable categorial features – that is, categorial Agree – also explains why lexical material is always merged first, 'at the bottom of the tree'. Finally, categorial Agree can explain how the label is decided in most instances of First Merge, possibly all of them: for instance, when a head – an 'LI', for 'lexical item', in Chomsky (2000, 2004) – merges with another head.

The ordinary character of categorial features as LF-interpretable will serve to solve the recurring problem in grammatical theory of how best to analyse mixed projections. The existence of functional categorizers, SWITCHES, consisting of one uninterpretable (hence 'functional') and one interpretable (hence categorizing) categorial feature is posited and their position and role are scrutinized – namely, what size and type their complements can be.

2 *Are word class categories universal?*

2.1 Introduction

A theory of categorial features cannot overlook the question of whether the lexical classes we recognize as nouns, verbs and adjectives are universal or particular to a subset of languages. This task becomes more important if one considers the frequent charge that categories like 'noun' and 'verb' have been analytically imposed by Eurocentric grammarians and linguists (mostly) onto non-Indo-European languages: this has been a matter of debate for at least the past 80 years.[1] This chapter critically reviews some of the points of contention in the literature on the universality of lexical categories, beginning with the need to make sure we know what we are talking about when we talk about nouns, verbs and adjectives. The reason such a caveat is necessary, followed by some preliminary clarifications and statements on methods and terminology, is because different scholars tend to mean different things when they talk about nouns, verbs and adjectives – especially, but not exclusively, when they use them in a mainly pre-theoretical fashion. After these necessary refinements, the universality itself is discussed, as well as a detailed justification of why it was decided not to include adjectives (and adpositions) among lexical categories in this book.

The universality question is introduced in Section 2.2, and two methodological guidelines – that is, to distinguish verbs from their functional superstructure and to use morphological criteria cautiously – are introduced and examined in Section 2.3. Section 2.4 reviews evidence from Tagalog and Riau Indonesian that has been claimed to demonstrate grounds for a single undifferentiated lexical category in these languages. Section 2.5 revisits the Nootka debate and Baker's (2003) treatment of it, further suggesting that the debate is

---

[1] This debate was recently vigorously revived, or rather 'updated', in the wake of Everett's (2005) claims that Pirahã is radically and profoundly different from other languages. See Nevins, Pesetsky and Rodrigues (2009) for a careful assessment.

possibly moot in a syntactic categorization approach. The resulting picture is reviewed in Section 2.7. Section 2.8 justifies the non-inclusion of adjectives in the discussion, and Section 2.9 does the same for adpositions. The final section concludes the chapter.

2.2 Do all languages have nouns and verbs? How can we tell?

We set out in the previous chapter to develop a UG theory of grammatical category. This entails making claims about the Language Faculty. More specifically, claims about the existence of (particular) categorial features within the purported 'pool' of UG-available features will be raised; we will then have to go beyond typological generalizations that could reflect (a) extralinguistic factors (e.g., all languages have a word for 'mother' or 'sun' for obvious reasons) or, worse, (b) a methodological bias that seeks to impose Indo-European categories on languages working in distinctly non-Indo-European ways.

If our desideratum of a theory of category founded on LF-interpretable syntactic features is to have any substance at all, we need to ensure first that differences between nouns and verbs are universal and subsequently to inquire as to whether the two lexical categories are indeed manifested in all natural languages.[2] This question is not a matter of pure data collection, however. If the noun–verb distinction is so persistent and fundamental, it needs to be shown why this is the case and what kind of conceptual distinction it reflects and encodes. Moreover, on the methodological side of things, we need to move away from the situation realized by languages like English: in languages like English, the noun–verb distinction is also one between two broad *syntactic* categories – that is, between two categories that regulate or, at least, affect syntactic distribution: whether X will appear in such and such a position depends (also) on its word category membership – see Rauh (2010, 325–39). However, as will be seen, this is not the case cross-linguistically: in some languages, verbs and nouns have a seemingly free distribution; in other languages nouns and verbs are embedded within layer upon layer of functional material, material which, typically, is morphologically attached to the lexical element. Finally, a great number of languages possess mixed projections. In this section we will examine cases of allegedly free distribution between nouns and verbs, as well as verbs and nouns embedded inside a lot

---

[2] This second statement would be highly desirable but it is not a *necessary* condition for the universality of categorial features.

of functional material. We shall leave a more detailed discussion of mixed projections for Chapter 6.

2.3   Two caveats: when we talk about 'verb' and 'noun'

Given the above, we first need to decide how we can tell whether a language *has* nouns and verbs in a quasi-pre-theoretical way. This is going to be useful for the discussion that will follow.

2.3.1   *Verbs, not their entourage*

A first point to watch is the following: it is always important and necessary to distinguish between a verb and the larger constituent within which verbs are typically contained. In other words, we need to separate the verbal element – let us call it V for the sake of exposition – from the verbal phrasal constituent it is embedded within: for example, Voice phrases, aspectual phrases, Tense phrases and even complete Complementizer phrases. Note also that this embedding is customarily morphologically mediated, in that Morphology rarely (if at all) expresses a V as a stand-alone word. This is not the case only in inflectionally rich languages, but also in English.

Let us begin with what is considered a periphrastic verb form in most pedagogical descriptions of English, *have been watching* (the 'present perfect continuous form of the verb *watch*'). Of course, *have been watching* is not a 'verb'; it is not even a constituent. The most appropriate way to describe *have been watching* would be to acknowledge that it is *part* of a Tense Phrase (TP) containing three Verb Phrases (VPs) embedded within each other – see, for example, Haegeman (2006, sec. 3.4). However, the object of *watch*, which would complete the TP constituent together with the subject, is left out.

(1)

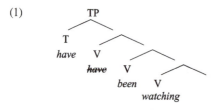

Although the above example certainly feels trivial, it does so because it is drawn from a familiar language. Moreover, it is indicative of the fact that similar considerations apply, and must be kept in mind, when we examine heavily inflected languages, even of the familiar sort, like Greek, Russian or Turkish: what we call a 'verb' in such languages usually contains the verb plus a lot more structure. Illustrating this, let us have a look at an equally straight-forward example from Turkish, a token of what traditionally is described as a 'verb'; notice that, as expected from an agglutinating language, it consists of a single word:

(2)   unut-   ma-   y-   acağ-   ımız
       forget   NEG   FUT   1ST.PL

Again, the 'verb form' packages together a part of a TP constituent. More accurately, the single morphological word *unutmayacağımız* packages together the heads of the TP projection line. So, as with the English example in (1) above, we must be very careful to tease apart the V from its functional environment, a functional superstructure that includes auxiliaries, modals, Mood, Tense, Aspect and Voice markers, agreement markers and arguments themselves, before we make any claims about V itself.

2.3.2   Misled by morphological criteria: nouns and verbs looking alike

A second point to watch, equally elementary but hardly trivial, is that the sharing of identical morphological forms – for example, affixes – and the fact that some inflectional morphology may be common to both nouns and verbs do not entail that there is no noun–verb distinction in a language. The sharing of, say, suffixes between nouns and verbs could be a sign of them being embedded within identical functional shells, when of course we are not simply dealing with a historical accident resulting in (extensive) morphological syncretism. Similarly, the lack of morphological distinction between nouns and verbs certainly does not entail that there is no verb–noun distinction in the grammar. An obvious example of this is the fact that English 'zero suffixation', whichever is the proper way to analyse it, does not neutralize the noun–verb distinction in English. Moreover, as Pesetsky (1995), Marantz (2000), Arad (2005) and Borer (2005) show, 'zero suffixation' effectively belies the wealth of structure present in examples like *certificate* (as a denominal verb) below.

(3)   work   do
       sleep   find
       fight   test
       play   poke
       water   certificate (vs certify)

To wit, observe English '*–ing*', to which we will return in Chapter 6. No matter what analysis we pick for it, we have hardly *one* category-neutral instance of *painting* in examples (4), (5), (6), (7) and (8), where *–ing* belies the varied roles the word *painting* can have in each of the sentences, the different categories it can belong to and the diverse structures it can participate in. Thus, whether there are two instances of *–ing*, an aspectual one and a nominalizer, or just one *–ing*, an aspectual marker, *painting* in (4) is a prototypical noun denoting an object concept, while in (8) it is a prototypical verb denoting a dynamic event, an activity. Even more interestingly, in the examples in-between, each instance of *painting* is embedded in rich (mixed) projections and involves complex and differentiated structures.[3] So, we have a process nominal, still a noun, in (5), a gerund with verbal and nominal properties in (6) and a verbal element in (7).

(4)   The painting is on the wall.

(5)   [Helena's painting of horses in her free time] proved more than a hobby.

(6)   [Helena('s) painting horses in her free time] proved more than a hobby.

(7)   I watched [her painting horse paintings].

(8)   She was painting horses.

2.3.3   What criterion, then?

Using well-described languages like English and Turkish to illustrate the two points above serves the purpose of highlighting not only the perils of exoticization on behalf of too eager field linguists and/or enthusiastic local informants, but primarily of relying on surface criteria to discuss category membership, especially when it comes to talking about less well-described languages. Moreover, the two points raised in this section are methodological mementos and cannot be used to stipulate noun–verb differences where there would be none. Indeed, a safe criterion that a language does not distinguish between nouns and verbs would be the following, from Baker (2003, sec. 3.9):

(9)   If a language can use all of its lexical elements interchangeably in all
       contexts, then it does not distinguish between nouns and verbs.

This means that in such languages we should be able to freely insert lexical elements in both 'nominal' and 'verbal/clausal' *functional* projections. We will see that this is most probably not attested in any natural language. Interestingly, however, we will argue that it appears that a slightly different state of

---

[3] Again, these matters will be looked at in detail in Chapter 6.

affairs could well be instantiated in some languages – that is, that we should be able to freely insert roots in both nominal and verbal *lexical* projections.

Summarizing, when we talk about the noun–verb distinction in a language and, consequently, the universality of nouns and verbs, we may discuss three very different empirical matters:

(10) *Noun–verb distinction in a given language*
   a. Whether there is extensive nominalization of verbs (denominal verbs and mixed projections) and extensive verbalization of nouns (deverbal nouns). This is a red herring: verbs and nouns are real in this language, although they can be morphosyntactically recategorized by a suitable functional entourage.
   b. Whether all roots can become both nouns and verbs. If yes, then categorization is certainly a grammatical process: nouns and verbs are grammatical constructs, syntactic categories, not specifications on lexical items (i.e., word classes). Essentially, the noun–verb distinction still stands.
   c. Whether (9) holds – that is, whether all lexical elements can be used interchangeably in all contexts. This would be an example of a language where a noun–verb distinction, and lexical categorization, would be pointless.

2.4 Identical (?) behaviours

Given the discussion in the previous section, the most radical challenge to the universality of nouns and verbs and to the noun–verb distinction would come from a natural language as described in (9), where any lexical element would be freely inserted in any grammatical context. Such languages would undeniably constitute genuine examples of the absence of a noun–verb distinction, languages with no noun–verb distinction either as word classes or as syntactic categories. Two languages have been famously claimed to fit the bill: Tagalog and Riau Indonesian.

Tagalog has been variously presented as a language whose roots 'are always [category-]neutral or "precategorial" and receive categorial specification via morphological specification' (Rauh 2010, 343). Even if this were true, it would not entail that Tagalog has *no* verb–noun distinction. It would only mean that categorization in Tagalog would be a purely grammatical process and that there would be no nouns and verbs as distinct *word classes* coming 'pre-packaged as nouns and verbs' from the lexicon. In other words, Tagalog would be like Nootka and Lillooet Salish (or St'át'imcets) (see Section 2.5 for details).

However, Tagalog is not even a language that illustrates the b. case in (10). Himmelmann (2008), cited in Rauh (2010, 343–5), observes that in Tagalog, as in Germanic languages like English or Dutch (Don 2004), some roots make better nouns or only nouns. In Tagalog, the version of this is slightly different: not all roots can be inserted in any morphological environment. Himmelmann (2008) illustrates this by discussing *ma–*, a polysemous prefix. The marker *ma–* expresses states (e.g., *magandá* 'beautiful' < *gandá* 'beauty') when affixed to a specific set of roots; however, it expresses accomplishments (e.g., *magalit* 'become angry' < *galit* 'anger') when affixed to a *different* set of roots. So, *magandá* cannot mean 'become beautiful'. The distinction between the two classes of roots appears to be arbitrary – that is, it is not the case that roots like *gandá* ('beauty') can only denote states. To wit, using a *different* marker, the infix *–um–*, *gandá* may also express an accomplishment: *g-um-andá* indeed means 'become beautiful'. Finally, using a different morphological process – stress shift – roots like *galit* can express states: *galit* ('anger') versus *galít* ('angry'). The above show that Tagalog roots cannot be freely inserted in any grammatical context. But what about categories like nouns and verbs? Is it meaningful to talk about such 'Eurocentric' (Gil 2000) categories in Tagalog? The answer seems to be affirmative. Himmelmann (2008), again as cited in Rauh (2010, 343–4), makes a very interesting point with respect to what he calls 'V-words'. Tagalog roots expressing things, animate beings *and* actions are nouns when used in isolation, and they become verbs, 'V-words', when they undergo Voice affixation.[4] Although it is unclear whether the resulting words are simplex or denominal verbs, I think that processes like Voice affixation make talking about a noun–verb distinction in Tagalog meaningful. Baker (2003, 185–9) follows a very similar path to show that a noun–verb distinction is meaningful in a number of languages, including Tukang Besi – whose behaviour closely resembles that of Tagalog.

There exists, however, an example of a language that has been claimed to exactly fit the bill in (9). Gil (1994, 2000, 2005, 2013) has consistently claimed that Riau Indonesian is a case of a language as described under c. in (10): all lexical material, *all lexical elements*, can be used interchangeably in all contexts; they can be freely inserted pretty much everywhere.[5] This purported radical state of affairs would render the noun–verb distinction in the particular language completely unnecessary and spurious, reducing it to a sort of analytical and methodological straightjacket. Consider the most famous example of this lack of lexical categories, as presented in Gil (2005, 246):

[4] The apparent 'default' nature of nouns will be examined in Chapter 4, Section 4.6.
[5] See Gil (n.d.) for a thorough and well-rounded presentation of the Riau Indonesian variety from a sociolinguistic viewpoint, a matter that has raised some controversy.

(11) makan ayam/ ayam makan
      eat chicken chicken eat
      'The chicken is eating.'
      'The chickens are eating.'
      'A chicken is eating.'
      'The chicken was eating.'
      'The chicken will be eating.'
      'The chicken eats.'
      'The chicken has eaten.'
      'Someone is eating the chicken.'
      'Someone is eating for the chicken.'
      'Someone is eating with the chicken.'
      'The chicken that is eating.'
      'Where the chicken is eating.'
      'When the chicken is eating.'

Gil (2005) claims that in Riau Indonesian *any* of the glosses above is an appropriate translation of the two-word sentence *makan ayam/ayam makan* – depending on the context, of course. So, indeed, Riau Indonesian is presented as a category-less language in the most thorough and dramatic fashion.[6]

Yoder (2010) put this claim to the test, going back to the original naturalistic data in Gil's publications, data originating from 'recorded spontaneous speech' (Yoder 2010, 2).[7] He went on to review the 154 examples presented in Gil's published work on Riau Indonesian until 2010 with a very simple goal: to detect whether there is any correlation between nouns, verbs and adjectives, on the one hand, and the syntactic functions argument, predicate and modifier, on the other (Yoder 2010: 7).

His methodology is simple but solid: departing from a comparative viewpoint, he took all the words in Gil's 154 examples and checked them against the category to which these words belong to in Standard Indonesian, an extremely similar and much better described variety, which does make categorial distinctions. Matching the Riau words to the Standard equivalents, he 'found a total of 271 nouns, 161 verbs, and 55 adjectives' (Yoder 2010: 7). He then revisited each of the 154 examples and examined whether items

---

[6] We must be very cautious with what could be called the 'Hopi fallacy' – that is, claims of exceptionality stemming from an exoticized (re)presentation of a language – on behalf of field linguists studying it. See, for instance, Nevins, Pesetsky and Rodrigues (2009) on the progressively exoticized grammatical descriptions of Pirahã.

[7] Gil does not seem to systematically ask for native speaker intuitions or to elicit responses. This is, to my mind, the major methodological obstacle in substantiating claims of Riau Indonesian being category-less.

categorized as nouns in Standard Indonesian functioned as arguments in Riau Indonesian; whether items categorized as verbs in Standard Indonesian functioned as Riau predicates; and whether adjectives in the Standard variety functioned as Riau Indonesian modifiers. If a verb, noun or adjective in the Standard variety had a different syntactic function in Riau Indonesian than the default one, he counted it as an exception.

His findings are pretty solid, as summarized in the table in (12), adapted from Yoder (2010: 7):

(12)   *Members of lexical categories and their functions in the Gil corpus*

	Default	*Non-default*
noun (default = argument)	244 (90%)	27 (10%)
verb (default = predicate)	160 (99%)	1 (>1%)
adjective (default = modifier)	27 (49%)	28 (51%)

Yoder proceeded to tackle the non-default cases and found that the majority thereof fall under five morphosyntactic patterns, which are also attested in Standard Indonesian: (i) nominal modifiers (belonging to all three categories) *following* the noun they modify; (ii) equative clauses with a nominal or an adjectival predicate; (iii) three instances of noun phrases headed by a phonologically null noun (like English *four reds and a yellow*); (iv) use of a verbalizing prefix *N-*; (v) use of a verbalizing suffix *–kan* attaching on adjectives.[8]

In the light of the above, I think we can safely consider Riau Indonesian as a run-of-the-mill language, at least as far as its lexical categories are concerned, pending a more in-depth investigation of its grammar, based on more empirical evidence, compounded by elicited responses and – crucially – speaker intuitions. Until then, Yoder (2010) makes a very convincing point that this variety has nouns, verbs and adjectives both as syntactic categories and as word classes, just like Standard Indonesian.

2.5   The Nootka debate (is probably pointless)

It has been extensively argued that there are languages where no distinction can be made between verbs and nouns. The most famous ones are Nootka and Lillooet Salish (also known as St'át'imcets), to the extent that the discussion on whether nouns and verbs are universal is termed 'the Nootka debate'. Very

---

[8] The three functions that do not fall under either the default cases or the five non-default patterns involve a noun in predicate position, a noun in verbal modifier position and a verb in argument position. None of these is typologically outlandish, let alone unheard of.

broadly speaking, most analyses arguing that languages like Nootka and Lillooet Salish do not distinguish between nouns and verbs are usually informed by the fact that lexical elements can all function as predicates in isolation and they can be differentiated with respect to their syntactic role only via particular functional elements. Evans and Levinson (2009, 434–5) eloquently summarize the case for the non-existence of a noun–verb distinction as follows:

> A feeling for what a language without a noun-verb distinction is like comes from Straits Salish. Here, on the analysis by Jelinek (1995), all major-class lexical items simply function as predicates, of the type 'run,' 'be_big,' or 'be_a_man.' They then slot into various clausal roles, such as argument ('the one such that he runs'), predicate ('run[s]'), and modifier ('the running [one]'), according to the syntactic slots they are placed in. The single open syntactic class of predicate includes words for events, entities, and qualities. When used directly as predicates, all appear in clause-initial position, followed by subject and/or object clitics. When used as arguments, all lexical stems are effectively converted into relative clauses through the use of a determiner, which must be employed whether the predicate-word refers to an event ('the [ones who] sing'), an entity ('the [one which is a] fish'), or even a proper name ('the [one which] is Eloise'). The square-bracketed material shows what we need to add to the English translation to convert the reading in the way the Straits Salish structure lays out.

There are two matters to review in the summary above, which echoes Jelinek's extensive work on Salish.

First, we have the fact that in most Salish languages arguments need a Determiner, as illustrated in (16) for Lillooet Salish and in (17) for Nootka.[9] This holds whether they are doubled by argument clitics on the predicate or not – that is, by whether they are true arguments or DP adjuncts (Jelinek 1996). However, does this necessarily entail that 'when used as arguments, all lexical stems *are effectively converted into relative clauses* through the use of a determiner'?[10] Should this be so, then it would be a strong argument for all lexical stems in Salish being inherently predicative. Not necessarily, however. In Romance, Determiners are generally necessary for nouns to function as arguments and predicate nouns may surface without a Determiner – this is what happens in Salish, too.[11] Moreover, we do not know what lexical stems

---

[9] In Makah, nouns like *waːqʼit* ('frog') can function as arguments with or without a Determiner suffix *-ºiq*; however, verbs *must* be suffixed with *-ºiq* in order to do so (Baker 2003, 179).

[10] Emphasis added.

[11] Of course, Salish is *not* Romance! All that is highlighted here is the obvious fact, also reviewed in Chierchia (1998) and elsewhere, that obligatory Determiners in argument positions, even with proper names, cannot be taken as *direct* evidence for the inexistence of nouns.

surfacing as nouns in other languages would do in 'other' Salish environments, because Salish seems to allow DPs *only* in adjunct positions. This restriction of Salish DPs to adjunct positions has profound consequences like the lack of *wh*-movement and A-dependencies (Jelinek 1996); it also forces these languages to resort to non-DP mechanisms of quantification (Matthewson 2001). At the end of the day, *the* in *the dog* is just a Determiner; in **(the) Paris of my youth* it introduces something like a reduced relative – Salish could be a little like that, as well.

The second matter is whether what Evans and Levinson (2009) call 'major-class lexical items' is actually anything more than bare *roots*. Should this be so, then Salish would eventually provide strong evidence for acategorial roots being categorized in syntax by the structure dominating them; in other words, we would have evidence for Distributed Morphology and Borer-style syntactic categorization: for the syntactic decomposition of nouns and verbs (see Chapter 3). In this case, Lillooet Salish would be a prominent example of a language where *any* root can be freely inserted inside any lexical environment to become a noun, a verb and so on – that is, a language falling under the b. case of (10).

Harking back to the caveats raised in Section 2.3.2 and the working principle in (9), it is precarious to assume that if a lexical element X takes the same type of affix as lexical item Y this makes X and Y identical. Again turning to languages more familiar for sociocultural and historical reasons, this point is nicely illustrated by the following situation in Turkish. Although few, if any, would argue that Turkish does not distinguish between nouns and verbs, nevertheless the suffix *–dI* can be found after verbal elements as well as after nominal ones:

(13)   muhtar-dı   bayıl-dı
        village headman-PAST   faint-PAST
        'S/he was village headman.'   'S/he fainted.'

However, this is possibly a case of allomorphy of sorts. First, as evident from the glosses, the interpretation of the noun above is distinctly different to that of a verb: the suffix *–dI* attaching to a noun functions as a past tense copula, but when it attaches to a noun it is simply a past tense marker. Second, stress patterns differ: the suffix *–dI* is stressed (marked in boldface above) only when attached to a verb. Finally, the picture becomes very different once we move away from the past tense:

(14)   *Copula versus Tense in Turkish*
        a. muhtar-dır   bayıl-ıyor
           village headman-COP   faint-PRESENT

    b. muhtar ol-acak   bayıl-acak
        village headman be.FUT   faint-FUT

Once we look at the present and the future tenses, it becomes obvious that the suffix *–dI* is the exponence of two different elements: of a past tense copula and of past tense. The conclusion is that we must be *very careful* before making claims of non-distinctness, given that the morphological exponence of functional categories within which nouns and verbs are embedded can mislead us. As repeatedly pointed out above, the essential task is threefold: first, to ensure that homophony of affixes is just that – a matter of exponence and forms; second, to correctly distinguish nouns and verbs from their functional entourage; and, third, to correctly tell whether the root embedded within the various functional structures is a categorized root (i.e., lexical noun or verb) or an uncategorized root.

    Let us, however, turn to some real data from Lillooet Salish and Nootka (Baker 2003, 173–89). Lillooet Salish can use any lexical category as a predicate, something to be expected if all lexical categories are indeed predicates (Higginbotham 1985), using the same (?) agreement-like suffix:[12]

(15)   *Lillooet Salish: predicates*
        a. Qwatsáts-kacw
            leave-2ndSG
            'You leave/left.'
        b. Smúlhats-kacw
            woman-2ndSG
            'You are a woman.'
        c. Xzúm-lhkacw
            big-2ndSG
            'You are big.'

So far, the situation could be similar to what happens with Turkish in (13). Nevertheless, as already mentioned, in Salish languages there is a determiner-like element that can nominalize anything, while whatever appears in the first position of a sentence can act as a predicate (Baker 2003, 175).

(16)   *Lillooet Salish: arguments*
        a. Qwatsáts-Ø   ti   smúlhats-a
            leave-3rdABS   the   woman-the
            'The woman left.'

---

[12] The examples are from Baker (2003, 175).

        b. Smúlhats-Ø   ti   qwatsáts-a
          woman-3^{rd}ABS   the   leave-the
          'The one who left is a woman.'

The picture is similar in Nootka:

(17)   *Nootka: arguments*
        a. Mamu:k-ma   qu:?as-?i
          work-INDIC   man-the
          'The man is working.'
        b. Qu:?as-ma   mamu:k-i
          man-INDIC   work-the
          'The working one is a man.'

What is worth observing above is that in (16), the predicate – that is, the first word in the sentence – takes a null subject agreement marker (third-person absolutive) that links it with a constituent nominalized by a determiner(-like element). Once more, the situation in (13) springs to mind, where –*dI* can be either a past tense marker (with the verbal stem *bayıl*) or a past tense copula (with the noun *muhtar*). Nootka in (17) is, on the other hand, much more interesting, as the suffix attaching on both 'work' and 'man' in the first position is one encoding indicative Mood.

    Abstracting away, the workings of roots illustrated above could in reality be no different to the ones in English: the category of lexical elements becomes visible through the morphology surrounding the roots and by these elements' syntactic position. If one goes for the view that some roots can make only nouns or only verbs, the true question here is whether there are Salish roots that *cannot* be made into first-position predicates, as, for example, *boy* and – for most speakers – *cat* cannot be made into verbs in English. Baker (2003, 177 et seq.) proceeds to 'isolat[e] the lexical heads from their functional support systems, to see if the noun-nonnoun contrast reemerges in those environments'. Revisiting candidate languages for a lack of noun–verb distinction, he shows that in Greenlandic and Nahuatl only nouns incorporate, despite the wide use of substantivized adjectives as nouns in other contexts; that in Kambera, Samoan, Tongan and Niuean (Austronesian) only true nouns can appear as arguments without a determiner (see also footnote 9). Revisiting Lillooet Salish, Baker (2003, 182) follows Davis (1999) in foregrounding a very important observation: while the determiner *ti–a* can nominalize anything, as shown in (16), only true nominals can take the demonstrative *ti7* plus the determiner *ku*:

(18)   a. Áts'x-en=lhkan   ti7   ku-sqaycw
              see-DIRECTIONAL=1stSG.SUBJECT DEM   DET-man
              'I saw that man.'
        b. *Áts'x-en=lhkan   ti7   ku-qwatsáts / ku-tayt
              see-DIRECTIONAL=1stSG.SUBJECT DEM   DET-leave / DET-hungry
              'I saw that leaving one/that hungry one.'

So, even in Lillooet Salish there are lexical elements that display an unambiguously nominal behaviour. This confirms our suspicions that in the b. example of (16) there is more structure than meets the eye; after all, subjects like *ti qwatsáts-a a* (DET leave DET) 'the one leaving' has been standardly analysed as a reduced relative.[13]

2.6   Verbs can be found everywhere, but not necessarily as a word class

Let us now turn to verbs. As will be extensively shown in the following two chapters, verbs are grammatically more complex than nouns, irrespective of whether one subscribes to the view that argument structure is syntactic structure: see Hale and Keyser (1993, 2002), Pylkkänen (2008), Ramchand (2008) and elsewhere. This pre-theoretical observation – namely, that verbs have more structure than nouns – apparently holds even if we abstract away from periphrastic forms that include more than just the lexical verb – recall the discussion of (1) – or affixes belonging to the functional entourage of the verb, as in (2). Beginning with Germanic, particle verbs are very common and particles are an integral part of the verbal predicate (Harley 2005b). Thus, the verb *cook* displays different selectional restrictions to the particle verb *cook up* (Basilico 2008):

(19)   a. the criminals cooked a meal/#an evil scheme
        b. the criminals cooked up an evil scheme

Complex verbs of a different type are Light Verb Constructions, in languages like Japanese, where verbal predicates are expressed by the combination of a light verb *suru* with an appropriate predicate. In Iranian languages, the picture is similar, with two additional factors that make them particularly interesting. Using Farsi to illustrate the above points, there are very few lexical verbs; Complex Predicates (to be discussed in Chapter 4) express all

---

[13] Or, perhaps, a mixed projection (see Chapter 6).

other verbal concepts, via the combination of a non-verbal element (also known as 'preverb') and one of the following fourteen light verbs, from Family (2008):

(20)   *Farsi light verbs*

kærdæn	'do'	keʃidæn	'pull'
ʃodæn	'become'	amædæn	'come'
zædæn	'hit'	aværdæn	'bring'
xordæn	'eat'	bordæn	'take'
dadæn	'give'	ræftæn	'go'
gereftæn	'get'	ændaxtæn	'throw'
daʃtæn	'have'	oftadæn	'fall'

The most exciting case of a language with complex verbs would be Jingulu, an Australian language discussed in Pensalfini (1997) and Baker (2003, 90–4). Jingulu possesses only three verbal elements – 'come', 'go' and 'do/be' – and there are no (other) lexical verbs, unlike Japanese and Farsi, which do possess a few lexical verbs. 'Come', 'go' and 'do/be' in Jingulu may stand as the only verbal predicates in a sentence and they are strictly obligatory; additionally, they are the only necessary elements in a sentence. In order for other verbal concepts to be expressed, one of these three elements must be combined with what looks like a bare root. Here are some examples from Baker (2003, 90–1):

(21)   *Jingulu verbs*
    a. Ya-angku
       3rdsg-will.come
       'He will come.'
    b. Jirrkiji-mindu-wa
       run-1stINCL.DU-will.go
       'You and me will run off.'
    c. Ngaruk   baka-nga-rriyi
       dive   1stsg-will.go
       'I'll dive down.'
    d. Ngaruk   baka-ngayi   arduku
       dive   1stsg-will.do   carefully
       'I'll submerge (something) carefully.'

Pensalfini (1997) argues that 'come', 'go' and 'do/be' are light verbs. I understand that 'light verbs' in this instance can possibly be equated to semi-lexical verbs (see Chapter 4). More concretely, they could be the lexicalization of verbalizers themselves, in the manner of Folli and Harley (2005), who claim that three flavours of v exist, v_{CAUS}, v_{DO}, and v_{BECOME}, each making different types of verbs.[14] This receives support by the differences in transitivity between examples c. and d. in (21), induced by the choice of 'go' versus 'do', the latter inducing transitivity. Baker (2003, 91–4), on the contrary, takes 'come', 'go' and 'do/be' to be inflected auxiliary verbs (like *have* and *be* in English) with roots like *ngaruk* ('dive') in (21) to be the actual verbs themselves. However, I am not convinced that something like *ngaruk* ('dive') in (21) is a verb instead of an acategorial root. Baker's (2003, 91–4) principal argument for the verbal nature of Jingulu roots like *ngaruk* ('dive') is that 'come', 'go' and 'do/be' do not *necessarily* affect transitivity and thematic properties and that the root, rather than 'come', 'go' and 'do/be', determines the verbal predicate's theta grid. This kind of debate is familiar from discussions on Farsi. The opening lines of Folli, Harley and Karimi (2003) are particularly enlightening about how to deal with the question of what part of the complex verb determines what:

> It has been argued in the literature that the argument and event structures of Persian *complex predicates* (CPr), as well as syntactic properties such as control, cannot be simply derived from the lexical specifications of the *nonverbal element* (NV) or the *light verb* (LV) ... In this paper, we show that the event structure of LV is not always the same as the event structure of its heavy counterpart. Furthermore, although LV determines the *agentivity* (*xordan* 'collide' versus *zadan* 'hit') and the eventiveness of the CPr, it fails to completely determine the event structure and the telicity of the CPr. Thus, depending on the NV element, the same LV may occur in different types of event structure.   (Folli, Harley, and Karimi 2003, 100)

Appealing to the Farsi case is valuable, because there is consensus that its complex predicates are made of light verbs and a *non-verbal* element. Nevertheless, both elements *contribute to the properties of the overall complex predicate*. In other words, although Jingulu roots affect the type of the complex predicate's thematic grid, this is no evidence that these roots are verbal. I therefore believe we can adhere to an analysis in the spirit of Pensalfini (1997); after all, even in inflected languages with solid lexical verb paradigms, like Greek, verbs may display an articulated structure in which the verbal or verbalizing element is kept distinct from the acategorial root material (Panagiotidis, Revithiadou and Spyropoulos 2013). At the same time, languages like Jingulu, Japanese and Farsi and many others lend support to the syntactic decomposition approach to lexical categories, which will be described and presented in Chapter 3.

---

[14] More precisely, Jingulu 'come', 'go' and 'do/be' would be the exponence of verbalizers *fused* with Tense heads, as glossed in (21).

2.7   An interim summary: verbs, nouns, roots

After the extensive overview of different flavours of the noun–verb distinction cross-linguistically, we can now revisit the hypotheses laid out in (10).[15]

Tagalog and Riau Indonesian do not seem to constitute cases of grammars where all lexical elements can be used interchangeably in all contexts. Languages claimed to possess a single undifferentiated lexical category and no noun–verb distinction cannot be claimed to have been discovered, at least not yet.

Nootka (pending more in-depth investigation) seems to be a language where all *roots* can be slotted in all category-defining syntactic contexts. In languages like this, evidence is very strong for roots being categorized by their syntactic context, and it makes no sense talking about nouns and verbs in Nootka as distinct word classes: lexical categories are syntactic categories. At this point it is worth remembering Baker's finding that where there is extensive nominalization of verbs (yielding deverbal nouns and mixed projections) and extensive verbalization of nouns (yielding denominal verbs), the verb–noun distinction may appear blurred. Still, this is a red herring: verbs and nouns are real in this language, although they are easy to morphosyntactically recategorize with the mediation of a suitable functional entourage.

In other Salish languages, and many more languages, some roots make better nouns than verbs (the reverse does not seem to hold – see also Chapter 3). Consider the Lillooet Salish example in (18), where 'man' is only a noun, and English roots like *boy*, *ball* and (perhaps) *cat*, all of which give nouns but no underived verbs, or, at least, not very good ones. These are empirical facts to be explained, possibly invoking grammar-external factors.

What about languages where nouns and verbs appear to form solid word classes? One possibility to explore is the following: in grammars where nouns and verbs form solid word classes, this is an illusion of rich morphology. This could be especially true in fusional languages like Romance. Consequently, it is not conceptually necessary for nouns and verbs to belong to different word classes if categorization is a syntactic process. More precisely, word classes like noun and verb could be the result of syntactic derivations and morphological processes and not necessarily constitute two classes of words distinguished by the root that these words are built around. We will look at these topics in detail in the next chapter.

---

[15] The interested reader is referred to the works cited in Baker's (2003) survey for further details and a more in-depth scrutiny of the matter.

2.8 What about adjectives (and adverbs)?

This monograph has so far exclusively discussed nouns and verbs and will continue to do so. Hence, the obvious category missing from the picture is adjectives. The question at this point is what adjectives are and why they are excluded from the present discussion.

I believe that adjectives are not a basic or fundamental word class, as I claim nouns and verbs to be. However, we have not looked at the mechanics of categorization yet, something we will do in Chapter 3. Therefore, in this section I will restrict myself to empirical and quasi-theoretical arguments in order to claim something less ambitious: first, that adjectives do not fall into the same categorial type as nouns and verbs; second, that adjectives are neither the unmarked category nor universal. I will tentatively conclude that adjectives involve more structure than nouns and verbs and that this structure is of quite a different nature to that 'making' nouns and verbs

2.8.1 *Adjectives are unlike nouns and verbs*

The idea that adjectives are not of the same ilk as nouns and verbs already exists as a sort of tacit understanding in a large part of the literature. This understanding stems from a number of descriptions and analyses, according to which there are languages that actually lack the category of adjective, with Dixon (1982) and Schachter (1985) figuring most prominently among them. In the generative literature, Amritavalli and Jayaseelan (2004, 19–20, 29–31) discuss the non-existence of adjectives in Kannada and Malayalam; Hale and Keyser (2002, 13–14) mention that Navajo 'adjectives' are verbs, whereas those in Warlpiri are nouns. Notably, in Baker (2003, 238–63), to which we will return, a whole section is dedicated to arguing *for* the universality of adjectives.

But before looking into the (non-)universality of adjectives, let us first review evidence with respect to a more modest goal – namely, showing that adjectives are qualitatively *different* from nouns and verbs, that they do not belong to the same class. Surprisingly, given his commitment to the opposite thesis, some grounds indicating this difference can be found in Baker (2003, chap. 4). In this chapter of his *Lexical Categories* monograph, Baker boldly argues that adjectives are the *unmarked* lexical category – that is, the word class category used whenever nouns and verbs cannot be used. As reviewed in the previous chapter, Baker (2003) considers nouns to bear referential indices, making them suitable to stand as arguments, and verbs as the only lexical categories that can stand as predicates by themselves – that is, without the mediation of a functional predicator. In this respect, adjectives, being unmarked, are restricted to two positions: (i) predicate positions, *with* the mediation of a functional predicator *Pred*, just like nouns and other syntactic constituents, yielding examples like *The flag is red*; *I painted the wall green*, and (ii) modifying positions: *The red flag*; *A house with green walls*.

In order to formalize adjectives as the unmarked lexical category, Baker (2003, chap. 4) is restricted by his two-membered privative feature system (i.e., [N] and [V]), so he has to argue that adjectives do not bear any categorial specification – that is, *no categorial feature* whatsoever. This claim has at least two consequences:

    a. They have no 'special characteristics' of their own as a category (Baker 2003, chap. 4), unlike nouns and their relationship with determiners and 'counting' or verbs and their argument structure and their relation with tense;[16]

    b. As practically admitted in Baker (2003, chap. 5), adjectives are essentially identical to roots: their categorial specification is precisely the lack of any categorial specification, if category is encoded by features like [N] and [V].

The above entail at least that adjectives are different from nouns and verbs. Of course, in Baker's theory they are different because they are the unmarked, basic lexical category. Even if this basic intuition is wrong, as I will propose, the fact remains that adjectives are different: either because they are categorially featureless roots (which I will disagree with) or because they are not a fundamental and universal lexical category like nouns and verbs (which seems to be going in the right direction).

2.8.2   *Adjectives are not unmarked*

Baker makes strong claims about adjectives which, as I postulated above, set them apart from the other two categories, nouns and verbs, one way or another. However, can it be the case that adjectives are unmarked, actually identical to free roots – despite the claim in Baker (2003, 269) that free uncategorized roots do not exist?[17]

Baker's claims, as we have seen, have two consequences: that adjectives are the unmarked lexical category and that they are identical to roots. Baker (2003,

---

[16] This decision is of course reminiscent of Déchaine's (1993) treatment of prepositions. See Section 1.3 in Chapter 1.

[17] After all, what would categorize a root into an adjective if no categorial features for adjectives exist?

230) calls them the 'elsewhere case' among lexical categories. Now, if adjectives are indeed the unmarked lexical category, expressing, say, pure properties, then we would expect

a. adjectives to be *universal*: if categorially unmarked roots surface as the category adjective, then all languages should possess this category, even more so than verbs: after all, in Baker's system, a language without [V] on lexical elements could potentially exist, having *all* predication mediated by the functional predicator *Pred*;
b. adjectives not to have any 'special' characteristics of their own whatsoever.

However, a lot of work on adjectives seems to be pointing in the opposite direction and evidence that adjectives are not a universal category is abundant. Besides those discussed in Dixon (1982), Schachter (1985), Hale and Keyser (2002, 13–14) and Amritavalli and Jayaseelan (2004), more languages seem not to possess an adjective category, let alone one that is the elsewhere case. If adjectives are indeed the unmarked category, what are we to make of Chichewa which has six adjectives (Baker 2003, 246–9) or of Hausa which is reported to possess no more than a dozen? And there also exist languages without an adjective category; in these languages, three scenarios are typically attested.

First, in languages like Japanese, the 'adjective category' is split in two (Miyagawa 1987) and adjective-like words behave as if they belong to two distinct classes with precious little in common. See also the discussion of Japanese 'adjectival nouns' in Iwasaki (1999, chap. 4).

In Korean (and Navajo) adjectives behave as a subclass of the verb category. Citing Haspelmath (2001, 16542), 'in Korean, property concepts inflect for tense and mood like verbs in predication structures [see (22) below], and they require a relative suffix ... when they modify a noun [see (23) below], again like verbs'.[18] The examples below (Haspelmath 2001, 16542) illustrate the situation:

(22)   a. salam-i   mek-ess-ta
          person-NOM   eat-PAST-DECLARATIVE
          'The person ate.'

---

[18] It is true that Korean property verbs do not take the present-tense suffix *–nun*, but I am not sure this is enough to make them a lexical category on a par with nouns and verbs, as opposed to a subclass of verbs or a verbal category.

b. san-i   noph-ess-ta
   hill-NOM   high-PAST-DECLARATIVE
   'The hill was high.'

(23)   a. mek-un   salam
          eat-RELATIVE   person
          'A person who ate.'
       b. noph-un   san
          high-RELATIVE hill
          'A high hill.'

Turning to Dravidian languages, they are also analysed as not possessing adjectives distinct from nouns incorporated into Kase, which typically surfaces as dative (Amritavalli and Jayaseelan 2004, 19–20, 29–31); this is illustrated below for Kannada and Malayalam:[19]

(24)   a. raama   udda-kke   idd-aane   *Kannada*
          Rama.NOM   height-DAT   be-3SG
       b. raaman-@   uyaram   uND@   *Malayalam*
          Raman- DAT   height   is
          'Rama(n) is tall.'

Chichewa also seems to overwhelmingly use nouns in the way other languages use adjectives.

Turning to languages with a distinct adjectival category that constitutes an open class, this does not possess any of the hallmarks of an unmarked lexical category, let alone of a category that is posited to be the direct manifestation of a root without any categorial features. In Romance, Germanic and Greek a large number of adjectives, if not the majority, are derived from nouns and verbs, as opposed to being derived directly from roots. A good case in point is that of Slavic, which makes extensive and productive derivation of adjectives via suffixes for a number of purposes – for example, for the resulting adjectives to function as possessives in lieu of simple genitives. This is elegantly exemplified in Russian, as described in Valgina, Rosental and Fomina (2002, sec. 145), which the review below follows closely.[20]

---

[19] Both examples are from Amritavalli and Jayaseelan (2004, 29), who also make the conjecture that 'there is … an implicational relationship between the absence of adjectives and the prevalence of the dative experiencer construction'. As in Chichewa, there are in Kannada 'a few indisputable underived adjectives, such as *oLLeya* "good"'.

[20] I am grateful to Svetlana Karpava and Olga Kvasova for discussing the Russian facts with me and for lending me their native speaker intuitions. Karpava kindly translated Valgina, Rosental

Russian has 'possessive adjectives' which indicate a possessor; 'typically, possessive adjectives are formed from animate nouns, with the help of the suffixes *–in, –nin, –n-ij, –ov, –ev, –sk-ij*' (Valgina, Rosental and Fomina 2002, sec. 145):

(25)   *Some Russian possessive adjectives*

Noun	Possessive adjective	Meaning
Liza	Lizin	Liza's
brat	bratnin	brother's
doch	dochernin	daughter's
otec	otcov	father's
Vladislav	Vladislavlev	Vladislav's

What is important here is that these adjectives indicate *referential possessors*, not properties. In other words, 'Ljuba's book' can be expressed either with a genitive possessor, as *kniga Ljubij* (book Ljuba.GEN), or with a possessive adjective derived from the name 'Ljuba': *ljubina kniga* (Svetlana Karpava, personal communication, April 2013). In a restriction reminiscent of those by which Saxon genitives in English abide, Russian possessive adjectives 'that are formed from inanimate nouns are very rare' (Valgina, Rosental and Fomina 2002, sec. 145). Moreover, they are better with some first names, odd or awkward with others, impossible with non-Russian names or surnames – and so on (Svetlana Karpava, personal communication, April 2013; Olga Kvasova, personal communication, April 2013). Finally, adjectives can be ambiguous between a possessive and an attributive reading.

(26)   *Ambiguous interpretation*

volchij	hvost	volchij	appetit
wolf.ADJ	tail	wolf.ADJ	appetite
'The/a wolf's tail'		'Wolfish appetite'	
		(cf. 'Hungry like a wolf')	

Generally speaking, it seems that adjectives in most languages involve more rather than fewer structural layers. For instance, in Romance, Greek and Slavic modifying (and also predicative) adjectives are obligatorily embedded within the functional structures that trigger concord and nominal agreement morphology. What is also worth noting here is that the other elements, besides

and Fomina (2002, sec. 145), from which examples are drawn, as well as from Karpava (personal communication, April 2013) and from Kvasova (personal communication, April 2013).

adjectives, that display concord with the noun inside a DP are all *functional* elements: quantifiers, demonstratives, possessives and articles. This is starkly illustrated in Modern Greek.

(27)   *Concord*

    a. olus   aftus   tus   neus   typus

       all.M.ACC.PL these.M.ACC.PL the.M.ACC.PL new.M.ACC.PL type.M.ACC.PL

       'All these new types.'

    b. oli   afti   i   nea   sodia

       all.F.ACC.SG this.F.ACC.SG the.F.ACC.SG new.F.ACC.SG crop.F.ACC.SG

       'All of this new harvest.'

Adjectives inside a DP are both dependent, agreement-wise, on nouns and actually often resemble quantifiers, demonstratives and possessives. I think that the above indicates that even in languages where adjectives look like a bona fide lexical category, they are indeed very hard to be taken to belong to the same type of lexical category as nouns and verbs.

Returning to the matter of the morphological complexity of adjectives themselves, naturally, morphological complexity on its own does not necessarily entail that adjectives as a category are non-basic: after all, deriving nouns from verbs (e.g., *place-ment*) and adjectives (e.g., *red-ness*) and deriving verbs from nouns (e.g., *en-shrine*) and adjectives (e.g., *trivial-ize*) is standard in a large number of languages, without this making 'noun' and 'verb' non-basic. However, there are two important consequences of morphological complexity when it comes to adjectives.

First, and as mentioned above, very few adjectives in Romance, Germanic and Greek are underived, leading us to the implication that Adjective is definitely not the unmarked category, especially one co-extensive with roots. Second, and far more problematic for Baker's (2003) approach: if adjectives are not marked for *any* categorial feature whatsoever, how are adjective-making derivational affixes marked?[21] For instance, if –*y* attaches to nouns to make them adjectives (e.g., *cloud-y*, *milk-y*, *water-y* etc.), what categorial feature is borne by –*y*? If none, how does the category change from noun (marked with [N]) to adjective? I think this is a very serious problem for any approach that takes adjectives to be categorial feature-free and, by extension, to approaches arguing adjectives to be the unmarked lexical category, of the same ilk as nouns and verbs.

---

[21] This is precisely Déchaine's (1993) argument for treating prepositions as not encoding any categorial features; see Section 2.9.

On top of their customary morphological 'heaviness', adjectives are also hardly unmarked in all other ways. Crucially, adjectives do seem to have *distinctive* characteristics as a category, but they look as if they possess their own functional category – namely, Degree. Work by Corver (1997) and Neeleman, van de Koot and Doetjes (2004) is particularly enlightening in this respect. Neeleman, van de Koot and Doetjes (2004) claim that English possesses two classes of degree expressions. Class 1 degree expressions are specific to adjectives:

(28)   *Class 1 Degree expressions*

Class 1 Degree expressions (*very, as, too, that, how*) c-select an Adjectival Phrase (AP), which they *must* precede: they take the AP as a complement. This suggests that Class 1 Degree *heads* are members of the adjectival projection line, possibly of the so-called Extended Projection of A.[22] Class 1 Degree expressions need *much* (a dummy A) in order to combine with non-APs: [[$_{DegP}$ Deg *much*] [XP]]; they tolerate neither topicalization nor freer linearization options – something to be expected if they take APs as complements *qua* heads which are members of the projection line of A. Class 1 Degree expressions can be claimed to be to the category A what D is to N and T to V.

In contrast, Class 2 Degree expressions (*more, less, enough, a little, a good deal*) have no c-selectional requirements and they also combine with Preposition Phrases (PPs), Verb Phrases (VPs) and so on, apparently as adjunct modifiers:

(29)   *Class 2 Degree expressions*

Class 2 Degree expressions, being phrasal adjuncts, may possess internal structure and they do not need any gradable predicate in order to modify the XP they are adjoined to. As we might expect, topicalization of Class 2 Degree expressions is possible, as well as their freer linearization.

A final point is this: basic nouns seem to be relatively simplex in structure. Verbs are usually not, but verbal predicates can be expressed – in languages like Japanese, Farsi and even Jingulu – by using a *light verb* plus something

---

[22] Grimshaw (1991, 2003).

else. On the contrary, *light adjectives*, making adjectival predicates and/or modifiers, do not exist. I think that this additional fact also seriously points to adjectives being not of the same ilk as nouns and verbs.

Concluding this short preliminary discussion on adjectives: they do not seem to be either identical to roots or universal (as plain roots, at least); they tend to be morphologically complex and they possess their own dedicated functional head, (Class 1) Degree, as part of their projection line.[23] When they appear as modifiers, they undergo concord precisely like functional elements such as quantifiers, demonstratives, possessives and articles. In any event, they stand apart from N and V.

2.8.3 *Adverbs are not a simplex category*

If adjectives are not of the noun and verb ilk, say because they are simplex uncategorized roots or because they are parts of speech complexly derived from nouns and verbs with the mediation of functional structure, it goes without saying that adverbs are certainly not candidates for a basic lexical category either. Of course, most languages do not visibly distinguish between adjectives and adverbs. In any case, the answer to what adverbs are depends on our story for adjectives, as even languages that distinguish adverbs from adjectives allow both to be modified by Class 1 Degree expressions – allegedly heads of the adjectival projection line/Extended Projection. This is acknowledged by Baker (2003, 230–7), who takes adverbs to be adjectives incorporated into an abstract noun, one whose exponence in English is the suffix –*ly*.[24] Recall also the well-known fact from Romance that adjectives becoming adverbs are in the feminine, as if the adverbial suffix –*ment(e)* is (still) a feminine noun with which they agree: for example, Spanish *guapa-mente* not **guapo-mente*. In other words, the morphologically simplex and apparently basic character of adverbs like *well* should not misguide us to consider the whole category on a par with nouns and verbs. Again, the fact that in some Indo-European languages adverbs are a word class tells us something about how Morphology works in these languages and not about adverbs as an independent lexical category. This is a lesson we can extend to adjectives and, almost certainly, to adpositions.

---

[23] The view that Class 1 Degree expressions are specific to adjectives will be qualified and revised in Chapter 5.

[24] Corver (2005), more reasonably in my view, takes –*ly* to be a copular element. This perhaps ties in nicely with the Davidsonian insights in Larson (1998).

2.9 The trouble with adpositions

'Adposition' is the cover term used to include *prepositions* and *postpositions* (typically in head-final languages like Korean, Turkish etc.). Adpositions are absent from the original feature system in Chomsky (1970) and were added later, to form the so-called 'Amherst system', filling in the [−N][−V] gap in it (see Chapter 1). Adpositions have been the focus of a lot of work and of varying and broad-ranging analyses. Besides having been treated as lexical items (Déchaine 1993), they have been assimilated to Complementizers (Emonds 1985, 156–7) or to instances of Kase (Baker 2003, 303–25). Other detailed treatments argue for the Adposition category to involve complex structure (actually, to *be* complex structures), akin to argument structure, as in Svenonius (2007, 2008) and, in a different way, Botwinik-Rotem and Terzi (2008) and Terzi (2010).

Although in most treatments adpositions are usually understood either as a lexical category or as functional elements, there are three reasonable ways to go. The first is to split them into two categories, a functional one and a lexical one; the second is to treat them as a hybrid category; and the third is to hypothesize that they are phrasally complex structures, involving both functional elements and lexical, possibly nominal, material.

As far as splitting the 'category' Adposition in two, looking at English data we can easily consider elements like *on, at, to, in, of, by* and so on to behave like functional elements. Perhaps equally easily, *over, above, front, behind, while, during* and so on can be understood to behave like lexical elements.

An approach acknowledging the Janus-like behaviour of adpositions, based on their hybrid behaviour in West Germanic, is that of van Riemsdijk (1998a, 31), where he is led to propose that (i) 'adpositions be characterized as [−N, −V]', as in the Amherst system, while (ii) 'they should . . . be considered (extended) projections of nouns, at least when they are transitive'; (iii) the possibility that 'there are also functional prepositions remain[s] fully valid', but (iv) in many cases adpositions are semi-lexical heads.

The complex structure solution consists of attributing each of the distinct properties of adpositions to a separate functional or lexical component participating in a complex adpositional structure. Such a solution is, for instance, the only one that makes sense in the case of Greek 'complex prepositions', where lexical and functional components thereof and the restrictions ruling their relative positions are plainly visible: see Botwinik-Rotem and Terzi (2008) and Terzi (2010).

However, there exists an added dimension of complexity – namely, that the selfsame form can sometimes act as functional and sometimes as lexical.

Consider the following examples from Panagiotidis (2003a), where the form *of* can behave both as lexical (a. examples) and as functional (b. examples):

(30)   a. My favourite picture is [of the Vice-Chancellor].
       b. * My favourite student is [of Chemistry].

(31)   a. [A photo _] was found [of the Vice-Chancellor drinking absinthe].
       b. *[A student _] was jailed [of Chemistry].

(32)   a. A (*Vice-Chancellor) picture (of the Vice Chancellor).
       b. A (Chemistry) student (of Chemistry).

Lexical *of* behaves like a θ-assigning lexical head and its phrasal projection does not have to be adjacent to the N, as shown in (30)a.; it can also extrapose, as in (31)a.[25] The reverse is true for functional *of* and its projection: its licensing depends on whether the N *student* in the b. examples can assign a θ role to it, as the alternation between *Chemistry student* and *student of Chemistry* in (32) also suggests. It is unclear how this state of affairs can be captured in a satisfactory and non-stipulative way in an analysis of adpositions as complex structures. However, both the solution of splitting the category Adposition in two and the one assuming adpositions to be a hybrid category in the best of cases give the impression of merely restating the facts at a more abstract level.

Déchaine (1993, 32–6), on her way to arguing for adpositions as the elsewhere lexical category, observes that there is no English compound headed by an adposition. So, although adpositions (or, perhaps, particles) may be part of a compound like *up-root*, *under-dog* or *over-cast*, they can never be the head of a compound, unlike nouns, verbs and adjectives. Her second generalization is twofold: on the one hand, there is *no* affix that derives adpositions; on the other hand, very few derivational affixes attach to adpositions. Déchaine (1993, 33) lists English words derived from an 'adpositional' stem: *off-ing*, *about-ness*, *under-ling*, *upp-ity*. However, she argues adpositions to be a lexical category, and not a closed-class either. At this point, we could say that adpositions are indeed not word classes but complex and articulated syntactic structures in which certain, one or more, lexical items are visible.

In this monograph, we will assume without any further discussion that, despite all the complications, adpositions are complex structures à la Svenonius (2007, 2008), which include both clearly defined functional heads like

---

[25] Oga (2001) independently reached the conclusion that there are two types of *of*. Tremblay (1996) shows exactly the same to be the case with *with*.

Kase, Figure, Ground, Path and so on and lexical material, possibly of a nominal nature, in the respective specifiers. So, oversimplifying, particles such as *at*, *in* and the like could be the realizations of a projection that relates two spaces and/or time intervals; such projections would be part of a larger functional complex fleshing out this and similar relations: 'heavy' prepositions of a nominal and/or adverbial flavour, such as *front*, *under*, *after* and so on, would be sitting in dedicated specifiers as arguments or modifiers. If this sketch is on the right track, adpositional projections would be akin to the system of functional structure supporting and realizing the expression of verbal arguments in Hale and Keyser (2002), Pylkkänen (2008), Ramchand (2008) and elsewhere. Alternatively, adpositional projections could be relational, like Tense structure as envisaged by Stowell (2007), a claim that is epigrammatically stated in Pesetsky and Torrego (2004, 506): 'the category P[reposition] is actually a kind of T[ense]'.

2.10 Conclusion

First of all, the noun–verb distinction is indeed universal: nouns and verbs are distinct syntactic categories and, in a large number of languages, they are also distinct word classes. Two examples of languages that have been claimed to possess a single undifferentiated lexical category, Tagalog and Riau Indonesian, turn out to actually make a distinction, at least between nouns and verbs. On top of this, and with the possible exception of Nootka, there are roots that can only become nouns, not verbs. A syntactic categorization approach, correctly calibrated, should capture this, together with the universal presence of nouns and verbs.

When we say that verbs are universal we do not necessarily refer to those exemplified by latinate verbs in English – for example, *donate*. Single-word verbs in inflecting languages already contain a lot of structure, structure that is actually visible in such languages as Japanese, Farsi and Jingulu: these and other languages combine a light verb with some lexical material to yield complex verbal predicates. The essential point here is that verbs, including light verbs, are universal. In Chapter 4 I will actually argue that it is v heads, verbalizers, that are universal.

Despite what surface descriptions may suggest (confounded and misled either by morphological complexity or by the radical absence of familiar morphological distinctions), verbs and nouns cannot be used interchangeably. Repeating the initial point here: roots may be inserted in a number of grammatical contexts categorizing them, but categorized nouns and verbs are not freely distributed, neither do they collapse into a single undifferentiated 'predicate' or 'lexical' category. In the following chapter I will argue that roots are categorized syntactically and in Chapter 4 that categorization is essential for roots to participate in syntactic derivations – explaining why categorized roots, as nouns or verbs, are universal.

We also looked at adjectives, which will be largely excluded from the discussion that follows, and we reached two tentative conclusions: adjectives are not the unmarked, elsewhere lexical category and they are not of the same ilk as nouns and verbs – and nowhere are they as fundamental and/or universal. On the contrary, they tend to be derived, they share a lot of characteristics with nominal functional heads, they can sometimes even stand in for possessive genitives, they tend to go either the way of verbs (Korean), of nouns (Chichewa, Dravidian), or both. Adverbs are possibly the result of adjectives being associated with even more syntactic structure.

Adpositions are still a kind of mystery. Although nouns, verbs and adjectives form word classes in a number of languages, adpositions usually resist inclusion in a single class. Moreover, when not manifestly pure functional heads, adpositions appear to be the (partial) lexicalization of complex functional structures that may host lexical material. The least we can say about adpositions is that they are not part of a $[\pm N]$ $[\pm V]$ system, not all of them at any rate.

Having established the fundamental character of nouns and verbs, which we will interpret in Chapter 4, we first need to discuss syntactic decomposition and syntactic categorization.

3 Syntactic decomposition and categorizers

3.1 Introduction

As already stated in the first chapter, the approach to category in this monograph is committed to conceiving of word classes as encoding different categorial features. These features are to be understood not as taxonomic ones creating word classes of a morphological nature – for example, like declension and conjugation classes – but as genuine LF-interpretable features, as instructions to the Conceptual–Intentional Systems. Put differently, we will be very serious in taking [N] and [V] to be ordinary syntactic features: interpretable, with uninterpretable versions, triggering syntactic operations and imposing syntactic constraints. In order to do this, we will embrace an approach to categorization which takes it to be a syntactic process. Arguing for syntactic categorization will enable us to work with categorial features as bona fide syntactic features and also to account for cross-linguistic typological data – for example, categorization behaviours such as the ones outlined in the previous chapter.

The following section poses the question of how words are made, of where morphology is located. The point of view assumed is that of a syntactician seeking to understand the workings of categorial features, and lexical and functional categories more specifically. After a brief and very sketchy critique of lexicalism the Distributed Morphology take on word-making is introduced. The following two sections, 3.3 and 3.4, zoom in on some details of this approach – that is, how Distributed Morphology can explain idiosyncrasies in the meaning of morphologically complex words, if all structure-building, including word-building, is done in syntax, a system typically conceived of as yielding compositional interpretations of the items it combines. Section 3.5 examines conversions in order to reveal how zero-derived verbs can have very different derivational histories, being either the product of root categorization, like the verb *hammer*, or of recategorization, like the denominal verb *tape*. Section 3.6 introduces the very basics of Phase theory in a simplified form and relates its implementation of cyclicity in grammar with respect to how we can explain the idiosyncratic character of some morphologically complex words. Roots are identified as the source of idiosyncrasy, and they are discussed in detail in Section 3.7, while in Section 3.8 we deal with the question of why 'word level' syntax does not appear to be anywhere near as productive as 'phrasal' syntax. In Section 3.9, we look at a different problem: we closely examine possibly the most convincing case for roots actually carrying categorial specifications. A concluding section finishes the chapter.

3.2   Where are words made?

The approach to syntactic categorization and syntactic decomposition of the main lexical categories 'noun' and 'verb' that we follow here is framed within Distributed Morphology: Halle and Marantz (1993), Marantz (1997, 2000, 2006), Harley and Noyer (1999, 2000) and elsewhere.[1] More specifically, Hale and Keyser (1993, 2002) introduced a *syntactic approach* to the construction of lexical categories, with an emphasis on verbs; the distinct version thereof developed in Marantz (1997, 2000) has gained considerable currency in the past ten years or so. The general outline of the Marantzian approach is that lexical categories such as 'noun', 'verb' and 'adjective' are not products of the combination of categorial features with roots in a lexicon: categories are not specified on lexical items in a pre-syntactic lexicon. On the contrary, roots are inserted bare in syntax, where the assignment of roots to categories takes place as a process of embedding the latter within categorizing projections: thus, categorization is a *syntactic process*; it is the syntactic environment that turns roots into 'nouns', 'verbs' or 'adjectives'. This is achieved by inserting roots inside the complement of *categorizers* – a nominalizer (n), a verbalizer (v) and an adjectivizer (a). On top of this, a categorizer may recategorize – that is, change the category of – an already categorized element: for example, in the cases of denominal verbs and deverbal nouns (e.g., *colony* → *colonize*, *colonize* → *colonization*).

---

[1] Although the analysis here is couched within Distributed Morphology, I believe that any consistently realizational morphological framework can be employed equally well, as long as it incorporates

    a. a separationist distinction (and/or a dissociation) between syntactic feature structures and their morphological exponence (Beard 1995) and,

    b. syntax-all-the-way-down, as in Marantz (1997) and Harley and Noyer (2000) – that is, taking the same combinatorial mechanism to lie behind both word-building and sentence-building.

As already noted in Chapter 1 (Section 1.4.1), where some references are cited, there exists an extensive body of research within the Distributed Morphology framework refining the mechanisms and categories at work as well as the empirical consequences of syntactic categorization, also exploring their implications from a cross-linguistic point of view. In the following chapter we will proceed to enrich the Distributed Morphology mechanism of syntactic categorization through categorizers by incorporating concepts and findings from Baker (2003), being indebted at the same time to the insights expressed in Langacker (1987) and Anderson (1997). More specifically, we will try to see what makes the categorizer n different from the categorizer v (we have already argued that adjectives are different from both, anyway), how n and v work and how they are interpreted. As should be clear by now, in order to do this, emphasis will be placed on categorial features, viewed as LF-interpretable features.

Before we can discuss the syntactic decomposition of category or, alternatively, syntactic categorization, we need to have a theory of word-making. If one abides by lexicalism and argues that (some or all) words come ready-made from a lexicon, then the behaviour of categorial features as syntactic ones is hardly evident or necessary: the noun–verb distinction could as well be one like that between hyponyms and basic category terms. Therefore, if we need a precise and falsifiable theoretical account of how and where nouns and verbs are made, we need first to answer the questions of how and where words are made.

It is conceded even in certain lexicalist models, the so-called 'weak lexicalist' models, that some word-making must be done in the syntax; see Baker (2003, sec. 5.2) and the discussion of Wasow (1977) and Dubinsky and Simango (1996) in Marantz (2000). This would mean that derivational morphology is not handled exclusively by the lexicon or by a morphological component separate from syntax. Indeed, some derivational morphemes must be attached on their host via a syntactic process. This renders word-making a non-unitary process and essentially falsifies most versions of the Lexical Integrity Principle, in that syntax is *needed* for the creation of at least *some* word structure.[2] The way Baker (2003, sec. 5.2) summarizes the resulting state of affairs, his version of weak lexicalism, is given in (1):

---

[2] Lieber and Scalise (2007) provide a very informative and thorough overview of the Lexical Integrity Principle and the different flavours of lexicalism.

(1)   *Word-making*

	Lexical/ 'morphological' word-making	Syntactic word-making
'Raw material'	any category *or* acategorial roots	a particular category
Meaning	idiosyncratic meaning	predictable meaning
Productivity	limited	full (allomorphy aside)
Examples	*–ful* attachment, compounding	*–ness* attachment

In the picture adumbrated in the table in (1) words can be created in three distinct ways (or, using a more Y-model-oriented metaphor, in three different *places*). First, there are roots already coming from the lexicon with a categorial specification. Thus, some nouns and verbs are *roots* specified for [N] and [V], as nouns and verbs, and their category is learned; it is *memorized*. Examples of such roots categorized in the lexicon would include *cat, dog, coffee, bake, run, kill* and so on. Second, some nouns and verbs are created via lexical word-making, via derivational morphology of a lexical nature – say, by combining roots with nominal ([N]) and verbal ([V]) affixes through non-syntactic, morphological processes: for example, *quant-ify, cert-ify, cert-ifi-cate, free-dom, geek-dom*, the denominal zero conversion giving the verb *water* and so on. Finally, syntactic word-making is also possible. Therefore, some nouns and verbs are assembled during the syntactic derivation by means of syntactic processes that combine nouns, verbs and adjectives with *category-changing* syntactic heads (which also may surface as affixes). Examples of this would be gerunds (*train-ing*) and adjectives like *kind-ness, bleak-ness* and so on, where *–ness* behaves like a nominalizing syntactic head according to the criteria in (1).

Weak lexicalism, exemplified by the picture presented in the table above, is a response to empirical necessity: strong lexicalism fails to capture important generalizations because it assigns all word-making to the lexicon or to the purported morphological combinatorial component. At the same time, weak lexicalism is not particularly desirable from a conceptual viewpoint, as there are now three distinct ways of making words; it is also empirically problematic as Halle and Marantz (1993) and Marantz (1997) discuss at some length.

Until the mid-nineties, most syntactic analyses in the major generative frameworks would assume that syntax manipulates words and/or morphemes. For instance, in most of Chomsky's work, such as in Chomsky (1957, 1995) (to name but two landmark cases), the syntactic derivation manipulates words and inflectional morphemes. Words would be constructed in some pre-syntactic morphological component and then be handed over to the syntactic derivation. However, in the nineties, syntactic theory took a turn in a new direction: first, it began to seriously consider the type of features and the requirements imposed on syntactic structures by the interfaces between the Language Faculty and the Articulatory–Perceptual systems, and between the Language Faculty and the Conceptual–Intentional systems. At the same time, syntactic theory paid close and serious attention to Economy of derivation considerations, with milestones such as Chomsky (1995, chap. 2), Collins (1997) and Fox (2000). The convergence of the above two research paths led a number of formal linguists to reconceive syntax as a system that optimally links two extra-linguistic systems: Articulatory–Perceptual and Conceptual–Intentional; Brody (1995) is an exemplar of both this drive towards Economy and of the endeavour to drastically eliminate superfluous levels of representation in the Language Faculty. The positing of principles such as Full Interpretation (Chomsky 1995) and the elaboration of the possible ways in which interface needs drive and/or shape syntax are indicative of this reconceptualization, nowadays termed 'minimalist'.

This turn towards 'virtual conceptual necessity' (Chomsky 1995, 169) made syntacticians more mindful of the place and the role of Morphology within the Language Faculty and of its precise relation and interaction with syntax. Beard (1995) and Halle and Marantz (1993) proved very influential in this context, as more and more syntacticians had to admit that syntax per se (or 'narrow syntax') cannot possibly manipulate fully formed words, or even morphemes, as pairs of sound and meaning. After all, words and morphemes contain both phonological and morphological features (such as declension and conjugation features) that are irrelevant for the syntactic derivation. In addition, lexical words carry descriptive content ('denotation'), which is irrelevant for narrow syntax. Given the well-established thesis known as the Autonomy of Syntax (Newmeyer 1998, chap. 2 and 3), the syntactic derivation is oblivious both to the morphophonological properties and to the meaning of the lexical items it manipulates. For instance, whether a verb in its past tense is regular (*play-ed*) or irregular (*ate*) is certainly of no consequence to syntax: either way it will syntactically behave in exactly the same way. Similarly, what matters when it comes to a noun is a [number:plural] feature, not whether it is expressed as a */-z/* plural or as an irregular form, like *children*.

One way to capture the above state of affairs is to posit that syntax manipulates roots and morphosyntactic *features*, rather than fully formed words or morphemes. Phonological features and, indeed, morphological forms would then be inserted *after* syntax, by a morphological component on the way to the interface with the Articulatory–Perceptual systems. The theories advocating the above state of affairs are *realizational* or *separational* morphological theories (see also footnote 1). One of these realizational frameworks, one tailored to the understanding of syntax as a derivational system, too, is Distributed Morphology.

According to Distributed Morphology, there is no such thing as lexical word-building: all forms (called 'Vocabulary Items') are inserted after syntax. Indeed, it is a syntax-all-the-way-down (see footnote 1) framework: the same combinatorial mechanism, syntax, responsible for phrase- and sentence-building, is also responsible for building words. Hence, all words are created syntactically.

At first sight, relegating all word-building to syntax is equally problematic with strong lexicalism: if strong lexicalism fails to capture important generalizations such as the ones outlined in (1), then perhaps syntax-all-the-way-down cannot explain the non-compositional and idiosyncratic character of (very many) morphologically complex words. The dichotomy between compositionality and productivity vis-à-vis idiosyncrasy and non-productivity can be captured in (1) because (at least) two distinct mechanisms are involved in word-making: a disciplined, compositional, predictable and fully productive syntactic one for the former and an arbitrary, idiosyncratic, non-productive lexical–morphological one for the latter. The kinds of words each one yields according to the table in (1) are therefore quite different: the relation of *rest-less-ness* to *rest-less* and *rest* is very different from that of *necess-ity* to *necess-ary* (and **necess* does not even exist as a word).

However, different 'ways' of making words do not necessarily entail different mechanisms (or different 'places') of word-making. In order to explain the differences between 'lexical' and 'syntactic' word-making within a syntax-all-the-way-down framework such as Distributed Morphology, first we need to focus on the meaning idiosyncrasies of 'lexical' word-making.

3.3   Fewer idiosyncrasies: argument structure is syntactic structure

A key argument against having syntax create all words, including simplex nouns like *cat*, is idiosyncrasy of meaning. It is too often the case that two words – say, a noun and a verb – deriving from the same root have completely different meanings and, certainly, these meanings cannot be related to each other through compositional processes, as one typically expects from the interpretation of syntactic output. Idiosyncrasy of meaning of words deriving from the same word is actually one of the arguments in Panagiotidis (2005) *against* the syntactic decomposition of nouns and verbs.

Let us look at a sample of verbs which are seemingly idiosyncratically related with corresponding nouns and adjectives, basing this on the line of inquiry inaugurated by Levin (1993), and loosely following Levin and Rappaport-Hovav (2005, 68–75):

(2)

Verb	Verb meaning	Type
sweat	*make/exude sweat*	
push *x*	*give x a push*	
clear *x*	*make x clear*	change of state verb
open *x*	*make x open*	change of state verb
box *x*	*put x in a box*	Location verb
butter *x*	*put butter on x*	Locatum verb
brush *y*	*put x on y with a brush*	instrumental verb

The picture is quite telling: there is no single relation between a noun and a verb. So, the verb *sweat* means 'make sweat' but the verb *butter* does not mean 'make butter'; the verb *box* means 'put in a box' but in the verb *brush* the root BRUSH is about the instrument of applying *x* on a surface *y* – and so on. In other words: there is a diverse number of types of verbs when it comes to the relation they have with co-radical nouns and adjectives. As Levin (1993) points out, these different types of verbs are systematic; they are most likely the result of where the verbal root appears in the argument structure of the verb (Hale and Keyser 2002). Thus, once we have a closer look, we realize that there is more regularity in the possible meanings of noun–verb pairs than is initially apparent. Broadly speaking, the root in the verbs in (2) behaves as a direct object in *sweat* and *push* and as a predicate designating an end state in change of state verbs like *clear* and *open*. Equally interestingly, in Location verbs (e.g., *box*) the root behaves something like the object of a Preposition Phrase, designating the background. In Locatum verbs (e.g., *butter*), however, the root behaves like the subject of a PP, the figure to be placed against a background. Finally, in an instrumental verb like *brush* the root acts as a manner adjunct, an instrument adjunct, more precisely.

One issue that can be noted already is the complexity of some verbs' argument structure: if we are to generate such structures 'morphologically', we must make sure we do not gratuitously duplicate the workings of syntax or, at least, those mechanisms familiar from the workings of phrasal syntax. For instance, it is very interesting that change of state verbs seem to embed a small clause consisting of the object *x* of the verb and the end state predicate, and that the end state predicate is the root that 'names' – to echo Harley (2005b) – the verb. The argument structure of an instrument verb such as *brush* seems to be even more complex: there, the root naming the verb is the instrument, the modifying adjunct. Moreover, the surface direct object of the verb *brush* sets the background: for example, we *brush the roast thoroughly (with a honey and mustard mix)* but we do not #*brush a honey and mustard mix thoroughly* although we can *brush a honey and mustard mix on the roast thoroughly*; such structural alterations strongly suggest that displacement of the syntactic sort is at play.

A second, and even more vital, point is that syntactic terminology like 'subjects', 'objects', 'adjuncts', 'predicates' turns out to be quite useful when talking about the position of a root within the verb's argument structure. Briefly, and following the lead in Hale and Keyser (1993, 2002), we can claim that different argument structures are actually different syntactic structures. Idiosyncrasy is only apparent, as the different types of verbs like those in (2) – and many more – boil down to where the root is to be found within the argument structure of the verb: that is, inside a bona fide syntactic structure. In this respect, we are justified in using syntactic terminology to discuss argument structure because it looks like (such) verbs contain some *hidden syntax*, what Hale and Keyser (1993) call *L-syntax* and Ramchand (2008) calls *First Phase Syntax*. Harley (2005b) and Marantz (2005) explain in considerable detail how to analyse verbs in this way, within a syntactic decomposition framework that embraces a realizational–separationist view on the syntax–morphology relation – that is, Distributed Morphology.

3.4   There are still idiosyncrasies, however

Showing that *some* lexical differences can be reduced to systematic argument structure patterns, which, in turn, can be conceived of as syntactic structures explains away a great deal of idiosyncrasy. However, this move hardly eliminates idiosyncratic readings from co-radical noun–verb pairs. Consider some well-known noun–verb pairs like the following:[3]

(3)   *deed–do, trial–try, action–act, revolution–revolve*

(4)   *chair–chair, ship–ship, egg–egg, book–book, castle–castle*[4]

---

[3] We are not looking at the whole panorama of lexical idiosyncrasy here – for example, the non-compositional interpretation of compounds – and we just focus on these aspects of the problem that are more pertinent to matters of syntactic categorization.

[4] Examples in (3) are from Chomsky (1970) and those in (4) are from Panagiotidis (2005) – originally from Clark and Clark (1977).

The above pairs (and many more) share a root, but it is extremely improbable that the meaning of the verb could be *guessed* – let alone be derived *compositionally* – by that of the noun, or vice versa, in the way things go with *sweat*, *push*, *box*, *brush* and so on above. Incidentally, as argued in Acquaviva and Panagiotidis (2012), examples like those in (3) and (4) render very problematic the idea that roots are underspecified but still meaningful elements which give rise to distinct interpretations depending on their immediate syntactic context (Arad 2005): 'even if we argue for impoverished and semantically underspecified roots, we are still left with the empirical problem … that roots too often do not capture a coherent meaning …. This renders unlearnable the purported "common semantic denominator" roots are supposed to express' (Acquaviva and Panagiotidis 2012, 109). To wit, what could be the 'common semantic denominator' between *revolution* (as 'uprising' or 'regime change') and *revolve*? Something as vague as 'change'? Surely this is hardly coherent, and the interested reader is again referred to Acquaviva and Panagiotidis (2012) and, also, Borer (2009).

The stand taken in Marantz (1997, 2000) and elsewhere on pairs like (3) and (4) is that they involve underlying syntactic structures which receive idiosyncratic interpretations. Now, idiosyncratic interpretations of variously-sized syntactic objects are not really an oddity: they are everywhere and they are called *idioms*. Trivially, *break a leg*, *kick the bucket*, *raining cats and dogs* are all syntactic phrases, *v*Ps according to Svenonius (2005). However, they have idiosyncratic meanings.

The idiom idea is definitely useful: lexical idiosyncrasies are not the result of a 'lexical/morphological' way of making words, but the result of idiomatic interpretation of otherwise ordinary structures. There are two questions, however: first, why can the meanings of words (nouns and verbs) made of the same root be so distinctly, even crazily, different and to such a considerable extent? Second, as Hagit Borer (personal communication, June 2009) pointed out, phrasal idioms can typically also receive a fully compositional interpretation when properly contextualized: *kick the bucket* may also simply describe a bucket-kicking event. However, the verb *castle* is impossible to interpret compositionally – for example, as a Location verb – and can only mean the chess move it idiosyncratically names. Why should such a difference between phrasal and 'lexical' idioms exist?

Panagiotidis (2011) seeks to answer both questions above by arguing the following points. If it is indeed the case that roots by themselves are characterized by impoverished or, perhaps, inexistent semantic content, then non-compositional and idiosyncratic interpretations of syntactic material directly involving roots are the *only* interpretive option: after all, how could compositional interpretation deal with the un- or under-specified meaning of roots? In other words, idiomaticity is the *only* way to interpret constituents containing roots, exactly because of the semantic impoverishment/deficiency of roots. This point is already alluded to in Arad (2005) and fleshes out the conception of the categorizing phrase in Marantz (1997, 2000) as the limit of (compulsory) idiomaticity. However, systematic idiomaticity of the categorizer projections is not due to the categorizer acting as some sort of a limit, below which interpretation is/can be/must be non-compositional. Rather, idiomaticity – that is, matching a structure with a memorized meaning stored in the Encyclopedia (Harley and Noyer 1998) – stems from the fact that the first phase (an *n*P or a *v*P)[5] contains a root, an LF-deficient element, which would resist any compositional treatment anyway. In other words, the semantically deficient character of the root blocks the application of a rule-based compositional interpretation. Therefore, inner versus outer morphology phenomena (Marantz 2006) are due to the semantic impoverishment of roots: once roots have been dispatched to the interfaces with the rest of the complement of the categorizer, compositional interpretation may canonically apply in the next phase up – see also the next chapter and Panagiotidis (2011, 378–9).

   Keeping these points in mind, we can now continue with the rest of this chapter, which will be dedicated to reviewing the literature on syntactic categorization. This will set the context in which the theory of categorial features to be posited applies.

3.5   Conversions

Syntactic decomposition can advance our understanding of why some verbs have a predictable, compositional relationship with their corresponding nouns (as discussed in Section 3.3 above) whereas others display only an arbitrary and idiosyncratic one (as reviewed in Section 3.4). The very short answer, which follows Kiparsky's (1982) analysis of the two levels of morphological processes, is that the former are denominal verbs, whereas the latter are root-derived. Staying with Arad (2003), whose account we will closely follow in this section, we will call (true) denominal verbs *tape*-type verbs and those verbs that are directly derived from a root *hammer*-type verbs. The structural differences between them will be argued to account

---

[5] See Chapter 4 for details.

for the idiosyncratic meaning of the latter, as opposed to the predictable and systematic meaning of the former.

Let us begin with root-derived, *hammer*-type verbs. In Arad (2003), verbs like *hammer* are directly formed from the root, just like corresponding nouns. Consider the schematic phrasal markers below.

(5)

In the tree to the left, the nominalizer head *n* takes a root complement, nominalizing it syntactically. In the tree to the right, the root HAMMER is a manner adjunct to an xP (schematically rendered) inside the *v*P, more or less along the lines of what was said about *brush* in Section 3.3 above, a configuration responsible for the manner interpretation of the root HAMMER within the verb *hammer*. Crucially, the verb does not mean 'hit with a hammer' but it takes up a broader interpretation, roughly 'hit in a hammer-like fashion' – maybe using a stone, a shoe, a fist, or similar.[6]

On the other hand, verbs like *tape* behave differently. These seem to be truly *denominal*, formed by converting a noun into a verb, by recategorizing the noun and not by categorizing a root. By hypothesis, the verbalizing head takes as its complement a structure that already contains a noun – that is, an *n*P in which the root TAPE has *already* been nominalized.

(6)

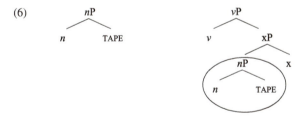

Again, in the tree to the left, a nominalizer *n* takes a root complement, nominalizing it syntactically. However, the verb *tape* is unlike the verb *hammer*: although it is also a manner/instrument verb, *tape* only means 'fasten

---

[6] Once more, this raises the question of roots' inherent content, if any, as an anonymous reviewer points out: what is the content of HAMMER? The answer I am partial to is 'none'; more on this line of reasoning and on ways the semantics could be executed can be found in Acquaviva (2009b), Borer (2009), Panagiotidis (2011) and, in detail, Harley (2012a).

with tape' – not with rope, pushpins, paperclips or even bandages. In other words, the meaning of the verb *tape* is not idiosyncratic but it wholly and predictably relies on the meaning of the noun *tape*, which it contains embedded in an adjunct position. This difference cannot be due to the verbalizer *v*, which is possibly the same in both cases. It therefore must be due to the fact that the verbalizer makes a verb out of root material in (5), yielding the verb *hammer*, whereas in (6) it makes a verb out of a ready-made noun, *tape*. This entails that *hammer*-type verbs can receive special meanings, whereas *tape*-type verbs do not.[7]

The general question here concerns the specifics of how these differently derived verbs, those categorizing a root and those recategorizing a noun, come to be. This question reduces in part to the whole issue of what is the limit of 'special meaning' in a syntactic tree. Inspecting the trees here, and as is the consensus in research, the limit of special, idiosyncratic meaning in a syntactic tree is *the first categorizer projection* as in Arad (2003, 2005) and Marantz (1997, 2000, 2006). Having said that, good arguments of an empirical nature are levelled against this thesis in Anagnostopoulou and Samioti (2009), Borer (2009), Harley (2012a) and Acquaviva and Panagiotidis (2012): the above seem to point towards the direction that, at least in the verbal/clausal domain, it is the Voice Phrase (or an even higher projection) that constitutes the 'limit' of idiosyncrasy.

If the first categorizer projection is the limit of idiosyncratic interpretation, then the verb *hammer* has a special meaning because categorization, brought about by the *v* head in (5), includes the *x* projection with its HAMMER root adjunct. On the contrary, the verb *tape* in (6) includes an *x* projection with an *n*P adjunct – that is, an already formed noun, an already categorized constituent. The *n*P has already received an interpretation of '(sticky) tape', so the range of possible interpretations of the *v*P containing it is significantly limited: 'stick *x* on *y* with tape'. The obvious problem that emerges now is why the first categorizer projection should be the limit of 'lexical' idiosyncrasy. Why is it not *the first* projection containing the root, like those indicated as *x*P in (5) and (6)? What is special about the first categorizer projection?

---

[7] I have deliberately chosen not to represent the position of the internal argument of *hammer* and *tape* in the diagrams (5) and (6) purely for reasons of exposition. I would, however, think they are merged as the specifier of *x* or *v*. The choice depends on the nature of the argument, as discussed in Marantz (2005).

3.6   Phases

In order to answer the question of why the first categorizer projection is the limit of 'lexical' idiosyncrasy, we need to appeal to cyclicity in syntax. The first syntactic cycle, which typically, but not necessarily, coincides with the word domain, manipulates impoverished roots; hence it is impossible for this first cycle to yield compositional interpretations. Once the interpretation of the first cycle is 'idiomatically' fixed, then its interpretive output may be used by higher cycles to yield compositional interpretations.

Let us follow the consensus in syntactic literature that syntactic operations are *local* and *cyclical*. A specific way to conceive cyclicity, one that makes precise and falsifiable empirical predictions, too, is through *Phase Theory*, as proposed and developed in Chomsky (2000, 2001, 2008) and a lot of subsequent work. Let us see how thinking in terms of phases may enable us to conceive the 'character' of the categorizer projection. According to Marantz (2006), a categorizer phrase (*v*P or *n*P) is a Phase. The other two phases are VoiceP[8] and Complementizer Phrase (CP). So, phases are both *interpretive* (meaning) units and phonological–prosodic ones – but see Hicks (2009) for solid arguments from binding that we need to separate LF-phases from PF-phases.

Let us turn to an example of a derivation with phases. Suppose we start building a tree – say, a clausal one:

(7)

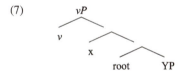

Given that *v*P is a phase, it is despatched to Morphology/PF and LF in order to be interpreted accordingly.

---

[8] There exists some terminological confusion on what the label *v* stands for. For the work cited and followed here, it is the verbalizing categorizer, the 'verbalizer'. However, in the work mainly concentrating on Phase Theory, beginning with Chomsky (2000), et seq., *v* essentially stands for Kratzer's (1996) *Voice*: a causative–transitive or passive head which hosts the external argument and of which the transitive version may assign accusative case, as per Burzio's Generalization. Now, *both* approaches take *v* (the categorizer or the Voice head) to be a phase head. Things become slightly more confusing in that Chomsky, and others, seem to consider the two elements, *v* and Voice, as one unitary head. I will here be concerned with the phase status of the categorizing *v* (and *n*) and will remain agnostic about that of Voice. However, see Anagnostopoulou and Samioti (2009) and Harley (2012b) for arguments on why *v* and Voice should be kept distinct.

(8)

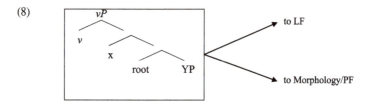

The syntactic derivation will from this point on only be able to see the *edge* of the phase: the topmost head – that is, *v* in (8) – and its specifier (none in the example above). The rest of the phase (shaded) will not be visible:

(9)

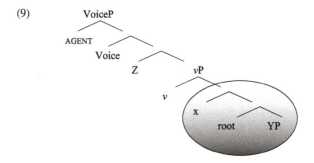

The derivation continues building structure until VoiceP is merged, which is the next phase; this in turn is also sent to Morphology/PF and LF:

(10)

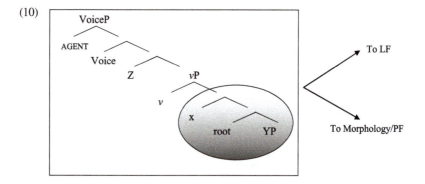

Once the VoiceP phase is interpreted, again, only its edge, the Voice head and the specifier hosting the Agent argument are visible for further syntactic computations. The derivation continues on to the next phase, CP, and so on.

In order to summarize how syntactic categorization interacts with the cyclic/phasal character of syntactic derivations, here are some essential points to retain from this very sketchy adumbration of Phase Theory:

1. Once a phase is completed, it is interpreted: therefore, its morphological form and its semantic interpretation become fixed.
2. The internal structure of a completed phase, except its edge, is invisible for the structure to be created higher up – that is, for the rest of the derivation.
3. The categorizer phrase (*n*P and *v*P) is the *First Phase*.

3.7   Roots and phases

Let us now apply the above to show how the 'lexical versus syntactic' difference in word formation can be explained away. In order to do this, we will revisit the denominal verbs *hammer* and *tape* (minus their internal argument; see also footnote 7) from Section 3.5:

(11)   *hammer* versus *tape*

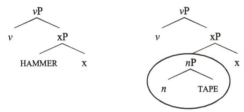

The verb *hammer* is made from root material (including some syntactic head *x*, as the root HAMMER behaves like a manner adjunct) and the verbalizer *v*; no interpretation or form is matched with the syntactic structure until *v*P, the first Phase, is completed. This is why *hammer* has an idiosyncratic meaning, exactly like any other word made directly out of a root, as opposed to words containing already categorized constituents in their structure. In the case of the verb *tape*, the root and the nominalizer *n* combine first (making a noun). This is a phase: it is sent to LF and Morphology/PF, where the meaning and the form of the *n*P *tape* are fixed. This *n*P phase can then participate in more syntactic structure: in (11) this *n*P merges as an adjunct with structure that is eventually verbalized.[9]

---

[9] The question here is whether we can embed the root TAPE *directly* under a *v* projection. The answer is that syntactically this is possible, and 'looser' usages of a verb *tape* are reported by some speakers; the whole thing boils down to whether Morphology makes available the form(s)

So, now we can explain why *v*P and *n*P are the limit of 'special meaning' in a syntactic tree: *v*P and *n*P are the first Phases. They are the first cycle after the derivation begins, provided of course that they categorize root material and not already categorized constituents – which of course would already be phasal constituents. Thus, far from acting as limits of idiosyncrasy, categorizer projections may receive a compositional interpretation if they recategorize already categorized material, just as is the case of denominal *tape* with its [ᵥ𝖯 *v* [ₓ𝖯 *n*P x]] structure. What causes idiosyncrasy is the semantic deficiency/impoverishment of roots within their first phase.

Further illustrating this point – namely, that verbs like *hammer* consist of a single phase – compare also the morphophonology and meaning of the near-homophones *dígest* (noun), *digést* (verb) and *dígest* (verb). The noun *dígest* and the verb *digést* are each derived directly by a categorizing head, an *n* and a *v* respectively, taking the projection that contains the root as its complement. Meanings of the respective noun (*n*P) and verb (*v*P) are distinct, as expected from the discussion above, each of them directly embedding the impoverished/semantically deficient root DIGEST. Stress, a morphophonological property, is also distinct (ₙ *dígest* vs ᵥ *digést*), a property decided and fixed at phase level, as well:[10]

(12)   *A root-derived noun and a root-derived verb*

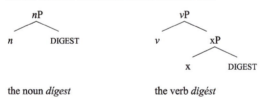

the noun *dígest*   the verb *digést*

Furthermore, the noun *dígest* can be converted into a verb, yielding the denominal verb *dígest*; this is a process identical to that giving the verb *tape*. Notice in the phrase marker below that the meaning of denominal *dígest* is again compositionally derived from the meaning of the noun and the contribution of *v*. The denominal verb *dígest* is therefore interpreted as 'make a *dígest*'; it also preserves the stress pattern, fixed after the *n*P phase was despatched to the interfaces:

---

necessary to express this direct verbalization of the root TAPE as a word. For discussion of blocking and gaps, see Embick and Marantz (2008) and references therein.

[10] Again, in (12) and (13) I have deliberately left out the internal argument. See also footnote 7.

(13)   *A denominal verb*

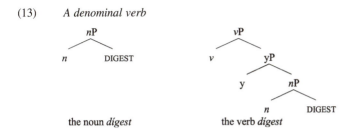

the noun *dígest*   the verb *digést*

Moving away from English and zero-derived conversions, let us observe the behaviour of two more elements as inner and outer morphemes and let us see how root deficiency and phases can capture their non-compositional behaviour when they are directly associated with roots below phase level. We begin with the Japanese causativizer –*(s)ase* (Marantz 1997). Next to compositional causatives, like *suw-ase* ('make somebody smoke') below, Japanese causativizers may also yield idiomatic, non-compositional interpretations, like *tob-ase* ('demote someone to a remote post') below. As illustrated below, the causativizing element –*(s)ase* in the case of *suw-ase* ('make somebody smoke') combines with a *v*P phase, whose interpretation has already been fixed as 'smoke', and the result is predictable and compositional. In the case of *tob-ase* ('demote someone to a remote post'), the causativizer merges with a root *tob-* (which also yields the verb 'fly') and derives an unpredictable and specialized verb *tob-ase* ('demote someone to a remote post') when it eventually becomes categorized by a *v* head.[11]

(14)   *Outer and inner causativizers*

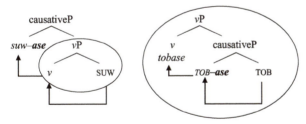

A similar picture emerges with Greek *syn-* (Drachman 2005). The interpretation of *syn-* (as an outer morpheme) can be described as comitative and it is

---

[11] As Marijke De Belder (personal communication, 2011) notes, even in idiomatic *tob-ase*, there is clear causation involved. This is interesting but, as will be illustrated for Greek *syn-*, inner morphemes need not preserve *any* of the meaning they have when they are used as outer, 'compositional', morphemes.

productively used to yield verbs and nouns that have a 'with X' interpretation. So, the verb *syn-trog-o* means 'eat with somebody', from the verb *tro(g)-o* ('eat'), and so on. Still, *syn-* is also used as an inner morpheme, with *no* discernible semantic contribution whatsoever. Hence, *syn-tax-i*, which means 'syntax' or 'pension'. Words like *syn-tax-i* belong to words that 'have morphological structure even when they are not compositionally derived' (Aronoff 2007, 819). Another example of this non-contribution is the noun *syn-graf-eas* ('author'), whose morphological structure is transparently related to that of *graf-eas* ('scribe') – still, *syn-graf-eas* cannot mean 'someone who acts as a scribe together with someone else'. To wit, 'co-author' in Greek would be something like *syn-[syn-graf-eas]*.[12] The diagram below illustrates the difference between *syn-* as an outer morpheme, with a compositional comitative interpretation, combining with a phasal *v*P in *syn-trogo* ('eat with sb'), and *syn-* as an inner morpheme in *syn-graf-eas* ('author'), where it combines with a root awaiting the phasal *n*P in order to receive its idiosyncratic interpretation.

(15)   *Outer* syn- *and inner* syn- *in Greek*

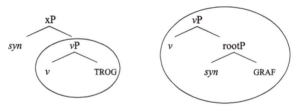

We have captured the differences between 'lexical' and 'syntactic' word-making as involving the merging of material inside the categorizing first phase versus the merging of material with already categorized material, with phasal *n*Ps and *v*Ps, which have had their interpretation and form already fixed. Before we look at a serious challenge towards acategorial roots, we can round up the discussion in this chapter by addressing the question of why syntactic derivations at the categorizer phase are not fully productive.

3.8   On the limited productivity (?) of first phases

If word-making, including what lexicalism understands as 'lexical' or 'morphological' word-making, is fully syntactic, if there is a single combinatorial

---

[12] When I was writing those lines I was confident that *syn-[syn-graf-eas]* was nothing but a slightly contrived coinage. While revising the chapter, I ran an exact Google search of *συν-συγγραφέας* out of curiosity: it yielded about 21,500 results.

mechanism that makes words and phrases, then we would expect word-making to be significantly more productive, whereas it is nowhere near so, compared with phrasal productivity. The short answer to this problem is the role of *stored* forms, Vocabulary Items in Distributed Morphology, associated (or not) with particular structures.

Indeed, syntactic composition at the first, categorial phase is unlike 'phrasal syntax' – that is, syntactic operations above the 'word level', involving higher phases. For instance, there are no verbs *cat*, *hair* or *tree*, for most speakers of English at least; there is a difference between *father* (which is only a 'becoming' verb) and *mother* (which is only a manner/instrument verb) and there is no verb #*father* meaning 'to treat as a father would' – see Clark and Clark (1977) for scores of similar examples; not all roots can be used to derive Location/ Locatum verbs; and so on.

Of course, productivity, or lack thereof, is a *morphological* matter:[13] whether Vocabulary contains an appropriate form to insert in a given structural environment. So, perhaps syntax is after all able to construct a *Location* verb 'butter', next to the well-known *Locatum* one, or even to construct a manner verb 'butter'. The problem in these cases would be whether Vocabulary (or Morphology, more generally) can make available the form(s) that will express such syntactic structures (see also footnote 9). Syntax is always free and always combinatorial; at the same time, a lot of Morphology is inevitably about a repository of memorized forms. It is very characteristic that in languages with few inflectional restrictions, such as English, spontaneous coinage of words – that is, novel morphological expressions of syntactic structures at the level of the word or whereabouts – is easier than in Romance or Greek, where all sorts of inflectional criteria must be met and where zero derivation is not available: in English, in the right context, even a manner verb *butter* is possible – for example, in a coinage like #*The vegetable oil was bad quality; it buttered* ('coagulated like butter').

Invoking morphological restrictions – that is, what is listed – is far from ad hoc. Indeed, there are gaps and morphological idiosyncrasies everywhere, even in the bona fide syntactic *inflectional* morphology: two well-known conundrums of this sort, hardly unique, from my native Greek are

---

[13] Aronoff and Anshen (1998, 243) raise a crucial point with respect to productivity – namely, that it is far from being an absolute notion: 'Some linguists treat morphological productivity as an absolute notion – a pattern is either productive or unproductive – but there is a good deal of evidence for the existence and utility of intermediate cases, ... so we will assume ... that affixes may differ continuously in productivity, rather than falling only into the polar categories of completely productive and completely unproductive ...'.

the general unavailability of a genitive plural form for Greek feminine nouns in –*a*, even of high-frequency ones like *mana* ('mother'), *patata* ('potato') and *kota* ('hen'), or the awkwardness of the majority of genitive singular forms for Greek diminutives in –*aki*. Once more, I refer the reader to (at least) Aronoff and Anshen (1998), Marantz (2000) and Embick and Marantz (2008).

Having said that, there is an additional factor that must be considered, one discussed amply and in careful detail throughout Ackema and Neeleman (2004). Recasting this factor in the framework employed here, we must remember that categorizing first phases (*n*Ps and *v*Ps) are typically matched with Vocabulary Items, with stored forms, *but not necessarily so*. To wit, there are few morphologically inexpressible VoicePs and probably no CPs; however, there are morphologically inexpressible *n*Ps and *v*Ps because these are typically matched with stored, word-like forms – or they are expected to be matched with word-like forms. Having said that, this is not the case in languages like Jinggulu, Farsi and, to a large extent, Japanese, where verbs are not expected to be co-extensive with a word – in languages possessing periphrastic verbal forms, light verbs and/or particle verbs, expressing verbal projections is much easier.

3.9   Are roots truly acategorial? Dutch restrictions

One of the assumptions underlying the workings of syntactic categorization is that free roots, or 'roots by themselves' so to speak, are category-less – a different term being 'acategorial'. This assumption goes part and parcel with roots being underspecified (or impoverished) semantically and/or bearing no UG features.[14] However, the assumption that roots bear no category is neither obvious nor uncontested. Already in the previous chapter we have mentioned the casual observation that some roots make better nouns than verbs. For instance, the roots CAT, DOG and BOY make good nouns in English but not great verbs, if at all. Moreover, verbs like *dog* and *cat* appear to be denominal verbs – that is, like *tape* – with the noun functioning like a manner modifier: *to dog* means 'to follow *like a dog*' and similar facts hold for *cat*, at least for those speakers that accept it as a lexicalized verb and not as a spontaneous coinage (Barner and Bale 2002). Moreover, as will be reviewed in the following chapter, languages like Farsi seem unable to verbalize most roots,

---

[14] These matters are discussed in more detail in the following chapter.

with Hindi/Urdu apparently working the same way (Rajesh Bhatt and David Embick, personal communication, October 2010). That is, the lack of verbs like *boy* and #*cat* in English is an empirical fact to be explained, possibly invoking grammar-external factors.[15]

More systematic and solid criticism of acategorial roots comes from Don (2004). He looks at conversions in Dutch to argue that 'the lexical category of roots should be lexically stored' (Don 2004, 933). More precisely, he claims that HAMMER-type derivations – that is, with a root directly yielding a noun and a verb – are not to be found and that all conversions involve denominal derivations (like *tape*) or deverbal ones (like the noun *throw*). Don makes two arguments, a morphological one and a phonological one. We will review them in turn.

Don's morphological argument against category-less roots (in Dutch) is very simple and comes from examining two properties of zero-derived noun–verb pairs in Dutch: irregular morphology on verbs and gender on nouns (Don 2004, 939–42). He first states that *four* logical possibilities present themselves when it comes to cross-classifying zero-derived noun–verb pairs, as follows:[16]

(16)   *Four possible verb–noun conversion pairs*
      a. regular verb – common gender noun
      b. regular verb – neuter gender noun
      c. irregular verb – common gender noun
      d. irregular verb – neuter gender noun

Interestingly, only the first three options in (16) are attested in the language:

(17)   Regular verb – common gender noun:
      fiets – de fiets   'cycle'
      ren – de ren   'run'
      tel – de tel   'count'
      twijfel – de twijfel   'doubt'

[15] This state of affairs is possibly different to the Romance and Greek cases, where the existence of 'nominal' and 'verbal' roots looks like an illusion of rich morphology, like the result of roots being embedded within 'their functional support systems', their morphological entourage. This is also suggested by Panagiotidis, Revithiadou and Spyropoulos (2013), where it is argued that *all* but a handful of verbal stems in Greek contain an overt verbalizing morpheme whose exponence depends on complex (sub-)regularities.
[16] Dutch has two genders: common (non-neuter), taking a *de* definite article, and neuter, taking a *het* definite article.

(18)   Regular verb – neuter gender noun:

werk – het werk   'work'
deel – het deel   'part'
feest – het feest   'party'
slijm – het slijm   'slime'

(19)   Irregular verb – common gender noun

val – de val   'fall'
wijk – de wijk   'flee'
loop – de loop   'walk'
kijk – de kijk   'look'

There are *no* verb–noun conversion pairs where the verb is irregular and the noun is neuter. Don (2004, 941) explains this gap in the following way:

1. V-to-N conversion renders common gender nouns;[17]
2. N-to-V conversion renders regular verbs;
3. There is no such thing as direct zero-derivation from acategorial roots.

From the above assumptions, it turns out that in (18) N-to-V conversion takes place, since V-to-N conversion would yield common gender nouns. In (19), V-to-N conversion takes place, since N-to-V conversion would yield regular verbs. A conversion pair 'irregular verb – neuter gender noun' is impossible: an N-to-V conversion would yield regular verbs; a V-to-N would yield common gender nouns.[18] Hence, according to Don, roots are stored with a category: if roots were category-less, then it should be possible to derive an irregular verb *and* a neuter noun directly from the same root, the HAMMER way, so to speak.

Looking to reinterpret Don's morphological facts from a point of view where roots are indeed category-less, one conclusion we can draw is that we are dealing with facts regarding the morphological exponence of categorizers in Dutch. Recall that the morphological realization of syntactic heads is decided post-syntactically (Late Insertion): morphological forms, Vocabulary items, are inserted late – that is, after syntax – to match the features on syntactic heads. Put succinctly, it seems that we are most likely dealing with morphological constraints on null nominalizers in Dutch. Reinterpreting the facts above, we can hypothesize that

---

[17] It is quite common for morphological processes to determine the gender of their output. Don (2004) cites Beard (1995) for examples of this in different languages.

[18] Crucially, *no statement* can be made on the pairs in (17): they could be V-to-N or N-to-V conversion pairs, verbs being regular and nouns bearing common gender. They could, for that matter, be directly derived from an acategorial root.

(20)   An *n* in an [$_{nP}$ *n* *v*P] syntactic environment cannot surface *both* as Ø
       and neuter;[19]

So, in (19), a *v*P (an irregular verb) with a Ø *v* is in the complement of a *n*
that is Ø and [common] gender – as per (20). Illustrating:

(21)   *A null nominalizer converting a verb surfaces with common gender*

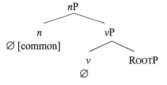

Note that there is no blanket ban on neuter gender nominalizers of verbs.
Don (2004: 941–2) discusses the neuter gender element *–sel*, which nominalizes verbs like *zaag* ('to saw'), giving *zaagsel* ('sawdust'). So, (20) is a
morphological constraint on *null* nominalizers with a *v*P complement.

However, and returning to the unattested conversion pair 'irregular verb –
neuter gender noun' in (16), what would prevent a Ø-exponence *n* bearing a
[gender:neuter] specification from taking a ROOT complement that also
derives an 'irregular' *v*? I think that, again, instead of invoking category
encoded on roots themselves, we had better examine the phenomenon from a
morphological and morphophonological point of view.

'Irregular' verbs in Dutch are not just verbs with deviant *inflectional*
paradigms, they are actually Germanic strong verbs – that is, verbs displaying
synchronically opaque stem allomorphy, what I would claim to be genuine
root allomorphy, resulting from Late Insertion of root forms, as in Galani
(2005, chaps. 5 and 6), Siddiqi (2006, chap. 3) and Haugen (2009). Here are
some examples from Don (2004, 940):

(22)   *Stem/root allomorphy in Dutch: irregular/strong verbs*

Present	Past	Past participle	
spijt(-t)(-en)	speet	ge-speet-en	'to regret'
val(-t)(-en)	viel(-en)	ge-val-en	'to fall'
bind(-t)(-en)	bond(-en)	ge-bond-en	'to bind'
sla(-t)(-en)	sloeg(-en)	ge-slag-en	'to beat'
koop(-t)(-en)	kocht(en)	ge-kocht-t	'to buy'

---

[19] See Lowenstamm (2008) for how gender defines different flavours of *n*.

A second generalization then seems to be that

(23)   A Ø-exponence nominalizer cannot bear the neuter gender when taking as its direct complement a root displaying allomorphy.

Putting (20) and (23) together, it turns out that

(24)   A Ø *n* head bearing a neuter gender specification can only take non-allomorphic root complements.

The above looks like the kind of morphological constraints we find in language after language, as opposed to being the offshoot of the purported categorial specification of roots. Additional evidence that the gap Don discusses is of a morphological and morphophonological nature comes from Don's (2004, 942–5) *phonological* argument for categorially specified roots. Reviewing evidence in Trommelen (1989), he observes an interesting constraint on Dutch verbal stems, summarized in (25):

(25)   *Phonological properties of verbs in Dutch*

	Simple syllable structure	Complex syllable structure
With identical noun	numerous: *bal, lepel, kat*	some: *oogst, feest, fiets*
Without identical noun	numerous: *win, kom, vang*	No examples

Apparently, verbs with complex syllable structure are *denominal*. Looking at the gap – that is, verbs with complex syllable structure but no corresponding nouns – we can perceive a picture where verbal stems can only have simple syllable structure – unless they are denominal conversions. Without getting too deeply into matters of Dutch morphology, two options present themselves.

    a.   The Dutch lexicon assigns a verbal category only to roots with a simple syllable structure. This claim is odd even within a lexicalist framework, because it regulates the category membership of a root, a matter ultimately tied to concepts (Acquaviva and Panagiotidis 2012), according to syllable structure.

    b.   Root forms are inserted late: roots in the complement of *v* are spelled out as forms with a simple syllable structure. Restrictions on the *form* of roots categorized as verbs are the result of Dutch grammar-internal requirements on *forms*.

If the latter is the case, then the Dutch restrictions, which have to do with the exponence of roots and categorizers in all cases, are not deep generalizations about the nature of roots but constraints that are morphological in nature: they are surface requirements, rather than the result of a universal principle that roots be lexically categorized.

3.10   Conclusion

Now that we have carefully separated the workings of syntax from those of morphology, we have a complete picture of how lexical decomposition and, more relevant to our topic of category here, syntactic categorization work: the picture is more or less complete. Thus, we can replace the outline in (26):

(26)

	Lexical/'morphological' word-making	**Syntactic word-making**
'Raw material'	any category or acategorial roots	a particular category
Meaning	idiosyncratic meaning	predictable meaning
Productivity	limited	full (allomorphy aside)
Examples	*–ful* attachment, compounding	*–ness* attachment

with something like the outline in (27):

(27)

Syntax:	**Working with roots (inside *n*P/*v*P)**	**Working with *n*P/*v*P**
'Raw material'	Roots	*n*P/*v*P
Meaning	idiomatic	usually compositional
Productivity	depending on Vocabulary	almost complete
Examples	*–ful* attachment, compounding, verbs *hammer* and *digést*, lexical causatives	*–ness* attachment, *tape*, verbs *tape* and *digést*, syntactic causatives

Now it is time to turn to what 'makes' *n* and *v*, to closely examine categorial features themselves.

4   *Categorial features*

4.1   Introduction

This chapter contains the core of the proposal presented here, one that weds
syntactic categorization with a new explanatory theory of categorial features
as LF-interpretable entities. Interpretable categorial features, borne by
categorizing heads, define the fundamental interpretive perspective of their
complement, thus licensing root material. The discussion begins in Section 4.2
with a recasting of the question regarding the difference between nouns and
verbs as one about the difference between n (the nominalizer) and v (the
verbalizer). Section 4.3 introduces categorial features [N] and [V] as
perspective-setting features and in Section 4.4 Embick and Marantz's (2008)
Categorization Assumption is used as a guide in order to explain the role of
categorization induced by categorial features, its nature as well as why it
is necessary to categorize roots. In Section 4.5, calling upon evidence from
semi-lexical heads, it is argued that categorizers are not functional heads but,
on the contrary, the only lexical heads in a grammar, as they are the only
elements that can categorize root material, setting a perspective on it. Perhaps
more crucially, it is also argued that categorizers are the only necessary
elements, even in the absence of any root, on which functional superstructures
can be built. Section 4.6 examines empirical evidence from languages like
Farsi in order to put to the test the view that perhaps [N] and [V] could be more
closely related to each other, with [N] possibly being the default value of a
perspective-setting feature.

4.2   Answering the old questions

In the previous chapter, we saw that the syntactic decomposition approach can
answer a number of questions regarding lexical categories: the source of
meaning idiosyncrasies in noun–verb pairs, the (im)possibility of conversion,
the kind of interpretations that nouns or verbs derived from already categorized

elements can and cannot have, the syntactic role of roots within the First Phase – and so on. We also saw that syntactic decomposition elevates categorizers such as *n* and *v* to a pivotal role in the derivation of nouns and verbs respectively. Consequently, what we call nouns and verbs are essentially (subconstituents of) *n*Ps and *v*Ps. Before moving on, let us illustrate this point, based on Marantz (1997, 2000, 2006) and as discussed in the previous chapter. Take a verb like *bake*. Essentially, the verb is a subconstituent of a *v*P.

(1)

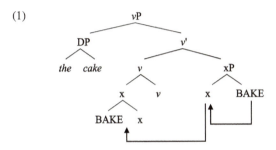

However, saying that nouns and verbs are really (parts of) *n*Ps and *v*Ps does not answer a fundamental question, the one we set out to answer in the first chapter. More precisely: suppose that a noun is a morphological unit created around the head of *n*P, an *n* constituent typically, and a verb a morphological unit created around the head of *v*P, a *v* node in typical cases as in (1) above. If the above is the case, then the problem of what distinguishes nouns from verbs now becomes one of what distinguishes *n* from *v*.

(2)   What distinguishes *n* from *v*? What is their difference at LF?

In other words, the long-standing conundrum of how lexical categories are defined and in what ways they differ from each other (Baker 2003, chap. 1) is now recast as what makes *categorizers* different from each other. Although this question is still one that has been largely overlooked, answering it is essential: otherwise we are merely rephrasing the problem of category as one of the *n–v* distinction. Plainly put, even if we conceive nouns and verbs as syntactically decomposable entities within *n*Ps and *v*Ps, the *syntactic* difference between 'nouns' and 'verbs' remains real and cross-linguistically persistent and apparently rooted in some essential property of language; therefore, this syntactic difference now needs to be expressed as a (fundamental) difference between categorizers *n* and *v*.

At this very point, we can obviously follow the received formalist approach to this kind of problem. Instead of looking for distinctive features of nouns and verbs, now that we have adopted categorizers and we have outlined a process of syntactic categorization, the simplest hypothesis would be to look for distinctive features that differentiate *n* from *v*. The most straightforward version of this approach would be that each categorizer (*n* and *v*) bears a distinctive feature (or a distinctive feature value). Therefore, we need to identify

a. the distinctive feature or feature values on categorizers and
b. its (or their) interpretation.

Keeping with the established notation in the research on categories, let us call these features [N] and [V] and let us take *categorial* features as the distinctive features on categorizers. Regarding this matter, an alternative methodological path to take would be to first seek the precise interpretation for each of the features on *n* and *v* – as we will set out to do in this chapter anyway – and *then* notate them accordingly, discarding the old [N] and [V] labels. However, I will adhere to [N] and [V] for mnemonic purposes, if nothing else.

Now, if categorial features [N] and [V] truly exist and act as the features distinguishing between *n* and *v*, they must also be interpretable at one of the two interfaces, according to a version of Chomsky's (1995) *Full Interpretation* and following current assumptions on features as instructions to the interfaces. Moreover, these features most probably somehow affect the syntactic derivation, given that features are understood not only as properties and instructions to the interfaces, but also as that which triggers (most) syntactic operations (Chomsky 1995). What we had better not argue for is [N] and [V] being purely taxonomic and otherwise syntactically inert 'features': this would bring us back to approaches criticized in Chapter 1, which simply take categorial features to be class-marking flags of no interpretive significance. This would also be empirically inadequate, as *n*Ps and *v*Ps do appear to have *syntactic* differences. Considering the above, the following options present themselves:

(3)   *Approaches to categorial features*
    a. Categorial features are PF-interpretable: the noun–verb distinction would be utterly superficial. This possibility can be easily discarded as, cross-linguistically speaking, there is no unambiguous, across-the-board phonological marking of the noun–verb distinction.
    b. [N] and [V] are purely morphological and/or post-syntactic features. In this case, categorial features would be like grammatical gender (under some approaches to gender). Appealing to better-studied examples, if categorial features were morphological and/or post-syntactic, they would be germane to morphological class (e.g., noun declension and verb conjugation) features, as these are analysed in Marantz (1991), Aronoff

(1994), Embick and Noyer (2001), Arad (2005, chap. 2).[1] However, the universal relevance and cross-linguistic significance of the noun–verb distinction extend well beyond both morphological exponence and – crucially – word-class membership. Nouns and verbs are not mere morphological epiphenomena: thus, a claim that [N] and [V] are morphological and/or post-syntactic features is a highly implausible one.

    c. All categorial features are uninterpretable, in a fashion similar to that in which Case features are analysed in Chomsky (1995). If this is so, then grammatical category would accordingly be a grammar-internal mechanism with no direct interpretive effect. In the same way that there is no uniform semantic interpretation for all nominative or accusative DPs, similarly there would be no uniform interpretive identity for *all nouns* or *all verbs*. As I will sketch below, and as implied in Chapter 1 already, this would be undesirable given the research on the semantic differences between (bare) nouns and (bare) verbs.

    d. [N] and [V] are LF-interpretable, as suggested in Déchaine (1993) and explicitly argued in Baker (2003). This looks like the option worth exploring, perhaps the only one. Of course, this is a take on word classes that has been more or less embraced by Anderson (1997) and linguists working in functionalist frameworks, as reviewed in Chapter 1.

Concluding, even more than in a model where categorial information is decided in the lexicon, it is necessary for categorial features to be syntactic LF-interpretable features, acting (at least) as distinctive features on categorizers *n* and *v*. Thus, there is no escape from categorial features (or from syntax, for that matter), a result already anticipated in the influential Chomsky (1970).

A second question that has to be answered – especially once we have committed ourselves to a syntactic decomposition approach to categories, and word-making in general – is why we cannot have bare roots inserted directly in the syntax; that is, why the *Categorization Assumption* (Embick and Marantz 2008, 6) is valid. Generally speaking, roots need to be assigned to a category and they cannot be freely inserted in syntax, as observed in Baker (2003, 268) and – from a slightly different perspective – Acquaviva (2009b). Why is it the case that roots can only appear embedded within the complement of a categorizer? An answer to why the *Categorization Assumption* holds, especially a principled one, is a basic desideratum of a theory of category. Continuing the discussion begun in Section 3.7 of the previous chapter, I will try to show here that such an answer is not only possible, but that it can be made to emerge from a theory of categorial features.

---

[1] See Alexiadou and Müller (2007) for an account of such features as uninterpretable *syntactic* features.

Before concluding this section, I must make a reference, albeit a brief one and without doing justice to it, to the system of lexical categories put forth in Pesetsky and Torrego (2004). More or less in the spirit of Stowell (1981) and Déchaine (1993), they conceive lexical categories noun, verb and adjective as grammar-internal entities that can be completely defined in a contextual way, bringing together the most interesting ingredients of approaches b. and c. in (3) above: so, nouns, verbs and adjectives *are* morphological epiphenomena and, consequently, a grammar-internal business. There are no categorial features; in which of the three forms a predicate manifests itself is regulated contextually – that is, by the superimposed syntactic structure, but also locally, according to the features and selectional requirements of a very low tense head, a T_O:

(4)   *Contextual determination of lexical categories* (in Pesetsky and Torrego 2004, 525):
       Predicates are morphological verbs when associated with a T_O that seeks uninterpretable Tense features (i.e., Case, in the Pesetsky–Torrego system); predicates are morphological nouns when associated with a T_O that seeks interpretable Tense features;
       otherwise, predicates are morphologically adjectives.

The approach is very elegant and simple; it also fleshes out the programmatic desire we briefly mentioned in Chapter 1 to strip lexical categories of all kinds of interpretive characteristics. However, I think that a fully contextual defin-ition of lexical categories, to the extent that it can be implemented in the way of (4) or otherwise, is undesirable for exactly this reason: it strips lexical categories of all interpretive characteristics, which – let me repeat this – results in missing generalizations of paramount importance. So, I will pursue the goal set out here, to discover the LF-interpretation of categorial features.

4.3   Categorial features: a matter of perspective

Let us now substantiate our hypothesis that [N] is the distinctive feature on the categorizer *n* and [V] the distinctive feature on the categorizer *v*.

We can start doing so by siding with Déchaine (1993) and Baker (2003) in stating that the features [N] and [V] must be *LF-interpretable*. Of course, if [N] and [V] are truly LF-interpretable features, then we have to consider their LF interpretation. So, we are finally facing the really tough question: what makes a noun a noun and a verb a verb?

Let us approach the problem first from the level of categorizers themselves. Apparently, an [N] feature is the one common to all different types of *n* head and a [V] feature the one common to all different types of *v* head. Hence, by hypothesis, different *n* heads, bearing [N], and different *v* heads, bearing [V], would also bear different additional LF-interpretable features. To wit, Folli and Harley (2005) claim that three 'flavours' of *v* exist – that is, v_{CAUS}, v_{DO} and v_{BECOME} – making different types of verbs; these would all share a [V] categorial feature, but each entry would bear different additional features. A similar state of affairs would hold for Lowenstamm's (2008) different flavours of *n*: they would all share an [N] feature but differ in their other, additional features. Therefore, [N] and [V] would encode at LF some interpretive instruction common to all *n* and *v* heads respectively: exemplifying on *v*, the interpretation of [V] is what remains when the differences among the purported v_{CAUS}, v_{DO} and v_{BECOME} are abstracted away from. Similarly, the interpretation of [N] would be what remains when the differences among the various types of *n* are abstracted away from.

Following the received path towards attacking the problem of the LF-interpretation of [N] and [V], we are brought back to the point of asking about the semantics of grammatical category: what it means to be a noun, what it means to be a verb. Quickly revising the discussion in Chapter 1, the table in (5) summarizes the differences between nouns and verbs:

(5)   *Nouns versus verbs*

NOUNS	VERBS
Number	Tense
Case-marked	Case-assigning
gender and so on	agreement with arguments
argument structure covert	argument structure overt
determiners	particles

From the discussion in Chapter 1 it is also worth recalling two simple but crucial points. First, 'prototypical' members of each lexical category (e.g., *rock* or *tree* for nouns) share exactly the same grammatical properties as 'non-prototypical' ones (e.g., *theory*, *liberty* and *game* for nouns); this is treated in length in Newmeyer (1998, chap. 4). Second, the same concept, as sometimes expressed by an identical root, like SLEEP, can appear both as a noun and as a verb.

As also announced in Chapter 1, and following Baker (2003, 296–7), we have to bear in mind that category distinctions must correspond to *perspectives* on the concepts which roots and associated material are employed in order to express: category distinctions are certainly *not* ontological distinctions, whether clear-cut or fuzzy. Crudely put:

(6)   conceptual categorization $\neq$ linguistic categorization

Thus, although all physical objects are nouns cross-linguistically, not all nouns denote concepts of physical objects (David Pesetsky, personal communication, September 2005): thus, *rock* and *theory* cannot belong together in any useful, or even coherent, conceptual category. The concepts expressed by *rock* and *theory* can, however, be *viewed* by the Language Faculty in the same way. This would entail that grammatical categories, such as 'noun' and 'verb', are particular *interpretive perspectives* on concepts, that there is a way in which *rock* and *theory* are treated the same by grammar, even if they share no significant common properties notionally. This stance is essentially taken in Langacker (1987), Uriagereka (1999), Baker (2003, 293–4) and Acquaviva (2009a, 2009b). Finally, understanding categorization as grammar imposing interpretive perspectives on concepts, we can tackle the question I raised in Section 1.2.6 of Chapter 1 – namely, what conceptual mechanism decides which category concepts are assigned to. The reply is 'grammar does the categorization', giving us *sleep* the noun and *sleep* the verb, built from the same concept (and root), but encoding different interpretive perspectives, or even cross-category near-synonyms like *fond* the adjective and *like* the verb.[2]

Building on the above points, we can now turn to the question of what the actual interpretations of [N] and [V] are. The question is of course now recast as one regarding the different interpretive perspectives that categorial features impose on the material in their complement. In principle, we could adopt Baker's (2003) interpretations of [N] as sortal and [V] as predicative. However, as discussed in the Appendix, there are several issues with the way Baker imports sortality into his system and links it with referentiality. Even more damagingly, [V] as a feature encoding predicativity that also forces the projection of a specifier is also multiply problematic. I am therefore departing from Baker's interpretation for the two categorial features and I am proposing the following alternative interpretations for [N] and [V]:

(7)   *LF-interpretation of categorial features*
       An [N] feature imposes a sortal perspective on the categorizer's
       complement at LF.
       A [V] feature imposes an extending-into-time perspective on the categorizer's
       complement at LF.

The statements above will now be explained and discussed thoroughly. To begin with, here I will diverge from Baker's interpretation of sortality, which

---

[2] I wish to thank an anonymous reviewer for comments on categorization.

principally revolves around the criterion of identity, and I will explore instead the notion of sortality as implemented in Prasada (2008) and Acquaviva (2009a).

Prasada (2008) notes that sortality incorporates three criteria: *application, identity* and *individuation*. The criterion of application 'means that the representation is understood to apply to things of a certain kind, but not others. Thus, the sortal DOG allows us to think about dogs, but not tables, trees, wood or any other kind of thing' (Prasada 2008, 6). In this respect, the criterion of application differentiates (sortal, but not exclusively) predicates from indexicals like *this* and from elements with similar functions. The criterion of application also incorporates the received understanding of bare nominal expressions as *kinds* in Chierchia (1998), as it 'provides the basis for thoughts like dogs, [which] by virtue of being dogs, remain dogs throughout their existence' (Prasada 2008, 7), for as long as external conditions permit them to maintain their existence (for a short time, like *puppy*, or for a long one, like *water* and *universe*). Very interestingly, this is precisely the meeting point with the intuitions in prototype theory and in functionalist literature (see Chapter 1) as far as the 'time stability' of nouns is concerned: while it turns out that concepts denoted by nouns are not themselves necessarily time-stable – as cogently pointed out in Baker (2003, 292–4) – nouns are, however, *viewed* by the Language Faculty as time-stable, irrespective of the actual time stability of the concepts they denote. This is where the notion of *interpretive perspective* becomes crucial.[3]

Regarding the criterion of identity, I will adopt its reinterpretation in Acquaviva (2009a). The discussion in Acquaviva (2009a, 4) goes like this: if we take a kind (e.g., the kind *person*), it has instances (i.e., persons) which are particulars and which do not themselves have instances. In this way, being a person is different from being tall: only the property *person* identifies a type of entity. At the same time, the property of being tall is characteristic of all the entities it is true of, but it does not define a *category* of being. This distinction leads us back to Baker's (2003, 101–9) discussion of the criterion of identity: the criterion of identity essentially defines something which may replace *A* in the relative identity statement '*x is the same A as y*'. Acquaviva (2009a, 4) continues by pointing out the following: a concept that defines what it means

---

[3] Acquaviva (2009a, 1–5) contains more detailed and in-depth discussion of nominal concepts as such, which goes beyond this sketch of the two criteria of application and identity. Here we will be satisfied with Prasada's (2008) two criteria of application and identity as being enough to define sortality for our purposes: namely, exploring what 'nominality' means in grammar and – crucially – what the interpretation of a nominal feature [N] is.

to be an entity of a *particular* kind functions as a condition of identity for the corresponding kind.[4] I would therefore argue that this is how the feature [N] imposes a sortal interpretive perspective: it enables a concept – say, *rock* or even *sleep* – to act as a condition of identity.[5] Summarizing and simplifying, the criteria of application and identity taken *together* adequately characterize the *sortal* interpretive perspective that [N] features impose on the concept they associate with, an association mediated by syntax.[6]

Let us now turn to the interpretation of [V]. We will once more be calling upon the intuitions framed within prototype theory and incorporated in the functionalist literature on word classes. In work by Givón (1984, chap. 3), who conceives categories as prototypes along a continuum of temporal stability after Ross (1973), verbs are placed at the least time-stable end of the spectrum (see also Chapter 1). The intuition that the temporal perspective seriously matters for the interpretation of verbs is also echoed in Ramchand (2008, 40; emphasis added): '*procP* is the heart of the dynamic predicate, since *it represents change through time*, and it is present in every dynamic verb'.[7] The very same intuition is explored in more detail in Uriagereka (1999). His approach to nouns and verbs can be encapsulated along the lines of both nouns and verbs corresponding to mathematical spaces of various dimensions; the difference between them is conceived as whether those spaces are *seen* as *permanent* or *mutable*. Uriagereka's approach incorporates three crucial ingredients: first, the temporal dimension argued for by functionalists as a crucial factor in the distinction between nouns and verbs. Second, Uriagereka also upholds and expands Langacker's (1987) introduction of spaces in our understanding of lexical categories – recall that he defines nouns as uninterrupted 'region[s] in some domain' (Langacker 1987, 189) and verbs as processes. Third, as the use of *seen* stresses in the précis above, Uriagereka conceives lexical categories as

---

[4] Acquaviva distinguishes between a criterion, which is a necessary and sufficient condition, and a condition. I am here using both terms loosely and interchangeably.

[5] When not associated with a concept, [N] would trigger a pronominal interpretation; see Panagiotidis (2003b, 423–6). As an anonymous reviewer points out, if [N] is about identity and if it is present inside pronouns, then it is hard to explain the workings of expletive pronouns, such as *it* in *it rains*. I have no coherent answer to this problem.

[6] The criterion of individuation – namely, that 'two instances of a kind are distinct because they are the kinds of things they are' (Prasada 2008, 8) – does not apply to mass nouns. However, it may play a role in the object bias in the acquisition of nouns (Bloom 2000, chap. 4) and the perceived prototypical character of objects over substances in terms of nominality.

[7] There is *no* one-to-one correspondence between Ramchand's (2008, 38–42) *process* projection and the verbalizer projection here. However, it is crucial that *procP*, which 'specifies the nature of the change or process' (40), is understood as the essential ingredient of every dynamic verb.

being different perspectives on concepts, as different 'grammaticalisations' of concepts, to recall Anderson (1997). Zooming in on verbs, Uriagereka begins his treatment with the more or less received lore that 'themes are standardly nouns' and that 'verbal elements [are] functions over nouns'. He brings these two statements together by claiming the following:

(8)   A verb expresses the derivative of its theme's space over time.

Here, then, we have two essential ingredients for the interpretation of categorial features: perspective-setting, and the relevance of temporality (as opposed to predicativity) for verbs and their distinctive feature.[8] In a similar vein, Acquaviva (2009a, 2) notes that because 'verbal meaning is based on event structure [...], it has a temporal dimension built in. Nominal meaning, by contrast, does not have a temporal dimension built in.' If we replace 'meaning' with 'perspective' in Acquaviva's quote, we can make the claim that [V] encodes an actual *perspective* over the concept with which it is associated and that this perspective is of the said concept as extending into time: this is why verbs and their projections are the basic ingredients of events. From this point of view, we can actually call Vs and VPs subevents, with the feature [V] contributing the temporal perspective to event structures.

Some consequences of the way features [N] and [V] are interpreted, if we go by (7), include the following: first of all, we can now explain why objects – but, also, *substances* – are typically conceived as sortal concepts in the way sketched above; they smoothly satisfy both criteria of application and identity. This is compatible with the canonical mapping of such concepts onto nouns cross-linguistically and – as already pointed out – object and substance concepts are typically expressed as nouns. At the same time, together with Uriagereka (1999) and Baker (2003, 290–5), we expect dynamic events (activities, achievements, accomplishments) to be conceived typically as extending into time, hence the canonical mapping of such concepts onto verbs. If, on top of everything, dynamic events are compositionally derived from states and states are, very roughly, equivalent to VPs, then a theory of event structure, such as the ones in Rappaport Hovav and Levin (1998), Borer (2005), Levin and Rappaport Hovav (2005) and Ramchand (2008), receives added justification along the lines of verbal constituents being

---

[8] I have long thought that Langacker (1987) and Uriagereka's (1999) understanding of nouns as regions and spaces could be unified with Acquaviva's (2009a) treatment of nominal *concepts* as 'unbroken' – that is, as having no temporal parts (as discussed below). However, I presently can offer no true insight on this prospect.

inherently (sub-)eventive by virtue of the temporal perspective contributed by the categorial feature [V].

Furthermore, Tense and Voice exclusively combine with verbal projections (Tonhauser 2007). This generalization can now easily be associated exactly with the kind of perspective a [V] feature imposes on the concept it is associated with, through syntactic categorization of the root material. The root, along with everything else within the complement of *v*, will be interpreted as extending into time. In a similar fashion, Number combines with nouns. This can now be linked with the perspective an [N] feature imposes on the complement (typically containing a root) of an *n*: that of a sortal predicate satisfying both the criteria of application and identity. Interestingly, the association with a Num head, or similar, guarantees that the sortal concept in question – for example, *tree* – will also fulfil the third sortal criterion, that of individuation, as individuation can be coerced upon a wide range of 'inherently' non-countable concepts by classifiers and Number (Borer 2005).

An informal example illustrating how this difference in interpretive perspective works can be glimpsed by looking at the pair *sleep* the noun and *sleep* the verb. Both words can be said to encode the same concept. However, the noun *sleep* forces the viewing of this concept to be a sortal one, which is to say that the perspective over the concept of sleep that the nominal category imposes is of sleep as some type of virtual object or substance. We can therefore *lose our sleep* (like we lose our keys or lose blood), *get more sleep* (like we can get more air, food or water); we can also talk about *morning sleep* being different or sweeter than *early evening sleep*, and so on. On the other hand, the verb *sleep* forces us to view the concept of sleep as a subevent, as extending into time, which readily offers itself to temporal modification and so on. Similarly, the perspective over the concept of sleep that the verbal category imposes is of sleep being expressible as a time interval, as something potentially having duration (long, short etc.). This nicely ties in with the following long quote from Acquaviva (2009a, 2–3) (emphases added):

> ... nouns allow speakers to describe events unfolding in time as if they were complete entities that acquire and lose properties over time. We know that *argument* or *wedding* describe events, but we can speak of them as if they could undergo changes in time, as in (1):
>
> (1) a. the argument was calm at first, then it became heated (Simons 1987, 134)
>
>   b. the wedding moved from the church to the bride's parents' house

Speakers know that only a part of the event had a property and another part had the other property, but this is disregarded in a structure which predicates two contradictory properties of the same subject. The nature of the nouns' referents as occurrents is only disregarded, not changed; this becomes obvious when we explicitly state that the whole subject is there at a given time:

(2) a. the iron became heated (all of it) $\neq$ the argument became heated (all of it)
b. the wedding moved from A to B $\neq$ they married first in A then in B

In (2a), *all of it* may not refer to all of the event's temporal parts . . . In (2b), the right-hand side is not a good paraphrase of the left-hand side because *marry* is a telic verb and so the sentence entails that the event is completed, first in A, then in B. To explicitly describe the referents of *argument* and *wedding* as lacking temporal parts, thus, conflicts with their lexical semantics. Yet the sentences in (1) are natural even though they sideline temporal constitution. Reference to temporal constitution is thus inessential for nouns referring to occurrents. This, then, is a clear difference: verbal reference has a temporal dimension built in (in terms of actionality, not tense; this applies to permanent states as well as to bounded events); nominal reference does not, and can do without such a dimension even when referring to occurrents.

In any case, the truly important part of (7) is that [N] or [V] on *n* and *v* encode different perspectives, rather than different *inherent properties of the concept itself* as expressed by the root. This is actually a most welcome consequence of syntactically decomposing lexical categories in the light of pairs like ₙ *work* – ᵥ *work*, which brings us to the answer of what distinguishes *n* from *v*:

(9) Categorial features [N] and [V] are interpretable on the *n* and *v* categorizers respectively.

As we have seen, categorial features provide the fundamental interpretive perspective through which the meaning of the categorizer's complement will be negotiated. This will become especially relevant in the context of discussing the behaviour of roots below and in deriving Embick and Marantz's (2008, 6) Categorization Assumption, a discussion that began in Section 3.7 of the previous chapter.

4.4 The Categorization Assumption and roots

4.4.1 The Categorization Assumption

We turn next to the Categorization Assumption and examine it from the angle of how categorizers – their categorial features actually – enable the inclusion of roots in syntactic derivations that can be interpreted at the interfaces. Illustrating the Categorization Assumption below, we see that a root cannot be directly merged with a functional head – say, a Number or a Voice head: such NumPs or VoicePs are illicit.

(10)

This generalization is supported by a cursory look at languages where roots are morphologically bound morphemes, like Italian and Spanish: they can never combine with any functional material in the absence of categorizing heads.[9] Consider the situation in Greek. Roots emerge as stems like *aer–* ('air'), which are bound morphemes in the language. The impossibility of a structure like *[$_{NumP}$ Num ROOT] is very difficult to demonstrate, because Greek is a fusional language and nominal endings are typically the exponence of fusion between *n*, Number and Case (or 'Kase'). However, there are two facts to consider with respect to (10). The first is this: Greek possesses a linking form, typically expressed as –*o*–, which satisfies the morphological requirement for Greek stems to be bound but encodes *no grammatical* (or other) content. It is typically used in root–root compounding, where two roots merge together and are subsequently categorized:[10]

(11)   aer-o-vol-a   AER-O-VOL- N.NEUT.PL   'airguns'
       aer-o-por-os   AER-O-POR-N.MASC.SG.NOM   'aviator'
       aer-o-gram-i   AER-O-GRAM-N.FEM.SG   'airline'

This –*o*– morph is an elsewhere form and its sole purpose is to satisfy the requirement that Greek stems be morphologically bound. Interestingly, if that was all that there was – that is, a morphological restriction on stems – acategorial roots could easily be part of syntactic structures by getting –*o*– attached onto them as stems: we would expect –*o*– to have a wider distribution. However, –*o*– is illicit in all environments where the root is expected to be categorized – that is, where the roots will then have to combine with functional structure. Thus we have pairs like the following:

---

[9] Perhaps it might be possible to correlate the cross-linguistic avoidance of roots as free morphemes with the Categorization Assumption itself; however, this is not a claim I would make here.

[10] N here stands for 'nominal'.

(12) vrox-o-lastix-a
      VROX-O-LASTIX-N.NEUT.PL
      'rain tyres'

      lastix-a   vrox-is
      LASTIX- NOM.NEUT.PL   VROX-N.FEM.SG.GEN
      'rain tyres'

Before protesting that (12) simply adumbrates the morphology–syntax competition (Ackema and Neeleman 2004), we must consider work by Panagiotidis, Revithiadou and Spyropoulos (2013), which discusses Greek verbalizers: these are overwhelmingly expressed morphologically, and they make distinct verbal stems out of roots.[11] In the case of the root AER, the verbalizer is expressed as *–iz–* and combines with the root, yielding the unambiguously verbal stem *aeriz–* ('to air'). So, although the fact that roots in Greek must emerge as morphologically bound stems can be bypassed by using *–o–*, roots still *also* need to be categorized as nominal and – visibly – as verbal.

Hence, the descriptive observation that roots must be categorized is already made in the literature but neither Embick and Marantz (2008) nor Baker (2003) before them provide an attempt to derive it from more general principles – as Embick and Marantz claim should be done. Now, at the beginning of this chapter we noted that the Categorization Assumption is equivalent to an understanding that *roots cannot be interpreted unless inside the complement of a categorizer*. Having decomposed lexical categories 'noun' and 'verb' to parts of *n*P and *v*P projections, we are left with at least the following elements for syntax to build structures with:[12]

   a. Roots
   b. Categorizers (e.g., *n* and *v*)
   c. Functional heads (e.g., Num, D, T, C . . .)

Therefore the statement that 'roots need category' can be expanded to the descriptive generalization below:

(13)   Roots can only be merged inside the complement of a categorizer, *never* inside the complement of a functional head in the absence of a categorizer.

---

[11] The caveat 'overwhelmingly' is inserted because I am not sure light verbs exist in Greek.

[12] The list is incomplete and will be revised and expanded: we need also to include inner, subcategorial, morphemes, which merge directly with root material, as seen in the previous chapter. See Chapter 5, footnote 12.

A more traditional way to express (13) is of course that functional heads, unlike categorizers, cannot support *real descriptive content*, as in Abney's (1987, 64–5) oft-quoted criteria. However, we must still address the real question of why configurations like those in (10) are impossible and why (13) holds.

In order to reach a principled answer, we need to weave together three threads:

(14)   the zero hypothesis that roots are syntactically unexceptional;

(15)   an examination of the conceptual content and of the interpretation of roots as *objects* – that is, by themselves;

(16)   the role of categorial features [N] and [V] in the licensing of roots.

First, we take seriously the hypothesis that roots are *unexceptional* syntactically, by being merged inside the complement of material below the categorizers or, perhaps, by projecting their own phrases, too, as in Marantz (2006) and Harley (2007, 2009) – but see De Belder (2011) for argumentation against roots projecting phrases. This is the zero hypothesis, as stated in (14): if roots are manipulated by syntax, then they should behave like all other LIs ('lexical items'), unless there is evidence to the contrary. Having said that, (14) goes against what we have in (10) and (13), unless of course we try to stipulate (10) and (13) via some kind of c-selectional restrictions. Still, it is not the case that all roots are *directly* selected by *n* and *v*: as seen in Chapter 3, some roots may be deeply embedded inside more material.

Second, the thread in (15) is about carefully considering the LF interpretation of roots in isolation, so to speak, about examining their own conceptual content; in this I will assume that the semantic content of the root is seriously underspecified/impoverished.

Third, (16) announces that we will employ our newly developed understanding of categorial features on categorizers as providing the necessary perspective (e.g., sortal or temporal) through which the root will be interpreted; we will also explain why the *absence* of such an interpretive perspective prevents roots from participating in legitimate syntactic objects. In other words, I argue that categorizers exclusively provide the grammatical 'context' of Marantz (2000) for the root to be assigned an interpretation and/or a matching entry at the interface with the Conceptual–Intentional/SEM systems.

Let us now look at the second and third threads, (14) and (15), in more detail.

4.4.2   The interpretation of free roots

Bare roots are sometimes thought of as standing for stative predicates (Alexiadou 2001), whereas Doron (2003) and Levin and Rappaport Hovav (2005) assume them to contain argument structure information. This would make roots the semantic core of verbs; for instance, a root like OPEN would be the 'core element' of the verbs in *The window opened* and *Tim opened the window*. However, Acquaviva (2009a, 2009b) argues against *any* semantic content for roots along the following lines, already familiar from Aronoff (2007):[13] as the same root can underlie a number of nouns, verbs and adjectives with significantly different meanings, lexical information must necessarily be *root-external* (Acquaviva 2009b, 5); this is something to be expected if lexical information is assigned to grammatical structures at the interface with the Conceptual–Intentional systems. Moreover, it is not the case that the 'meaning' of the root can be a (proper) subset of that of the nouns, verbs and adjectives in the derivation of which it participates. To wit, Aronoff (2007, 819) observes that 'words have morphological structure even when they are not compositionally derived, and roots are morphologically important entities, [even] though not particularly characterized by lexical meaning.' He supplies the example of the Hebrew root KBš (typically rendered as bearing a meaning like 'press'):

(17)   KBš
    Nouns:
    keveš ('gangway', 'step', 'degree', 'pickled fruit')
    kviš ('paved road', 'highway')
    kviša ('compression')
    kivšon ('furnace', 'kiln')

    Verbs:
    kavaš ('conquer', 'subdue', 'press', 'pave', 'pickle', 'preserve', 'store', 'hide')
    kibeš ('conquer', 'subdue', 'press', 'pave', 'pickle', 'preserve')

We realize that there is no way in which 'step', 'degree', 'furnace', 'pave', 'highway', 'pickle' and 'conquer' can be *compositionally* derived from a root with conceptual content along the lines of 'press', or similar. If the words in (17) are all 'lexical idioms', then we are better off arguing, as Marantz (2000), Aronoff (2007) and Acquaviva (2009a, 2009b) essentially claim, that *all* lexemes are idioms. In Levinson's (2007) analysis of roots as polysemous,

---

[13] Acquaviva also discusses the issue of morphological class membership information and the problems arising if we argue that it is (not) encoded on the root.

all these words with their diverse and unrelated meanings should be listed as possible interpretations of the root KBŠ. However, if roots themselves are polysemous, then a root (say, KBŠ) must also lexically encode information on *which* of its many meanings is available in which syntactic environment.

Whatever the precise amount of semantic content that characterizes roots, what is important for the discussion here is that roots on their own have minimal semantic content or, as Arad (2003; 2005, chap. 3) proposes, that they are severely underspecified. This could be understood to result in free roots not being adequately specified to stand on their own as legitimate LF objects.[14] Consider that syntactic objects at LF – say, a *v*P phase – consist purely of interpretable and/or valued UG features *and* roots. Now, by hypothesis, syntax uses the operation Agree in order to eliminate uninterpretable and/or unvalued UG features before the phase is completed (i.e., before the derivation is sent off to the interface). But what about roots? Roots are possibly UG-extraneous elements. Even if this claim is too strong, roots do not form part of UG, as they can be borrowed or even coined, pre-theoretically speaking, at least. Roots are essentially 'imported' *into* the syntactic derivation. However, FLN (the Faculty of Language in the Narrow sense) *must* somehow manipulate roots, apparently in order to be able to express a variety of concepts. If no roots are manipulated by FLN in a particular derivation, we get expressions made up exclusively of UG features like 'This is her', 'I got that', 'It is here' and so on (cf. Emonds 1985, chap. 4). Therefore, the ability of FLN to manipulate roots enables it to denote concepts and, ultimately, to be used to 'refer' (Acquaviva and Panagiotidis 2012).

However, roots being possibly extraneous to FLN, and given that they probably do not contain any UG features (as is the emerging consensus), they need to be somehow dealt with by FLN: categorization is exactly the way this is achieved. In a nutshell: uncategorized roots are FLN-extraneous; either just because of this or also because they are semantically underspecified themselves, uncategorized roots would not be recognized at the interface between syntax and the Conceptual–Intentional/SEM systems.

---

[14] The semantic underspecification of (uncategorized) roots can be understood as the reason they are not legitimate objects at LF, but more needs to be said on the matter. For instance, Horst Lohnstein (personal communication, 2010) points out that a root like SPIT could still be interpretable in some sense even if it is underspecified, unlike KBŠ; the 'basic meaning' of SPIT as a root is more clearly circumscribed. However, even a relatively straightforward root like SPIT means much less when it is uncategorized than, for example, the verb it names. See Rappaport Hovav and Levin (1998) for discussion; see also Acquaviva and Panagiotidis (2012).

The specific claim made here is that syntax does not use a special operation to 'acclimatize' roots but embeds them within a categorizer projection, whose categorial features provide an interpretive perspective in which Conceptual–Intentional systems will associate the root with conceptual content. The short of it is that

(18)   (Free/uncategorized) roots are not readable by the Conceptual–Intentional/ SEM systems.

4.4.3   The role of categorization

Let us now take up the third thread, that in (16), and look at how categorial features license roots. In (18) we concluded that free roots are unreadable by the Conceptual–Intentional/SEM systems and in (13) we had rephrased Embick and Marantz's Categorization Assumption as a need for roots to always appear inside the complement of a categorizer. We now must clarify how categorization – that is, embedding roots inside the complement of a categorizer – cancels out the roots' LF-deficient character and allows them to participate in LF-convergent derivations.

By (7) and (9), the way this is achieved is that the categorial feature [N] or [V], on *n* or *v*, provides the interpretive perspective in which to interpret the root. At the same time, (13) is trivially satisfied because no functional heads bear interpretable categorial features (more on this in Chapter 5).[15] This picture is completed by what is pointed out in the very definition of the Categorization Assumption (Embick and Marantz 2008, 6): 'If all category-defining heads are phase heads ... the categorization assumption would follow from the general architecture of the grammar ...'.Given that roots cannot be directly embedded in the context of a *functional* phase head like C – compare the discussion of (10) – I would be tempted to think that the phasehood of categorizers ('category-defining heads') is not a sufficient condition for the categorization of roots.[16]

The argument goes as follows: roots are semantically impoverished when they are free. However, we have already noted that they are syntactically unexceptional objects: they may merge with elements such as low applicatives,

---

[15] This is already stated in Marantz (2000): 'To use a root in the syntax, one must 'merge' it (combine it syntactically) with a node containing category information.' I of course take [N] and [V] to be the said 'category information' here.

[16] Non-phasal heads could also provide a context for the interpretation of roots; categorizers could in principle be non-phasal heads. Note that if the objections in Anagnostopoulou and Samioti (2009) are correct, this is exactly the way things are: categorizer phrases are *not* phases but they are (inside) the complements of phase heads.

low causatives, abstract prepositions, particles and what we call 'inner morphemes'. Roots can also participate in small clause structures and, perhaps, they can project their own phrases, according to Marantz (2006) and Harley (2007, 2009). Nevertheless, the resulting structures would still contain an offending item, the LF-deficient root itself. In this sense, a 'free' root is simply an uncategorized root. In order to supply a concrete example, consider the configuration in (19), adapted from Marantz (2000, 27):

(19)

Merge creates a syntactic object from the root and its object 'tomatoes', with the root projecting: a syntactically unexceptional object. However, if this is embedded under functional structure without the licensing 'intervention' of a categorizer, then the resulting syntactic object will lack interpretive perspective, because of the SEM-deficient root GROW. This is why the categorial feature on the categorizer, [V] on *v* or [N] on *n*, is necessary: it assigns an interpretive perspective to the object as extending into time or as sortal, therefore enabling the resulting *v*P or *n*P – the so-called First Phase – to be interpreted. At the same time, the root-*categorizer* object, associated with an interpretive perspective, can be matched with a vocabulary item (*grow* or *growth*) and an appropriate 'lexical' concept, a 'meaning' (cf. Aronoff 2007).

(20)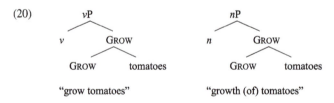

Summarizing, categorial features on the categorizer *close off* material associated with the root; they do so by providing this material with a fundamental perspective for the conceptual systems to view it in. No such perspective can be supplied by a (phase) head without categorial features: it is [N] or [V] on *n* or *v* that provide the necessary perspective, the 'context', for the root to be interpreted. Therefore, the association of root material with categorial features [N] and [V] enables the former to be interpreted at the interfaces and beyond. The categorization of roots is consequently not a narrow-syntactic requirement, but one of the interface between syntax and the conceptual–intentional/ SEM systems. It indeed follows "from the general architecture of the grammar" (Embick and Marantz 2008, 6).

4.4.4   nPs and vPs as idioms

Before turning to the status of categorizers – that is, whether they are functional heads – a note on the systematic idiomaticity of *n*Ps and *v*Ps is in order. To begin with, the interpretation of the First Phase is *canonically non-compositional*: in Section 3.4 of Chapter 3 we had a cursory look at well-known pairs such as $_N$ *water* – $_V$ *water* – $_A$ *watery*, $_N$ *dog* – $_V$ *dog*, $_N$ *castle* – $_V$ *castle*, $_N$ *deed* – $_V$ *do* and so on. Moreover, as argued in that same section, meanings associated with material such as root-*v* and root-*n* in (20) are invariably *listed* and almost always *idiosyncratic*. This is a well-known and widely examined fact, and recall that it is one of the key arguments supporting the analysis of word-formation in ways different from phrase-building.[17] This canonical idiosyncrasy/non-compositionality is what tempts one to think of the First Phase as a somehow *privileged* domain for non-compositional interpretation and to correlate idiomaticity of material with the fact that this material appears *below* the categorizer, within the categorizer's complement. However, we need to consider two factors, extensively discussed in Chapter 3:

a. Idiomaticity, non-predictability and non-compositionality are *in part* explained away once the role of subcategorial material ('inner morphemes' and the like) and argument structure are spelled out in more detail.

b. Given the impoverished or (even) inexistent semantic import of roots themselves, having non-compositional and idiosyncratic interpretations of material in *n*P and *v*P is the *only* option: no function yielding compositional interpretations could take a root as one of its operands.

Furthermore, as has been argued in the literature, idioms larger than the First Phase do exist: see, for instance, the discussion in Nunberg, Sag and Wasow (1994) and McGinnis (2002) – *pace* Svenonius (2005). So, although an idiomatic interpretation may be associated with syntactic constituents (phases perhaps) of various sizes, idiomaticity is the *only* option for first phases, exactly because of the semantic impoverishment/deficiency of roots.

Let us then summarize the conclusions of the previous chapter in the light of this chapter's analysis of categorizers. The systematic idiomaticity of first phases – that is, of categorizer phrases containing root material – is not due to the categorizer acting as a limit, below which interpretation is or must be non-compositional. On the contrary, idiomaticity is due to this projection

---

[17] For overviews, see Ackema and Neeleman (2004) and Marantz (1997, 2000, 2006).

(an *n*P or a *v*P) containing a root, an LF-deficient element by (18), that would resist acting as suitable input for *any* compositional function anyway. The categorial features on categorizers supply the complement of *n* or *v* with an interpretive perspective, within which the whole projection will be matched with a concept when the phase is interpreted. The perspective-setting categorial features are *necessary* for the matching of root material with a concept at LF, as no other phase head can take a free (i.e., 'uncategorized') root as its complement. Therefore, inner versus outer morphology phenomena (Marantz 2006) are due to the semantic impoverishment of roots: once roots have been dispatched to the interfaces, along with the rest of the complement of the categorizer, compositional interpretation may canonically apply in the next phase up.

4.5   Categorizers are not functional

Based on the above discussion, we can distil our analysis of categorial features on categorizers as follows:

(21)   Categorial features
        a. contribute the interpretive perspective phase-internally, and
        b. identify the whole phase externally (as 'nominal', 'verbal' etc.).

So, categorial features on categorizers enable roots to participate in the derivation, essentially empowering FLN to manipulate *concepts not encoded by UG-features* – that is, the vast majority of them. Furthermore, categorial features form the basis on which functional structure is built on, as will be demonstrated in the following chapter.

Although they are phase heads, categorizers are by no means functional heads, like Complementizer or Determiner. At the first level of empirical inquiry, it already becomes evident through the fact that no functional head can categorize roots and root material. This is true both for 'major' functional categories such as Voice, Aspect, Tense, Complementizer, Number or Determiner (recall (10) above) and for those subcategorial elements that Marantz (2000, 2006) terms 'inner morphemes'. I think that precisely here lies the difference between 'lexical' and functional': only the former can categorize a free root in its complement. So, effectively

(22)   There is only one class of 'lexical elements' that qualify as atomic
        'verbs': *v* heads.

(23)   There is only one class of 'lexical elements' that qualify as atomic
        'nouns': *n* heads.

Hence, contrary to the received perception of them, categorizers are *not* functional heads; they are the *only* lexical heads in existence. A way to systematically capture the above observations is to adopt Categorial Deficiency for 'major' functional categories (Panagiotidis 2002, 170–83), something to be scrutinized in the next chapter. However, the distinction between lexical and functional can already be recast as follows.

(24)   Lexical heads can support roots, by categorizing them. Functional heads *cannot* categorize roots; therefore they cannot be directly associated with roots.[18]

The fact that what we used to classify as 'lexical heads' are in reality the categorizers themselves can be glimpsed from a very privileged angle once we consider *semi-lexical categories* (Corver and van Riemsdijk 2001). Semi-lexical elements are lexical nouns and verbs that do not carry any descriptive content, including English *one* (as in *the right one*), 'empty nouns' (Panagiotidis 2003b) and at least some types of light verbs. Emonds (1985, chap. 4) already analyses semi-lexical elements – which he calls *grammatical nouns* and *grammatical verbs* – as instances of N and V heads without any descriptive, concept-denoting features. This line of analysing semi-lexical heads is taken up and developed in van Riemsdijk (1998a), Haider (2001), Schütze (2001) and Panagiotidis (2003b). I think it is very interesting that Emonds' definition, dating from 1985, of such elements as lexical elements that only bear *formal* features is exactly what we would think *categorizers themselves* are in a lexical decomposition framework: consider, for instance, Folli and Harley's (2005) postulation of three *v* heads CAUS, DO and BECOME. Indeed, Emonds (1985, 159–68) claims that different lexical entries of grammatical nouns and grammatical verbs can be distinguished from each other by virtue of their formal features only, as they are completely devoid of any descriptive content.

It seems, then, that when we deal with semi-lexical elements, the root supplying the descriptive content – whichever way it does it – is absent. So, a first straightforward conclusion would be that in order to have a 'noun' (*n*P)

---

[18] As a consequence, adpositions and functional elements such as determiners should not contain roots. Received lore within Distributed Morphology would indeed take all functional elements to be bundles of features realized by Vocabulary Items. As for adpositions, the lexical material they contain – that is, the 'heavy' nominal and adverbial material briefly mentioned in Section 2.9 of Chapter 2 – must already be categorized. I am grateful to Carlos de Cuba (personal communication, April 2008) who first raised this question in 2008, and to an anonymous reviewer.

or a 'verb' (vP) a *root* is not necessary, whereas categorizers always are. This is a conclusion that Harley (2005a) arrives at, in her treatment of *one*: she convincingly shows that *one* is, precisely, the Vocabulary Item inserted when an *n* head is not associated with a root, under certain morphosyntactic conditions.

The above strongly suggests that (category-less) roots and subcategorial material are – syntactically speaking – optional and that a well-formed syntactic representation can be constructed using just categorizers and a functional structure superimposed on them: we can build syntactic structures using only a categorizer as its 'seed'; roots are not necessary. We will return to this observation in the next chapter.

4.6   Nouns and verbs

According to the account presented in this chapter, a nominal feature [N] is completely different from a verbal feature [V]. [N] and [V] are presented as different attributes, as also suggested by the different interpretive perspectives they impose, rather than different values of the same feature. But is this really the case? Is there a principled reason to prevent them from being the two values of a categorial feature, a [perspective] feature, more concretely? Alternatively, what prevents nominality from being the default perspective, resulting from a [−V] feature or from the absence of a [V] feature?[19]

Kayne (2009) makes a very interesting proposal along the lines of nouns being the unmarked category. He applies antisymmetry (Kayne 1994) to the lexicon to argue that there are lexical items of category *x* and lexical items of the category *y*. Lexical items of the category *x* form an open class, they only contain valued features and are not the locus of parametric variation – these are the nouns. Nouns, by virtue of having no unvalued features, are also the only lexical elements that can denote. Lexical items of the category *y* form a closed class, they enter the derivation with unvalued features and are the locus of parametric variation – these are 'non-nouns': that is, a category containing at least verbs and aspectual heads. Effectively, Kayne (2009) takes nouns to be the only (open) lexical category, whereas verbs are made of light verbs (a closed class, akin to *v*) with nominal complements, as in Hale and Keyser's (1993, 55) proposal concerning *laugh* and similar items: '*laugh* is a noun that in some sentences co-occurs with a light verb that is unpronounced, giving the

---

[19] Some relevant options had already been explored by Déchaine (1993) in her three-feature system for lexical and functional categories.

4.6 Nouns and verbs

(misleading) impression that *laugh* in English can also be a verb. Strictly speaking, though, *laugh* is invariably a noun, even when it incorporates (in some sense of the term) into a (silent) light verb' (Kayne 2009, 7). In a nutshell, English 'verbs' are all denominal, nouns are the only lexical category and something like *v* (Kayne's *y*) verbalizes them. Of course, we saw in the previous chapter that deriving *all* verbs from nouns is not the right way to go and adopting such a thesis would both entail missing a number of generalizations (beginning with the *hammer–tape* contrast) and blurring the very useful (if not absolutely vital) distinction between nouns and acategorial roots. Finally, I think it would not be far removed from the spirit of Kayne's proposal to claim that roots are nominal by default. This is, however, a point Acquaviva (2009a) extensively argues against.

The questions of whether [N] and [V] are simply values of a single [perspective] feature and whether one of them is unmarked and/or default present a rather intricate conceptual matter, and relevant empirical evidence can be very hard to come by. What I will do in the remainder of this chapter is (a) provide arguments for keeping the [N] and the [V] features separate and (b) debate to what extent [N] shows signs of being the unmarked categorial feature.

4.6.1   Keeping [N] and [V] separate?

Although both [N] and [V] impose interpretive perspectives, perhaps supplying the grounds for treating them as merely different values of a [perspective] feature, a sortal perspective and a temporal one are quite different from each other. Moreover, once we have a proper theory of syntactic categorization from roots in place, we do not need to automatically think of nouns as more basic/elementary than verbs or to think of verbs as more marked than nouns. Finally, the impairment of nouns and that of verbs in aphasia are doubly dissociated (Caramazza and Hillis 1991), as would be expected if the distinction underlying the noun–verb distinction involved different features.

However, there are some facts that could point towards understanding [V] and [N] as different values of the same feature, with [V] – or whatever its proper notation would be – appearing to be more marked than [N]. An initial piece of data pointing in this direction comes from Arad (2005, chap. 3), who discusses the fact that nominal and verbal morphology seem to be of a different nature in languages such as Hebrew and Russian, both inflectionally rich languages. I will exemplify the phenomenon she discusses using Greek examples, as the facts seem to be identical in this language.

In Hebrew, Russian and Greek nouns can be borrowed exactly as they are, modulo phonological adaptation. Observe, for instance, the following loanwords into Greek:

(25)   *Loanwords into Greek: nouns*
         rok   'rock music'
         solo   'solo'
         zum   'zoom'
         indriga   'intrigue' – from Italian *intriga*

At the same time, when borrowing roots to make verbs, special verbalizing morphology must be added to these root forms in order to turn them into legitimate verbal stems – recall the discussion in Section 4.4.1:

(26)   rok-ar-o   'I rock.'
         sol-ar-o   'I do a solo.'
         zum-ar-o   'I zoom in.'
         indrig-ar-o   'I intrigue sb.'

On the basis of similar evidence from Hebrew and Russian, Arad argues that this asymmetric behaviour is the result of a *VoiceP* (as opposed to a bare *v*P) being the *minimum* verb. She goes on to argue that although a nominalized root is a noun, a verbalized root is not a verb: this results in the paradox of a verbalized root being smaller than a verb. Corroborating this is the fact that, in Hebrew, 'roots make nouns more easily than verbs' (Arad 2005, 56), a fact that also seems to hold true for Greek, even beyond the domain of borrowing.[20] However, taking a better look at (26) above, it turns out that the extra morphology, the *–ar–* form, attached to (borrowed) roots to make verbs is not an exponence of Voice but, rather, of *v* itself. Panagiotidis, Revithiadou and Spyropoulos (2013) observe that the *–ar–*-type elements that make verbal stems out of roots co-exist with Voice, Aspect, Tense and Agreement morphology, and they are obligatory, even when combining with native roots: it is impossible to form verbs from roots without one of these pieces.[21] Even so, the fact that verbalizers, *v* heads, overwhelmingly tend to be morphologically expressed in Greek (and, possibly, in Hebrew and Russian, too), unlike the *n* head, is something that in turn must be explained: the issue of the markedness of verbs re-emerges.

---

[20] Nouns vastly outnumber verbs in any given dictionary, after all.

[21] There is actually a very limited number of verbs, all of Ancient Greek origin, that do not show an overt piece of verbalizing morphology; these include *graf-o* ('I write'), *vaf-o* ('I paint/dye'), *trex-o* ('I run'), *idri-o* ('I found/establish').

Given this apparent markedness of verbs, would we perhaps have to express this asymmetry by keeping the [V] feature while replacing [N] as [−V], the unmarked 'elsewhere' value? If this is the case, then nouns would be the default category, exactly as we saw Kayne (2009) predict, taking nouns to be the default category. A language that looks ideally suited to test the claim that nouns are the unmarked lexical category is Farsi.

4.6.2   *Do Farsi verbs always contain nouns?*

Farsi is known for having only 100 simplex verbs (Karimi-Doostan 2008a), although far fewer are reported to be commonly used (Peyman Vahdati, personal communication, 2005). All other verbal concepts are expressed via periphrastic constructions made of preverbs, predicative elements, which combine with fourteen light verbs (Family 2008) to give Light Verb Constructions known in the literature as Complex Predicates (Folli, Harley and Karimi 2003). This is illustrated in the examples below (from Family 2008):[22]

(27)   *Farsi Complex Predicates with nominal preverbs*

hærf zædæn	word hit	'talk'
xun ændaxtæn	blood throw	'cause to bleed'
kæm ʃodæn	few become	'be diminished'
qæbul daʃtæn	assent have	'maintain as true'
arameʃ dadæn	calmness give	'calm'
jæʃn gereftæn	party obtain	'celebrate'
tʃopoq keʃidæn	pipe pull	'smoke a pipe'
qorbæt keʃidæn	remoteness pull	'long for home'

Farsi Complex Predicates, substituting for verbs, are multiply exciting. What we are going to focus on here, however, is the categorial status of the preverbs. The preverbs in (27) all look like nouns, making Farsi Complex Predicates apparently similar to English periphrases like *have/take a shower, have/take a look, make a call/a statement/a mistake, take a picture* and the like. The Farsi situation is much more intricate. Karimi-Doostan (2008a, emphasis added) explains why:

> Some of the [preverbs] are adverbs, adjectives, prepositions or nouns but some of them lack any lexical category and will be called *Classless Words* (CWs) …. The adverbs and adjectives can be used in superlative and comparative forms and they can be modified by intensifier adverbs like

---

[22] Farsi is a subject–object–verb (SOV) language.

'very'. The nouns can be pluralized and selected by D, demonstrative adjectives and prepositions and they can function as subject and object. However, CWs do not have any of the properties of adverbs, adjectives and nouns referred to here. CWs are different from prepositions and simple verbs too. Prepositions can directly select DPs, but CWs cannot. Simple verbs may co-occur with verbal inflectional items, but CWs may not.

Karimi-Doostan (2008a) goes on to show that Classless Words are listed as independent lexemes, behave unlike nouns with respect to *ezafe* – that is, a type of nominal agreement (see Larson and Yamakido 2008), cannot be the input to nominalization and cannot function as subjects or objects or – of course – verbs:[23]

(28)   *Farsi Complex Predicates with Classless Word preverbs*

faraamush kardæn	forgetting do	'forget'
mahsub kardæn	taking into account do	'take into account'
haali kardæn	understood do	'cause to understand'
moraxas kardæn	releasing do	'let leave, release'
vaadaar kardæn	persuading do	'persuade'
kansel kardæn	cancel do	'cancel'
gom kardæn	losing do	'lose'

There is an interesting issue here. Complex predicates in (28), involving the purported Classless Words, seem to mostly have predictable, possibly compositional, meanings. This would discourage us from pursuing an analysis in which they are subcategorial uncategorized roots, merged in the derivation as the complements of a categorizing *v* head. After all, as Karimi-Doostan (2008b, 3) shows in detail, *all* other preverbs in Farsi Complex Predicates, whether they yield compositional or idiosyncratic interpretations, are fully categorized: Preposition Phrases, adjectives, adverbs, nouns. If this observation is on the right track, then in Farsi there also exists a *default lexical category* that is neither verbal nor nominal. Its distribution is restricted inside Complex Predicates, by virtue of this 'Classless' default lexical category encoding neither a sortal perspective, a contribution of [N], nor a temporal one, a contribution of [V] – Classless Words lacking either categorial feature. At the same time, I think that the existence of Classless Words constitutes evidence that nouns are not the default lexical category.

Where would the above leave us with respect to whether [N] and [V] are different features or different values of a [perspective] feature? An initial answer would be that [N] should perhaps be recast as [perspective:sortal], [V] as [perspective:temporal], while Classless Words would perhaps be introduced by a categorizer with an *unvalued* [perspective:] feature. [N] and [V] will still be used, as mnemonically convenient flags, but the question of unvalued and, crucially, uninterpretable features takes us into the next chapter and the status of functional categories.

5 *Functional categories*

5.1 Introduction

Arguing for two privative/unary categorial features, [N] and [V], as setting particular interpretive perspectives marks a significant step in our understanding of the workings and status of categorizers n and v respectively. However, the theory developed here goes well beyond providing an interpretation for the behaviour of categorizers. In this chapter I will put forward the hypothesis that *uninterpretable* categorial features are borne by functional heads. In Section 5.2 the case against dedicated 'category' features for functional elements is made and in Section 5.3 the idea that functional heads are satellites of lexical ones, members of a lexical category's functional entourage, is rehearsed, an idea familiar from such analytical concepts as Grimshaw's (1991) *Extended Projections*, van Riemsdijk's (1998a) *M-projections* and Chomsky's (2001) supercategories. Section 5.4 correlates this idea with the notion of biuniqueness – namely, that functional elements may appear in the superstructure of only one lexical head and in Section 5.5 I argue against the claim that biuniqueness entails that functional heads bear the categorial specification of the lexical head in their 'Extended Projection'. Categorial Deficiency, the hypothesis that uninterpretable categorial features flag functional heads, is introduced in Section 5.6 and is refined in Sections 5.7 and 5.8. In Section 5.9 we review the crucial consequences of Categorial Deficiency: how uninterpretable categorial features triggering Agree operations can account for some well-established characteristics of phrase structure and how uninterpretable categorial features are the Agree probes that regulate labelling of (some) projections after the application of Merge. The final section concludes the chapter.

5.2 The category of functional categories

In the previous chapter a theory of category was introduced in which categorial features

106

(1)   a. are LF-interpretable;
        b. are borne by categorizers;
        c. define the interpretive perspective of the categorizers' complement.

The above represents an attempt to make clear predictions with respect to resolving the question of what makes nouns nouns and verbs verbs, suggesting what their difference is, clarifying the interpretive role of categorizers and, more precisely, the interpretive function of the features on categorizers that are responsible for the categorization of roots or the recategorization of already categorized constituents. If this is the picture regarding *lexical* categories, the evident thing to ask next is 'what about *functional* categories'?

Functional categories are certainly peculiar beasts. The very detailed survey in Muysken (2008) is particularly revealing in this respect. Muysken extensively examines the theoretical status of functional categories and their role in grammar; he also studies their behaviour in diachronic processes (e.g., *grammaticalization*), their acquisition and their processing, as well as their vulnerability in language breakdown and language death, and in a variety of contact situations. Repeatedly throughout the book he observes that there exist no unambiguous criteria for functional category membership. Hence, he concludes that 'indeed there is an overall correspondence between the functional status of an element and its form, but that this correspondence cannot be captured by structural principles' (Muysken 2008, 41). To this Muysken adds that 'very few semantic features, if any, unambiguously characterise a class of elements that may be reasonably termed functional categories' (2008, 52). A central problem with any pre-theoretical definitions of what functional categories are stems from the lack of any isomorphism between the phonological, the morphosyntactic and, say, the parsing behaviour of the purported class of functional elements. Muysken (2008, chap. 18) eventually opts for a multi-factorial model in order to capture what he conceives as a symmetrical lexical–functional schema, heavily based on formal criteria nevertheless; the multi-factorial model turns out to be useful in teasing apart the different entwined strands characterizing phenomena like grammaticalization and borrowing. The overall conclusion is that the lexical–functional distinction is real but, ultimately, one that must be made theory-internally, as happens with most of the important analytical distinctions in scientific enquiry.

One can, therefore, take a variety of approaches towards establishing this distinction formally. The first is to argue that next to [N] or [V], there should also exist dedicated *categorial* features for functional categories such as [T] for Tense, [C] for Complementizer or Chomsky's (1995) [D] for Determiner. These features would define functional categories as word classes, whereas the features themselves (e.g., [T], [C], [D] etc.) would be interpretable at LF. Again, this appears to form among theoretical syntacticians the received, albeit largely unexamined, view, a view made explicit, for example, in textbooks such as Adger (2003). Still, in the spirit of looking for an explanatory theory of category, as opposed to settling for a purely taxonomic grouping of grammatical elements, we must seriously ask the question of what kind of interpretation features like [T], [C] or [D] would have.

(2)   What is the interpretation of categorial features on functional heads?

Answering this question is both easy and difficult: easy because one can straightforwardly come up with specific ideas on the interpretation of the [T] feature – for example, anchoring in time; [C] would most likely encode illocutionary force and [D] would encode referentiality and, possibly, also deixis. However, if we are guided by a desire for thoroughness, we will soon stumble upon the fact that answering (2) can be a rather complex affair, punctuated by a number of complications.

An initial complication involves the categorial features of functional categories beyond Tense, Complementizer and Determiner – that is, of categories such as Focus, Topic, Mood, Aspect, Voice (in the clausal/verbal projection line), and Quantifier, Number, Classifier (in the nominal projection line). Surely, these are all natural classes with identifiable LF interpretations. Adopting a coherent theory of features where features consist of an *attribute* and a range of *values*, we could easily capture functional categories as natural classes defined by their features. In the case of Complementizer, for instance, the [C] feature could be reformulated as an 'illocutionary force' attribute with declarative, interrogative and so on being different values thereof. Adger (2010) offers a cogent and detailed discussion on the details of implementing a system like that. Hence, we could treat categorial features for functional categories as ordinary LF-interpretable features consisting of an attribute and possible values. Different attributes – for example, 'illocutionary force', 'reference/deixis', 'anchoring in time' – would define different functional categories, Complementizer, Determiner and Tense respectively. The above would give us the following: (a) the LF-interpretable content of functional categories, and (b) why, for example, a [Q](uestion) head and the Complementizer *that* belong to the same natural class: because they bear the same illocutionary force feature, albeit differently valued.

However, would these features truly be our categorial features? If we answer this in the affirmative, then we actually commit ourselves to a view, one with some currency, that a functional head bears at most *one* interpretable feature:

this hypothesis is formulated as Kayne's (2005, chaps. 8 and 12) *Principle of Decompositionality*. A version of this principle informs Cinque (1999) and the cartographic approach in general, and forms the impetus of Starke's (2009, 2011) nanosyntax, where 'features are terminals' (Starke 2009, 2). If this were the case, then in a given grammar there would be as many functional heads as the interpretable features that can be encoded on them. Essentially, in this view, each interpretable feature *makes* its own functional head. A second matter is whether or not *all* UG-features are available in *all* grammars. If all UG-features are active in every natural language grammar, then the repertory of functional heads is also universal under these assumptions – making functional categories such as Classifier, Topic and Mood universal. This is presupposed in the influential Cinque (1999) and much subsequent work in Cartography, with the added assumption that there is a *fixed order* of these functional heads.

Here I wish to take a very different stand. Building on work by Thráinsson (1996), Bobaljik and Thráinsson (1998), Hegarty (2005) and Panagiotidis (2008), I wish to claim that the repertory of functional categories may vary from grammar to grammar.[1] According to this approach, the learner builds grammar-specific functional categories drawing from a *subset* of the feature pool that UG makes available: Focus, Topic, Force, Mood, Aspect, Voice Quantifier, Referentiality, Deixis, Number features and so on. To illustrate the consequences of this view, let us take Referentiality and Deixis features as an example. Whereas Grammar A may possess a functional head Det bearing Referentiality features and a separate functional head Dem bearing Deixis features, Grammar B may possess a single, unitary head bearing both Referentiality and Deixis features: English Determiner seems to be one of them (for discussion, see Panagiotidis 2008). If a functional head may host two or more LF-interpretable features – say, Referentiality and Deixis – it automatically follows that such features cannot act as categorial features. This becomes a very serious issue if one considers the possibility that (at least) some languages conflate the Complementizer Field (Rizzi 1997) into two Comp-type heads (Preminger 2010) or, even, a single, unitary Complementizer head (cf. Newmeyer 2004): would Focus, Topic or Force features together act as the

---

[1] There is some debate even about which would be the zero hypothesis, especially from an acquisition perspective: a universal fixed repertory of functional categories which are encoded in UG or forced by the Conceptual–Intentional systems, or a pool of UG features for the learner to assemble her own repertory of functional categories. See also Borer (2005) for insightful discussion.

categorial features of such a unitary Comp-head? Similar problems arise when, for example, we have languages with a conflated Quantifier–Determiner head – and so on.

A second reason for choosing this path – that is, positing grammar-specific functional categories assembled from a *subset* of the UG feature pool – has to do with the functional–lexical distinction and with 'biuniqueness' in the special sense that the term is used in Felix (1990). Both are examined below.

5.3   Functional categories as 'satellites' of lexical ones

A common way to deal with the difference between lexical and functional categories is to think of functional elements as bearing no descriptive, concept-denoting features; alternatively – and very similarly – functional elements are conceptualized as unable to assign θ-roles. This is an idea that has been around for some time, although it has hardly ever been defended explicitly. Still, it has gained some currency; for instance, Haegeman (2006) invokes it exactly with the purpose of distinguishing lexical from functional categories: the latter are unable to assign thematic roles.

However, distinguishing lexical from functional on the basis of θ-assignment and/or semantic content becomes much less convincing once *semi-lexical* elements are considered. Recall from the previous chapter these are typically lexical heads, lexical nouns and verbs, which do not seem to carry any descriptive content: still, they are not functional elements; see also the treatment in the following section.

The functional–lexical conundrum is extensively and insightfully discussed in Chametzky (2000, 22–32; 2003, 213–19) and Hinzen (2006, 174). Both Chametzky and Hinzen essentially take functional elements to be satellites of lexical ones; functional elements are understood to belong to the same 'supercategory' (Chomsky 2001, 47) as the lexical categories of which they form the functional entourage: hence, no matter how many functional categories are hypothesized, motivated and discovered, no actual proliferation of the number of *stricto sensu* parts of speech is necessary. An extension of this view of functional elements as 'dependencies' of lexical ones, as members of a lexical 'supercategory', is the even more radical and exciting approach that functional categories *do not exist* as primitives of the grammar at all. In this view, functional elements are perhaps just collections of features (either feature bundles or feature structures) in the Numeration which are flagged by a feature, just like Hegarty (2005) claims, in order to stand as a functional head during the derivation. This view essentially echoes the insights in Chametzky (2003, 213–19).

5.4   Biuniqueness

Besides their acting as satellites of lexical heads, there is a second property of functional elements that a proper account of their categorial features should capture – namely, what Felix (1990) calls *biuniqueness*, harking back to at least Martinet. Biuniqueness, according to Felix, is a general require-ment that functional elements merge in the projection line of only one kind of lexical head. For instance, D can only merge in the projection line of N, T in that of V, and so on. For mixed projections, which constitute a principled exception to this, see Bresnan (1997), Alexiadou (2001) and the following chapter.

There is a recurrent theme in the generative literature with respect to how to best capture biuniqueness, while also successfully addressing the question of the category of functional categories. Ouhalla (1991), Grimshaw (1991) as well as van Riemsdijk's (1998a) *Categorial Identity Thesis* all converge on the following hypothesis:

(3)   Functional categories bear the categorial specification of the lexical head in their projection line.

Illustrating, Aspect and Tense heads will all bear a [V] feature, whereas Number heads and Determiners must also bear an [N] feature. Any version of feature matching consequently guarantees that D (an [N] category) will never select V; T (a [V] category) will never select N – and so on.

But why only talk about nouns and verbs in (3)? We have of course discussed a number of objections to the uniformly lexical status of adpositions and even to their forming a coherent category in Chapter 2, Section 2.9; we have also argued in Section 2.8 of the same chapter that adjectives, even if they are a uniform lexical category, are not of the same ilk as nouns and verbs. However, these objections are not enough if we wish to exclude adpositions and adjectives from the discussion of biuniqueness: we would now need to show that there are no functional categories biuniquely associated with P and A. Interestingly, it has already been argued that what makes biuniqueness essentially a relation between nouns and the nominal functional layer and between verbs and the verbal/clausal functional layer is the fact that 'while V[erb]/N[oun] are uniquely selected by Functional heads, P[reposition]/A [djective] aren't' (Déchaine 1993, 32).

Let me begin with adpositions, which are relatively easy to deal with. Déchaine (1993, 34) puts it curtly: 'I know of no examples of P c-selected by a Functional head.' Assuming that some adpositions are indeed lexical – say, *behind, aboard, underneath, opposite, regarding* and the like – these are typically related to nominal functional material; they are probably specifiers of functional elements in a nominal superstructure, therefore of satellites of N. This is one of the main topics in van Riemsdijk (1998a), who examines the behaviour of Germanic 'lexical P-DP-functional P' structures like *auf den Berg hinauf* ('on the mountain upon'), the c-selection relations of prepositions with both the verbs selecting them (e.g., *depend on*) and the nouns inside their complement (e.g., *in 1996, on Sunday*). He concludes that prepositions 'should, in a sense yet to be made precise, be considered (extended) projections of nouns, at least when they are transitive. One aspect of this decision is that a nominal projection embedded in a prepositional shell does not constitute a maximal projection DP; instead, there is a transition from D' to P', induced by the prepositional head' (van Riemsdijk 1998a, 31). Sticking with this conclusion and not going into any more detail here, as in Chapter 2 the reader is referred to Emonds (1985, 156–7), where Prepositions are equated to Complementizers, to Baker (2003, 303–25), who considers Adpositions to be instances of Kase, to Svenonius (2007, 2008), Botwinik-Rotem and Terzi (2008) and Terzi (2010), for whom adpositions are complex structures parallel to argument structures.

Turning to adjectives, and in order not to repeat the discussion in Chapter 2, Section 2.8, on Degree Phrases and the question of the extent to which they are part of an Extended Projection of adjectives, I think a point made by Déchaine (1993, 35) actually sheds a lot of light on Degree heads, as opposed to Degree adjuncts:[2] 'any stative predicate can take a degree modifier, as long as it is gradable'. This generalization is already captured in Maling (1983) and becomes a reasonable working hypothesis when one considers Greek Degree expressions. Recall from the discussion of Neeleman, Doetjes and van de Koot (2004) that we have to distinguish between two classes of Degree expressions. On the one hand, we have what they call 'Class 2' Degree expressions – Degree adjunct modifiers like *more, less, enough, a little, a good deal* – which are promiscuous in that they adjoin to PPs, VPs and so on. Contrasting with them, we also have 'Class 1' Degree heads like *very, as, too, that, how*, which appear to belong

---

[2] See Section 2.8.2 in Chapter 2.

to the Extended Projection of an Adjectival Phrase, to the adjectival projection line, taking APs as their complements, as sketched below:

(4)   *Class 1 Degree expressions*

Let us turn to Class 1 Degree expressions in Modern Greek and see if we can indeed make the case for them being functional heads in a biunique relationship with adjectives, as is the claim in Neeleman, Doetjes and van de Koot (2004). Like English, Greek also seems to possess at least one Class 1 Degree expression: *pio* ('more'). Like *very* in English, *pio* needs to be embedded in a structure with a dummy adjective like *poly* ('much') in its complement, in order to combine with *most* non-APs: [[$_{DegP}$ Deg *poly*] [XP]]. Compare the behaviours of Class 1 expression *pio* ('more') and Class 2 expression *toso* ('that much/little'), which does not need a dummy adjective *poly* ('much) when it modifies non-adjectival expressions:[3]

(5)   *Class 1 ('pio') and Class 2 ('toso') Degree expressions in Greek*
    a. With adjectives and adverbs:
       pio kryo (more cold) 'colder'
       pio kato (more down) 'further down'
       toso kryo (that cold) 'that cold'
       toso kato (that down) 'that far down'
    b. With verb phrases:
       efaye pio *(poly) (ate more much) 's/he ate more'
       efaye toso (poly) (ate that much) 's/he that much'
    c. With preposition phrases:
       pio *(poly) sto kryo (more much in.the cold) 'more in the cold'
       toso (poly) sto kryo (that much in.the cold) 'that much in the cold'
    d. With nominal phrases:
       pio (poly) anthropos (that much human) 'more of a human being'
       toso (poly) anthropos (that more human) 'that much of a human being'
       pio #(poly) spiti (more much home) 'more of a home'
       toso (poly) spiti (that much home) 'that much of a home'

---

[3] Although it translates as 'more', *pio* is not a morpheme purely for the formation of periphrastic comparatives: it combines with indeclinable adverbs like *kato* ('down'), *mesa* ('inside'), *pera* ('far away') and *ektos* ('outside') which are not derived from adjectives. Moreover, its behaviour is identical to that of a number of Degree prefixes intensifying the adjective: *kata-* ('over'), *olo-* ('all'), *pan-* ('total'), *theo-* ('god'), *yper-* ('super'), *tris-* ('thrice'), *tetra-* ('fourfold'), *penta-* ('fivefold') and so on – which I will not discuss here for the sake of brevity.

The behaviour of the two expressions with VPs and PPs is as expected in Neeleman, Doetjes and van de Koot (2004). However, when it comes to noun phrases, the picture changes. If the noun is inherently gradable, then *pio* is felicitous on its own, without a dummy adjective *poly* ('much') as its complement, suggesting that this Class 1 Degree expression can actually take a nominal complement, as long as it is plausible to perceive it as gradable (Déchaine 1993, 35). *Anthropos* ('human being') is such a gradable noun, so '*pio anthropos*' ('more of a human being') in (5)d. can be felicitous either in the context of discussing evolution (e.g., *homo erectus* is more of a human than *homo habilis*) or moral qualities and/or being humane. Even more interestingly, just as Number can coerce the nominal in its complement into a kind and/or countable reading (cf. the ambiguous 'we need three coffees here'), the Degree expression *pio* can coerce an inherently non-gradable noun to behave as such, just like *spiti* ('home/house') in (5)d. above, which can be uttered comparing the appearance of a particular residence (a converted warehouse, a hut etc.) to a prototypical home or house.[4] So, at least in Greek, Class 1 Degree expressions cannot be claimed to be to the category A what D is to N and T to V. In other words, the relation between Degree and Adjective is not a categorial one; better put, to the extent that the Degree–Adjective relation (somehow) refers to category, it is not a biunique one between Degree and Adjective. Putting this together with the brief review on adpositions, we can argue for the following.

(6)   Biuniqueness is a relationship only between nouns and the nominal functional heads (D, Num etc.) and between verbs and the verbal/clausal functional heads (Voice, Asp, T, Mood etc.).

Now, the thesis in (3), a more articulated version of the intuition about 'supercategories', effectively captures the insights in Chametzky (2000), Hegarty (2005) and Hinzen (2006) that functional elements are satellites of lexical ones, and that functional categories *do not exist* as primitives of the grammar. However, a solution to the problem of 'the category of functional categories' like the one in (3) leads to a rather undesirable result – namely, that we cannot distinguish *functional* from *lexical* categories on the basis of categorial features only: we hardly want to say that, for example, T or Asp are *verbs* by virtue of their [V] feature. In other words, the very same feature

---

[4] Identical facts hold for the intensifying prefixes in footnote 3, with a lot of room for innovation and speaker variation – morphophonological matters, allomorphy and the usual morphological idiosyncrasies notwithstanding.

that is supposed to distinguish verbs from other categories, a categorial feature, fails to discern verbs from functional elements inside the clausal/verbal projection line, in their own 'Extended Projection' (Grimshaw 1991). Identical facts hold for [N] as a feature of 'nominal' functional elements.

As already mentioned, attempts to distinguish lexical from functional elements on the basis of the latter not supporting conceptual content and/or θ-roles stumble upon the existence of *semi-lexical* elements, these being lexical heads, typically lexical nouns and verbs, which do not carry any descriptive content (Panagiotidis 2003b). At the same time, the claim that functional heads cannot assign thematic roles made good sense in frameworks where lexically listed θ-roles were assigned by lexical verbs (and, perhaps, nouns, adjectives and prepositions, too) as a projection of their lexical properties. However, this makes little sense in a more syntacto-centric approach to argument structure, where, for instance, Voice and applicative heads (both definitely functional) also assign θ-roles. Whether this approach to θ-assignment is correct or not, semi-lexical elements, clearly not functional heads, also assign no thematic roles.[5]

Suppose, then, that we attempt to overcome this problem via trying to capture the lexical–functional distinction in a more up-to-date fashion, and that we state that functional elements cannot bear any descriptive, concept-denoting features. Clearly, this makes C, D, T or Asp different from *roots*, commonly assumed to bear descriptive content, but not different from *n* and *v* themselves. Finally, a formulation along the lines of 'functional elements cannot support (uncategorized) root material in their complement' seems accurate (see the discussion on the Categorization Assumption in the previous chapter). However, as already detailed there, this generalization is an explicandum not an explicans: it is merely a generalization and not an explanation.

Thus, capturing biuniqueness as the sharing of a categorial feature between lexical and functional elements in a projection line effectively blurs the lexical–functional distinction.[6]

---

[5] Panagiotidis (2003a) links the semi-lexical elements' lack of denotation to their inability to θ-mark.

[6] In Ouhalla's (1991) analysis lexical and functional categories can only be distinguished according to their position: lexical categories occupy the bottom of a projection line – an important matter we will return to. Similarly, in Grimshaw (1991), a numerically valued feature F stipulates the different position of the head within an Extended Projection: a value of 0 places the head at the bottom, rendering it both lexical by definition and the head of the Extended Projection, a value of 1 places it higher and a 2 value places it at the top of the Extended Projection. The role of this $F_0 \ldots F_n$ feature is then purely one of deciding the order of con-categorial heads within an Extended Projection, while its interpretation at LF is at best unclear.

5.5   Too many categorial features

Analyses according to which functional heads bear an [N] or a [V] feature proliferate the number of identical categorial features in a projection line, inside an 'Extended Projection', to use Grimshaw's term. Consider a concrete example like the one below:

(7)   They will probably not finish it.

Taking *will* to be a Tense head here, *probably* to be an adjunct, *not* to be the head of a Neg projection and *finish* to be a verb head-moved into a Voice head, and by both Ouhalla's and Grimshaw's analyses, we can count at least four [V] features in the projection line. Let us visualize this state of affairs in the form of a schematic phrase marker:

(8)   *Too many [V] features?*

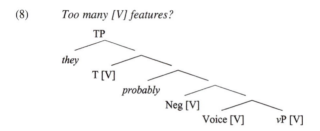

According to the idea that functional categories bear the categorial specification of the lexical head in their projection line, the above tree should contain four [V] features, and we are now facing the puzzle of how *all* of them are to be interpreted at LF. In other words, if we take (3) at face value, we end up treating categorial features exactly like taxonomic markers that are there purely to guarantee biuniqueness, which is nothing but a special case of c-selection (more on this below). Put differently, what is important is the fact that, according to (3), all three functional elements and the lexical verb in (7) are specified for a categorial [V] feature. If [V] is not a taxonomic feature and, in accordance with the discussion in the previous chapter, if it encodes an extending-into-time perspective, what happens at the interface with the Conceptual–Intentional/SEM systems, where this interpretive perspective is encoded *four* times inside a TP? To what end would this happen?

Summarizing, if we follow the path indicated in (3), then we must also explain what the role of categorial features on functional heads is; furthermore, we also need to suggest a general enough and language-independent way in which to capture the fundamental lexical–functional distinction. Hence, accounts invoking identity between the categorial features of lexical and functional elements in order to account for (biunique) selectional relations between them, as in (3), suffer from two drawbacks: they proliferate the instances of a categorial feature within a projection, and they come with the tacit entailment that such features are purely selectional, rather than LF-interpretable. This second matter is quite serious, and arises from the discussion of what possible interpretation at LF a feature repeated on virtually every head of the projection can have. Evidently, something more needs to be said.

5.6   Categorial Deficiency

A way to resolve the problem in the previous section is the following:

(9)   **Categorial Deficiency**: functional elements bear the uninterpretable version of the categorial feature of the lexical head at the bottom of their projection line (cf. Panagiotidis 2002, chap. 5).

Let us clarify the above: if v, the categorizing head, bears a [V] feature, then Asp, T and so on will all bear an uninterpretable [uV] feature. Identical facts hold for the nominal functional heads Num and D: they must also bear an uninterpretable [uN] feature. It follows that not *all* categorial features are interpretable: those on functional heads are not. The following diagram, a reinterpretation of the hypothetical state of affairs in (8), illustrates Categorial Deficiency:

(10)   *One [V] feature, three [uV] features*

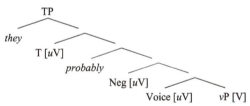

Essentially, Categorial Deficiency is in the spirit of Chomsky (1995), but takes further his discussion of (i) categorial feature strength as driving movement and (ii) 'affixal features' (269) on functional heads. Both these points will be discussed below but let us just indicate here that we are using 'affixal' features, uninterpretable categorial features, in order to guarantee the uniformity of 'supercategories' (Chomsky 2001, 47): such nominal and verbal supercategories consist of a lexical element, bearing an interpretable categorial feature, and the functional elements merged in its projection, bearing uninterpretable categorial features. Adger (2003, chap. 3) and Matushansky (2006)

have also called upon the uninterpretability of categorial features, but in different ways, which I will discuss in the following section.

Let us now review some welcome consequences of Categorial Deficiency, beginning at the conceptual level. A first consequence has to do with functional category membership. More specifically, no matter how many functional categories are hypothesized, motivated and discovered, no proliferation of the number of parts of speech *stricto sensu*, is necessary – of course, this is already, a consequence of (3). In other words, perhaps only Complementizer, Tense, Voice and Determiner exist, or maybe more functional categories, or maybe even the functional category forest of Cinque (1999) and cartographic approaches. At the end of the day, this does not matter: we do not need dozens of categorial features for functional categories, depending on our theory: verbal/clausal functional heads will all be marked as [uV], nominal ones as [uN]; they will be distinguished from each other by virtue of their interpretable features, such as [voice], [tense], [aspect], [(illocutionary) force] and the like.

On top of this, we may now implement, at the level of features, the radical and exciting proposal that functional categories *do not exist* as primitives of the/a grammar at all. Functional heads are bundles of features assembled in the Numeration, each flagged by an *uninterpretable categorial feature*. Again, this is in accordance with the logic of Chametzky (2003, 213–19) and, as already mentioned, brings us back to an analysis of functional heads developed in Thráinsson (1996), Bobaljik and Thráinsson (1998) and Hegarty (2005). For the sake of clarity, I will present below how this analysis is reprised in Panagiotidis (2008): the core idea is that Universal Grammar (UG) provides the learner with a fixed repertoire, not of categories, but of *features* from which to choose in order to build functional heads. What Categorial Deficiency in (9) would add to this is that each head would bear either [uN] or [uV]. Let us sketch how this would work by way of an example:

Suppose, for the sake of argument, that UG makes available three feature attributes for the nominal domain – say, [foc(us)], [ref(erentiality)] and [ind (ividuation)]. Given the above, it follows that the possible number and types of nominal functional heads in grammars would be the following:

- a single 'hybrid' [uN] [foc] [ref] [ind] functional category;
- two heads: an independent nominal focus category [uN] [foc] and a 'hybrid' [uN] [ref] [ind] Determiner–Number category;
- two nominal functional categories, again, but this time a 'hybrid' [uN] [foc] [ref] Focus–Determiner and an independent [uN] [ind] (a Number category);

- three nominal functional categories, with each head hosting one feature: nominal focus [*u*N] [foc], Determiner [*u*N] [ref], and Number [*u*N] [ind];

and so on. We may therefore speculate that, although all languages contain nouns and verbs, the repertory of functional heads can *in principle* be varied from grammar to grammar – contra Cinque (1999) and Borer (2005). Whether this is true or not is ultimately an empirical matter.

Moving on, according to categorial Deficiency, the functional–lexical distinction is captured as one of *interpretability* of categorial features:

(11)   Lexical heads bear interpretable categorial features, either [N] or [V].
        Functional heads bear uninterpretable categorial features, [*u*N] or [*u*V].

As a consequence of this, we do away with all ad hoc systems stipulating the lexical–functional distinction on the basis of dedicated 'lexical' and 'functional' features – for example, the system supporting *Extended Projection* (see also footnote 6). We also do away with the necessity for any notational variants of the Extended Projection system, at the same time capturing its main intuition: namely, that lexical heads are the prominent elements in their respective Complete Functional Complexes (Chomsky 1986), the elements *around which* functional structure is organized. Functional heads are indeed the *entourage* of lexical categories, to use a turn of phrase from Chapter 2.

Less theory-internally, by invoking Categorial Deficiency for functional elements we can reaffirm the intuition that the lexical–functional distinction is real and sharp, and that there is no such thing as a lexical–functional gradient. Now, there are claims in the literature that a more or less smooth continuum between lexical and functional may exist – for instance, in the process of language change and grammaticalization, as in Traugott (2007) and Francis and Yuasa (2008); I believe that the illusory effect of a lexical–functional continuum is the result of the existence of semi-lexical elements.[7] All in all, a principled way to uphold the existence of a sharp lexical–functional divide must certainly be good news: in the study of language acquisition it has been observed that functional categories tend to be acquired later in L1 – among others, see Radford (1990, 1996), Guilfoyle and Noonan (1992), Vainikka (1994). Functional categories are also harder to acquire during the course of L2 acquisition, while experimental studies in Psycholinguistics and Neurolinguistics reveal that functional elements may be

---

[7] I wish to thank an anonymous reviewer for raising this matter.

selectively impaired in Specific Language Impairment or in cases of trauma – see Muysken (2008, chap. 8–11) for a survey of the above two matters. Explanations for this lexical–functional dissociation can now be framed as explanations regarding the differential acquisition or impairment of uninterpretable (categorial) features: uninterpretable (categorial) features would be both tough(er) to acquire and more vulnerable. This is interesting, because it links the acquisition and breakdown of functional elements to that of uninterpretable features; the importance of feature interpretability in language acquisition and language breakdown has been discussed extensively: see Hawkins and Chan (1997), Tsimpli (2003), Hawkins and Hattori (2006) and Tsimpli and Dimitrakopoulou (2007) for L2 acquisition; Friedmann (2006) and Fyndanis (2009) for language disorders resulting from trauma; Clahsen, Bartke and Göllner (1997), Tsimpli and Stavrakaki (1999) and Tsimpli and Mastropavlou (2007) for Specific Language Impairment; Tsimpli, Sorace, Heycock and Filiaci (2004) for language attrition.

Finally, the long-standing intuition of considering functional heads as grammar-internal elements can now be tangibly captured. In a model of grammar where uninterpretable features are conceived as derivation-internal atoms, we expect whatever involves them to be a grammar-internal affair and not some kind of interface-induced requirement. A very sketchy example would be the contrast between Focus movement, Quantifier Raising and Binding, on the one hand, all of which satisfy requirements of the interface with Conceptual–Intentional/SEM systems, and Case, Verb Second and types of scrambling, on the other, all of which seem to be purely syntax-internal. In the former operations, an interpretable feature is the trigger; in the latter we probably have an interplay between uninterpretable features. Functional heads, essentially expressing nominal and verbal/clausal properties, are also now understood to be flagged by a grammar-internal atom: uninterpretable categorial features.

5.7   Categorial Deficiency ≠ c-selection

Ideally, Categorial Deficiency captures something fundamental, if not elemental, about functional heads: that they do not exist as members of *independent* categories or as independent elements but exclusively as satellites of lexical material, as subconstituents of a nominal or a verbal supercategory. Put differently, according to (9), functional heads are outlying feature bundles or feature structures – that is, heads – necessary for the interpretation of lexical material: not only do they contribute interpretable features to the Conceptual–Intentional/SEM systems but they also can host specifiers, supporting intricate structural relations. Whatever the ontology of functional elements is, Categorial Deficiency has as its consequence that a functional head such as an imperfective Asp head belongs to the same syntactic category as a perfective Asp head not because they belong to the same 'functional category' Asp, or due to some '*categorial* [Asp] feature', but because both bundles of features (the imperfective Asp head and the perfective Asp head) bear interpretable features with the same attribute, [asp:], albeit with different values. Categorially speaking, both aspectual heads bear a [uV], an uninterpretable verbal categorial feature, which guarantees that the aspectual heads will be part of a verbal supercategory and not of a nominal one.

If this picture is close to accurate, then uninterpretable categorial features are only *incidentally* responsible for a type of c-selection – namely, the biunique relation between lexical and functional elements. The main role of uninterpretable categorial features [uN] and [uV] is to mark (functional) bundles of features (= heads) as belonging to one or the other supercategory (nominal or verbal); their uninterpretability has as its principal consequence that heads bearing them may not categorize roots, as discussed in the previous chapter.[8]

Now, Adger (2003, chap. 3) employs uninterpretable categorial features to do *all* c-selection. So, for instance, in *letters to Peter*, the noun *letters* is argued to contain a [uP], an uninterpretable prepositional category feature, which will be checked against a [P] feature on the prepositional head *to* of *to Peter*; *to* will in turn contain [uN], an uninterpretable nominal category feature, which will be checked against the [N] feature of *Peter*, and so on. Adger extends this mechanism so that he can capture the selectional restrictions of *wonder* versus *ask*: unlike *ask*, *wonder* would bear [uC], an uninterpretable Complementizer category feature, which would force *wonder* to select clausal but not nominal complements. At the same time, *ask* has no such feature, hence no similar restrictions, and it can take both clausal (*I am asking what happened*) and nominal (*I am asking the time*) complements.[9]

In a similar vein, Matushansky (2006) uses the same mechanism to capture c-selection *and* head movement, as already discussed in Panagiotidis (2000, 2004). The problem in invoking Categorial Deficiency in order to cast head movement as the overt checking of uninterpretable categorial features is that in this manner only lexical-to-functional X^0 movement can explained: lexical-to-lexical head movement, where no categorially deficient heads are involved, inevitably remains unaccounted for. This entails that head movement

---

[8] See also Section 5.8 below.
[9] I am grateful to David Willis for raising and discussing this matter.

operations such as N-to-V incorporation would remain a mystery – see Baker (1988; 2003, 305–11) and Li (1990) on lexical-to-lexical head movement. Additionally, and perhaps far more seriously, if V-to-T movement is driven by the [*u*V] feature on T, there is no principled way to prevent XP movement of *v*P to T, with the [V] feature of the *v*P head pied-piping the whole projection with it.[10]

Returning to Adger's view of something like Categorial Deficiency under-lying *all* c-selection, I think it is problematic on at least two levels: first, it requires a full menagerie of categorial features of the type and taxonomic shallowness we have been arguing against – for example, a [P] feature for prepositions, a [C] one for Complementizers, and many more; why this is undesirable should have been made entirely clear by now. On a second level, suppose that the basic idea behind Adger's analysis is correct and that instead of uninterpretable *categorial* features, like [*u*P] or [*u*C], it is the uninterpretable versions of exactly the features that a functional head bears – say, [force] for C or [relation] for P – that drive c-selection. Elaborating, suppose that *wonder* bears not [*u*C], an uninterpretable Complementizer category feature, but an uninterpretable (or unvalued) illocutionary force feature; this would suffice to capture the c-selectional requirements of a verb like *wonder*, which c-selects CPs, as clausal and not nominal constituents are headed by a Force head, a Complementizer.

I think that even this version is tough to support, although it both looks far more attractive and leaves Categorial Deficiency as a property solely of functional elements. The reason is that it requires lexical elements to encode uninterpretable features, which is a rather unattractive option for reasons discussed in Chomsky (1995), reasons that range from the nature of parametric variation to that of uninterpretable features themselves.

5.8   Categorial Deficiency and roots (and categorizers)

In the previous chapter we had a look at the fact that only categorizers can have root material in their complements. Elaborating on Embick and Marantz's Categorization Assumption, we also spelled out the germane generalization that a root cannot be directly merged with a functional head – say, a Number or a Voice head. We looked at an explanation for why roots must be categorized;

---

[10] Of course, this is not a problem in analyses such as Jouitteau (2005) and Richards and Biberauer (2005), where the whole *v*P might be pied-piped to SpecTP, at least for EPP purposes – but much more would need be said on the conditions under which this may happen, if at all.

we also explained the categorizers' exclusive privilege of hosting root material in their complements as a result of only categorizers having a perspective-setting role, due to the interpretable categorial features they bear.

Functional heads, by (9), bear uninterpretable [uN] and [uV] features and, consequently, they cannot impose interpretive perspectives on their complements. This by hypothesis prevents them from hosting root material in their complements, unless embedded within a categorizer projection. So, Categorial Deficiency can explain away the Categorization Assumption, and answer the original question in Baker (2003, 269): free roots, and their projections, cannot appear in the complement of anything but a head bearing interpretable categorial features. Therefore, roots cannot be merged directly with functional heads, which are categorially deficient and bear uninterpretable [uN] and [uV] features.

In view of the above, there may arise at this point a valid conceptual objection to Categorial Deficiency, as a consequence of applying Occam's Razor: why have something – that is, an uninterpretable categorial feature – if one can have nothing? Expanding this objection: even though there are good arguments for the existence of LF-interpretable categorial features on categorizers, why can the Categorization Assumption not be captured along the lines of functional heads bearing *no* categorial features at all? If functional heads encode no categorial features, as opposed to encoding uninterpretable ones, the prediction that roots *must* be embedded within a categorizing projection still stands: functional heads, being devoid of categorial features, would fail to provide an interpretive perspective for the roots. Simply put, in order to show that the following structures (repeated from Chapter 4) are impossible, one does not necessarily need *uninterpretable* categorial features on Num and Voice: having *no* categorial features on Num and Voice would yield the same results.

(12)

Hence, if Num, Voice and all other functional heads *lack* categorial features altogether, they would be unable to set interpretive perspectives on root material. Everything else we said about functional heads as satellites of lexical ones, as parts of a supercategory, would most probably still hold, as well. Given these considerations, and the purported explanatory benefits of Categorial Deficiency, the question is framed thus: is biuniqueness, which potentially could be worked out on purely semantic and/or conceptual terms, a sufficient condition to justify positing uninterpretable categorial features on functional heads?[11] More epigrammatically: when it comes to functional heads, do we need Categorial Deficiency or is it enough to say that they are acategorial?[12]

Addressing this objection, in the section below I will provide some arguments for the usefulness of Categorial Deficiency that go well beyond the questions of biuniqueness and categorization.

5.9   Categorial Deficiency and Agree

5.9.1   On Agree

If categorial features are ordinary interpretable features, as claimed in Chapter 4, and if uninterpretable versions thereof exist on functional elements, as claimed in this chapter, then we would expect these features to enter into Agree relations. I am going to show below that Agree relations between uninterpretable categorial features as Probes and interpretable categorial features as Goals can capture a number of facts about phrase structure. This hopefully will render the Categorial Deficiency hypothesis a tool that possesses explanatory value that goes beyond what it was devised to address – that is, the lexical–functional distinction, biuniqueness and categorization restrictions.

We begin with an informal working definition of Agree, purely in order to illustrate categorial Agree, based on Chomsky (2000, 2001, 2004) as well as the summary in Baker (2008, 48):

(13)   An element F (the 'Probe') agrees with F' (a 'Goal') if:
   a. F c-commands F' – *the c-command condition* (Chomsky 2000, 122);
   b. there is no X such that F c-commands X, X c-commands F', and X has φ-features – *the intervention condition* (Chomsky 2000, 122);
   c. F' has not been rendered inactive by the Phase Impenetrability Condition – *the phase condition* (Chomsky 2000, 108).

---

[11] Emphasis here should be placed on 'worked out': on a more personal note, I have heard this objection raised several times since Panagiotidis (2000). Fleshing out exactly how biuniqueness can be reduced to semantic requirements and/or conceptual restrictions remains at a programmatic stage in most cases, with the exception of Borer (2005). However, in order to embrace Borer's execution, one would also have to fully embrace her system on the workings of functional material in its entirety – no grafting of her solutions onto other analyses is possible.

[12] There is a potentially important distinction to be made here; however, I will not pursue it in detail. If functional heads are bundles of UG-features flagged by [uX], an uninterpretable categorial feature, then we could hypothesize that *inner morphemes* (see Section 3.7 of Chapter 3) – that is, subcategorial elements like low applicatives, low causativizers, particles and the like – are precisely *acategorial* bundles of UG-features *not* flagged by any categorial features, interpretable or uninterpretable. There is a lot more to be said on this conjecture, so I will leave it as is in this work.

Further clarifying for the purposes of the discussion here, 'Probe' and 'Goal' can be understood either as bundles of features or *as the features themselves*, but we will take Probes and Goals to be features here. We will also assume that we do not need an unvalued feature (Case or other) to flag the F' (the Goal) as *active*: simple matching between F and F' should be enough (at least for our purposes here) to guarantee the possibility of Agree between them, if all other conditions are respected.[13]

At this point something needs to be said about the c-command condition in (13). If we seriously subscribe to a bottom-up model of structure-building via successive applications of Merge, the c-command condition must be adhered to:

(14)   The Probe must always c-command the Goal – never the other way round: Chomsky (2000, 122), Richards and Biberauer (2005, 121) and Donati (2006).

In the reverse scenario, if Agree could occur with the Goal c-commanding the Probe, we would have derivations where a *potential* Probe is merged and has to 'wait' for a suitable Goal. Of course, as mentioned, 'waiting' is in principle possible until phase level is reached: until the spell-out of a phase, all syntactic operations are system-internal and not evaluable at either level of representation – that is, at either interface. Thus, phase-internally, the relative structural configuration between F and F' is of no consequence: see Richards (2004), Baker (2008) and Hicks (2009, chap. 2). However, here we will adhere to a strict version of the c-command condition – that is, for F to c-command F' as in (14). The reason we adhere to this stricter version is because we conceive it as a more special case of the following requirements, already in Chomsky (2000, 133–4; 2004, 109), Hegarty (2005, 32) and Donati (2006):

a.   that the Probe is always a head: a lexical item (LI) rather than a syntactic object (SO);[14]
b.   that the Probe (F) projects.

Thus, after the application of Merge:

(15)   The Probe, a head, projects.

The above can resolve labelling in a large number of cases (and, if further refined, possibly in all of them). Here the focus will be on how (15) works in

---

[13] Although 'matching' should be clear, on an intuitive plane at least, it is true that a formalization of the notion of matching is indeed needed: see Hegarty (2005), Adger (2006).
[14] That is, an object already assembled by a previous application of Merge.

resolving the label in those cases where two LIs (lexical items) merge in order to 'begin a tree'.

Let us now turn to Agree relations between uninterpretable [uX] and interpretable [X] categorial features. Let us informally call this instance of Agree 'categorial Agree' and make it explicit:

(16) If [X] is an interpretable categorial feature, [uX] serves as a Probe for the Goal [X], and not vice versa: [X] cannot ever act as a Probe for [uX] and [uX] can never act as a Goal.

5.9.2 *Biuniqueness as a product of categorial Agree*

A first effect of categorial Agree is, of course, biuniqueness. Biuniqueness reduces to the Probe–Goal matching requirement of (categorial) Agree: functional heads marked for [uV] will only appear in the Extended Projection of V (i.e., of v), which itself bears an interpretable [V] feature; at the same time, those marked for [uN] will only appear in the Extended Projection of N (i.e., of n), which itself bears an interpretable [N] feature. Hence, a derivation like the one below would crash due to *feature mismatch*.

(17)   *

    [uN]

       [uV]   [V]

The above straightforwardly derives 'Extended Projections' in Grimshaw (1991; 2003, chap. 1) as a result of (categorial) Agree, more specifically the feature-matching requirement thereof.[15]

Conceiving biuniqueness as a result of categorial Agree raises the following issue: in principle nothing rules out beginning a derivation by just merging all the lexical heads together and afterwards adding the functional heads on top, giving projection lines with heads arranged like this:

(18)   [uN]...[uV]...[V]...[N].

This unattested, and presumably impossible, state of affairs can be ruled out if it is independently impossible to merge all the lexical heads together in the absence of functional structure (see also footnote 19). Perhaps even more elegantly, it can be claimed that [uV] in (18) creates a defective intervention effect by preventing [uN] from probing beyond it.[16]

A more general problem is that concerning Agree as a feature valuation process. Given the situation in (17), we are forced to argue for *uninterpretable*

---

[15] On the ordering of functional heads, see Hegarty (2005).

[16] I wish to thank an anonymous reviewer for raising this matter.

versions of [N] and [V] in order to ensure matching with their interpretable versions on lexical heads and, consequently, biunique projection lines. Arguing for an unvalued [*u*CAT(egory)] feature on functional heads will not derive the desired empirical results, as this [*u*CAT] feature could be valued by either [N] or [V], assuming these to really be [CAT:N] and [CAT:V]. I of course understand that, unless we adopt the framework in Pesetsky and Torrego (2004, 2005), the notion of valued uninterpretable features such as [*u*N] and [*u*V] sits uncomfortably with current notions on *Agree as feature valuation* (rather than feature *checking*). Here, however, it seems necessary to argue for [*u*N] and [*u*V] in order to preserve biuniqueness – that is, in order to prevent, for example, Tense heads from appearing in the projection lines of nouns and the like.[17]

5.9.3   Why there are no mid-projection lexical heads
Now we move to a more intricate empirical question, one that the existence of categorial Agree can resolve without any additional assumptions. This question concerns the fact that lexical categories always appear *at the bottom* of a projection line and never somewhere in the middle. Although this is a state of affairs evident in tree diagram after tree diagram, it curiously has, to the best of my knowledge, only attracted the attention of Baker (2003, 269).

Before addressing the absence of mid-projection lexical material, let us first resolve a much easier issue: why we *must* have lexical material in a tree – that is, why there are no purely functional projections, no syntactic structures without a lexical head (i.e., without a categorizer) (see also the previous chapter). Suppose we build a tree without any lexical material – for example, something like the phrasal marker below:

(19)   *

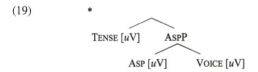

By (16), this structure would contain no Goal for the three Probes, the [*u*V] features, on each of the three functional heads. Although details and (im)

---

[17] At this point, a serious empirical question emerges – namely, what we are to make of functional elements like Aspect, which appear in the projection line of both verbs and nouns. The account developed here can accommodate such marginal cases under the idea that particular grammars allow the inclusion of a [*u*N] feature in bundles containing aspectual features. Alternatively, whenever we encounter aspectual heads within a nominal, we can perhaps demonstrate that we are dealing with a mixed projection (see the next chapter).

possible scenarios to salvage a derivation like the one in (19) are discussed below, the bottom line is that there can be no syntactic structure without lexical material, without a categorizer encoding an interpretable categorial feature.

We now turn to explaining how categorial Agree can also exclude mid-projection lexical heads sandwiched by functional material. Let us construct the beginning of a simplified sample derivation which would eventually yield a mid-projection lexical verb, one sandwiched by functional material:

(20)   *   ?

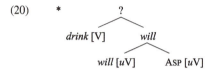

A first answer (to be revised below) to why (20) is impossible can be given as follows. Both *will* (e.g., a Tense head) and the Aspect head are Probes for categorial Agree, as they bear [uV], uninterpretable [V] features. However, they do not c-command a suitable Goal – for example, a lexical verb *drink* bearing the interpretable [V] feature. Consequently, there is a violation of (14) – and (16): of the two potential Probes, neither *will* nor ASP c-command their potential Goal *drink*; an Agree relation cannot be established and the derivation crashes. A welcome result of an explanation along these lines is that the impossibility of mid-projection lexical heads can now be expressed without seeking recourse to a templatic schema, cartographic or similar, where lexical heads 'must' be stipulated to appear at the bottom of the tree.

5.9.4   *How projection lines begin*

The above issue – that is, the position of lexical heads inside the tree – opens up a broader issue, that of how projections begin. This is what we are now going to have a better look at: the *first* application of Merge on a given Numeration, in a given workspace. Let us begin with the scenario where this first application involves merging two Lexical Items (LIs) and consider a simplified instance of the beginning of a nominal constituent:

(21)   DP

Assume that both D and N are LIs – that is, monadic elements drawn from the Numeration and not previously constructed by an application of Merge. By (15) above, either of them may project because they both qualify as potential heads of a projection; thus, between the two, it is the Probe of an

Agree relation that must project. Put otherwise, the label will be decided on the basis of which of the two LIs, D or N, is a Probe for Agree. Of course, it has been common knowledge since the formulation of the DP-hypothesis that in a case like (21), it is the Determiner that projects, which in turn suggests that, by (15), D is the Probe in some Agree relation. However, it is not self-evident *what* kind of Agree relation could hold between a Determiner and a Noun. It is at this point that categorial Agree turns out to have explanatory value. Determiners, being functional, bear [uN] features; lexical nouns by definition bear [N] features.[18] So, the answer to the question of why D is a Probe – so as to project – is because it hosts an uninterpretable categorial feature. This feature makes it a Probe for categorial Agree and the noun, bearing [N], is its Goal. Therefore, D, the Probe, projects after it is merged with N, because the Determiner is functional, thus bearing a [uX] categorial feature, a [uN] more specifically:

(22)

$$
\begin{array}{c}
\text{DP} \\
\diagup \quad \diagdown \\
\text{D } [u\text{N}] \qquad \text{N } [\text{N}]
\end{array}
$$

In a nutshell, a Determiner, like all *functional* LIs, is a Probe for (categorial) Agree, as per (15) and (16). When merging with a *lexical* LI, its (categorial) Goal, the functional LI will invariably project. The emerging picture is interesting in that it potentially resolves the question of labelling when a functional and lexical LI merge:

(23)   When a functional [uX] LI and a lexical [X] LI merge, the functional LI, a Probe for categorial Agree, projects.

The Categorial Deficiency of functional heads triggering categorial Agree can automatically be extended to also resolve labelling when a functional LI and a lexical Syntactic Object (SO) merge, too: the lexical SO will of course be headed by an element bearing an interpretable categorial feature [X], thus making it a Goal for categorial Agree.[19] Furthermore, we can now also predict the label in a (run of the mill) scenario where a functional LI merges

---

[18] Well, nominalizers, actually.

[19] However, categorial Agree obviously cannot predict the headedness of cases where two *lexical* LIs merge. Could this be because *directly* merging two lexical LIs is an impossibility? The ubiquity of applicative heads (Pylkkänen 2008), subordinating conjunctions (Cormack and Smith 1996), relators (Den Dikken 2006) and the like might suggest so, but I wish to remain agnostic here.

with a functional SO. Consider the following structure, where the LI *the* merges with the nominal SO *three little ducks*:

(24)

Let us assume the following structure for (24):

(25)

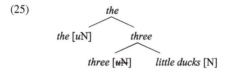

Once more the Determiner *the* is a Probe for (categorial) Agree, because it bears an uninterpretable categorial feature [*u*N]. The functional SO (e.g., a Number Phrase) with which it merges contains only one instance of an interpretable categorial feature, [N] on *ducks*. This is because the [*u*N] feature on *three* has already been checked off and eliminated after the previous application of Merge that created the SO *three little ducks*.[20] Therefore, *the*, a Probe for (categorial) Agree, projects. If this story is correct, then when a functional LI and an SO merge, the functional LI will always project: this straightforwardly predicts that functional LIs merging with a syntactic object *can never be specifiers*. Epigrammatically put:

(26)   When a functional [*u*X] LI and an SO merge, the functional LI, a probe for
        categorial Agree, projects as the head of the new constituent;

(27)   When a functional [*u*X] LI and an SO merge, the functional LI, a probe for
        categorial Agree, cannot be a specifier.

At the same time, when two functional SOs merge, headedness of the resulting object, its label, cannot be decided on the basis of *categorial* Agree. This is because both SOs will, by hypothesis, each have had all their uninterpretable categorial features already checked. Hence, a different instance of Agree will be relevant for deciding the label of the resulting object.

5.9.5   *Deciding the label: no uninterpretable Goals*
The above account, capitalizing on Agree relations between categorial features, has yet another important consequence. To illustrate, let us return to the phrase marker in (20), repeated below:

---

[20] Actually, in all probability *three* is the specifier of a Number Phrase with a null Num head, but
this is immaterial to the point made here.

(20)

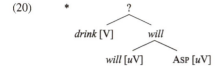

On the basis of (14), it was argued that (the [V] feature of) *drink* cannot act as a Goal for (the probing [*u*V] features of) *will* and ASP. However, there may be a way to account for the impossibility of structures like (20) in a more principled way. First, consider the fact that the phrase marker above is the result of *two* applications of Merge. Let us then backtrack to the first application of Merge that putatively gave the SO [*will* Asp], with which *drink* is supposed to merge.

(28)
```
        ?
      ⁀‾‾‾‾⁀
will [uV]   ASP [uV]
```

Looking at (28) the following question emerges: the exclusion in (16) notwithstanding, why is it actually the case that (the [*u*V] feature of) *will* cannot probe (that of) ASP? Or vice versa? Both *will* and the aspectual head are probes for Agree. What prevents the [*u*V] feature of ASP or that of *will* from serving as a Goal for categorial Agree? The condition in (14) would not be violated, as *will* and ASP c-command each other.

The short answer to the above question in a conception of Agree as a valuation process is that unvalued (and, presumably, uninterpretable) features cannot serve as Goals, as they cannot provide the Probe with a value; recall that this is stipulated in (16) but stems in a principled way from Chomsky (2001, 6; 2004, 113) and much subsequent work. However, it is perhaps useful to examine what would happen in examples like (28) if it *could* indeed happen to be the first application of Merge in a workspace.[21]

The first problem in a situation like that in (28) would be which of the [*u*V] features on each LI is the Probe. This cannot be resolved, as, in principle, both [*u*V] features can be Probes for categorial Agree. Therefore, in principle, both *will* and ASP would be possible to project. This in turn would result in (a) optional labelling for the resulting constituent, or (b) an intrinsic failure *of the system* to determine the head, or (c) co-projection of both *will* and Asp. I take it with Chomsky (1995, 244) that the last two options are impossible and

---

[21] I am grateful to Marc Richards and an anonymous reviewer for discussing interpretability of Goals with me.

I would think that the first one, that of optional labelling, is highly undesirable, too. In other words, the above scenarios run afoul of the received understanding of how labels are set after Merge: when merging X and Y, we expect either X or Y to project, as discussed in detail in Chomsky (2000, 2001, 2004). Moreover, if Hinzen (2006, 187–9) is correct in saying that the label is determined by lexical properties of the elements involved and that label determination is not part of the definition of Merge, then it is plausible to think that such relevant properties would interact with Agree and that there would exist no context-independent mechanisms to decide the label of a newly merged constituent.

Therefore, the relevance of the Probe–Goal relationship for determining labels – (15): *the Probe, a head, projects* – and the ubiquity of (categorial) Agree due to categorial Deficiency in (9) lead us to the following empirical generalization:

(29)   We cannot begin a tree by merging two functional LIs.[22]

Let us summarize the effect of Categorial Deficiency on deciding the label after an application of Merge in the table in (30):

(30)   *Labelling predictions with categorial Probes and Goals*

	Predicted result	Example
[uX] LI merges with **[uX] LI**	*	*[T Asp]
[uX] LI merges with **[X] LI**	[uX] LI *projects*	[$_{DP}$ D n]
[uX] LI merges with **SO** (always [X])	[uX] LI *projects*	[$_{DP}$ D NumP]
[uX] LI merges with **ROOT**	*	*[Num CAT]
[X] LI merges with **[X] LI**	?	?[23]
[X] LI merges with **SO** (always [X])	?	[$_{vP}$ v nP]
[X] LI merges with **ROOT**	?	[$_{nP}$ n CAT]
SO merges with **SO** (both always [X])	?	[$_{TP}$ [$_{DP}$ the cat] [$_{TP}$ meows]]

[22] This has as a consequence that the claim in Abney (1987) – and much subsequent work – that pronouns are bare – that is, nounless, Determiner constituents – must be false: a pronoun like [$_{DP}$ D Num], in the absence of an n, will be impossible. However, following Panagiotidis (2002) and Déchaine and Wiltschko (2002) in that all pronouns contain at least a minimally specified nominal head, the tension is resolved in favour of the generalization here.

[23] In the framework followed here I am not sure that two lexical LIs – that is, two categorizers – can merge. What would something like an [n v] be? This is why no example is provided in the '[X] LI merges with [X] LI' row. See also footnote 19.

By the categorial Agree account, all these characteristics of syntactic structures (the projection of functional heads after the application of Merge, the presence of a lexical element at the bottom of a syntactic structure, the existence of Extended Projections/M-Projections) derive from the fact that uninterpretable/unvalued features cannot act as Goals for Agree.

5.10   Conclusion

In this chapter I have proposed that functional heads are essentially category-less. On top of that, I have argued against categorial labels for functional heads and against functional categories as word classes like nouns and verbs are, claiming that functional heads are flagged by uninterpretable categorial features, that they are categorially deficient. Building on this hypothesis I have managed to derive the Categorization Assumption, the part where functional heads cannot directly merge with roots, more specifically. Biunique relations between functional and lexical elements as well as the nature of nominal super-categories/Extended Projections/M-Projections also fall out from Categorial Deficiency. Finally, the categorially deficient nature of functional heads – that is, their encoding uninterpretable categorial features – was argued to make them Probes for Agree relations with lexical heads; these Agree relations can shed light on labelling and the position of lexical material inside a tree, as well as on the impossibility of purely functional structures without any lexical material.

6 Mixed projections and functional categorizers

6.1 Introduction

The problem of mixed projections – that is, projections combining both nominal and verbal/clausal functional subconstituents – is discussed in this chapter. Our theory of categorial features combined with the existence of uninterpretable categorial features can capture the existence and function of mixed projections without novel theoretical assumptions. Section 6.2 introduces the problem and Section 6.3 presents two empirical generalizations on mixed projections: Categorial Uniformity and Nominal External Behaviour. The following section reviews evidence against freely mixing nominal and verbal functional elements – that is, without any concerns regarding categorial uniformity or biuniqueness. Section 6.5 introduces functional categorizers, SWITCH elements, as heads that both recategorize their complement, bearing an interpretable categorial feature, and belong to the functional projection of a lexical head. In Section 6.7 the type and size that the complement of a functional categorizer can take is examined, as well as the phasal status of SWITCH heads. Whether mixed projections all behave externally as nominals is reviewed in Section 6.8, on the basis of the behaviour that verbal nouns in Korean and Japanese display. Section 6.9 attempts to explain away differences between mixed projections that consist of the same type of subconstituents – say, Tense Phrases – by appealing to the different feature specification of the heads within the verbal/clausal functional subtree. The need for functional categorizers next to the better-known ones – that is, n and v – is addressed in Section 6.10 and the last section concludes the chapter.

6.2 Mixed projections

So far I have proposed a theory of categorial features and I have examined some of its consequences. I started off with a commitment to a theory according to which categorial features are LF-interpretable features. These features 'make' categorizers (*n* and *v*), the same way one can argue that temporal relation features make Tense heads. Categorial features are interpreted as fundamental interpretive perspectives on the material in the categorizers' complement. Uninterpretable versions of categorial features flag functional heads and give rise to a number of familiar phrase-structure phenomena: the biunique relation between lexical and functional elements and the position of lexical material at the bottom of a projection line, they also play a central role in labelling after the application of Merge.

Given all of the above, we might expect syntactic projections to be either *nominal* or *verbal/clausal*. In other words, we expect biuniqueness all the way up the tree: essentially, the categorial feature [N] or [V] of the categorizer should guarantee the categorial uniformity of the *whole* projection line. Graphically expressed, we expect, for instance, that projections be exclusively made up of functional elements with a [*u*V] specification, forming the verbal/clausal entourage of a lexical verb.

(1)

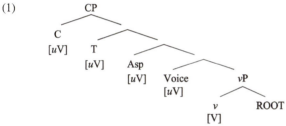

The obvious question is how this system can accommodate *mixed projections*. Generally speaking, mixed projections are a problem for *any* system of phrase structure that (implicitly or, as in this case, explicitly) admits total categorial uniformity of projections. At the same time, most conceptions of phrase structure would, for instance, prevent a D taking a TP complement or a T taking a DP complement, and they would do so for very good reasons, *pace* Alexiadou (2001) and (in a sense) Borer (2005). This is why the existence and properties of mixed projections must be seriously addressed.

Of course, mixed projections have already been variously addressed, time and time again; they have indeed posed a serious problem for syntactic theories. In order to get a sample of the ways mixed projections have been dealt with, let us briefly review the types of analyses proposed for Poss–*ing* gerunds (after Hudson 2003), maybe the best-studied mixed projections.

A first analysis comes from Jackendoff (1977), who develops an insight in Chomsky (1970): Poss–*ing* gerunds are exocentric NPs consisting of a VP. This could be roughly understood as an NP without an N head but dominating a VP, a state of affairs that was possible given the labelling and bar-level conventions in the 1970s and, more importantly, something that captures a key intuition: that POSS–*ing* gerunds, like most mixed projections, ostensibly behave externally as nominal, despite their having a verb at their heart – this is an intuition we will extensively scrutinize here. Baker (1985) argues that gerunds are NPs headed by –*ing*, an affix which is then lowered onto the verb, via a version of Affix-hopping; the underlying suggestion is that –*ing* is nominal, which is a commonly shared assumption. Abney (1987), updated and refined in Yoon (1996a), claims that in gerundive projections Det directly selects IPs or VPs.

A more elaborate solution for the violation of biuniqueness in mixed projections like gerunds is offered in Pullum (1991), who, within the HPSG framework, proposes the weakening of the Head Feature Convention, thus allowing the mother phrase and its head to have different values for N and V. In a similar vein, in the HPSG account of Lapointe (1993), the NP and VP nodes have 'dual' lexical categories <X|Y>, where X and Y determine external and internal properties respectively: nominal externally and verbal internally. Finally, in Bresnan (1997) – to which we will return – an LFG account is offered, in which a single c-structure N (the gerund) maps to both an N and a V position in f-structure.

Summarizing, the old chestnut of mixed projections has been attacked from two viewpoints: either writing categorial duality into their head, as in Jackendoff (1977), Pullum (1991), Lapointe (1993) and Bresnan (1997), or arguing for a structure where an abstract nominal element selects a VP, as in Baker (1985), Abney (1987) and Yoon (1996a). Here we will combine both lines of reasoning in order to tackle the problem: thankfully, treating categorial features as ordinary LF-interpretable features (and not as flags merely identifying grammar-internal entities) combined with Categorial Deficiency enables us to do exactly that.

Before presenting the analysis, let us first look at mixed projections in a descriptive way and let us adumbrate the generalizations we can extract from looking at empirical evidence.

6.3   Two generalizations on mixed projections

Mixed projections combine characteristics from more than one category. This is what makes mixed projections different from Complementizer Phrases ('clauses'), which contain a series of 'verbal' functional categories and a verb (at least a verbalizer), and from Determiner Phrases ('nominal phrases'), which contain a series of 'nominal' functional categories and a noun (at least a nominalizer). Typically (and expectedly) mixed projections combine

    a. verbal/clausal *and* nominal characteristics (like gerunds), or
    b. verbal/clausal *and* adjectival characteristics (like participles)

Following the practice here to ignore adjectives (see Chapter 2), we will concentrate only on mixed projections bringing together verbal/clausal and nominal characteristics.[1] Three examples (among many) of such mixed projections are English Poss–*ing* gerunds (2), Spanish nominalized infinitives (3) and Greek D+CP constructions (4).

(2)   [Bob's insulting them all] annoyed us.

(3)   [El cantar yo La Traviata] traerá malas consecuencias.
        The sing.INF I La Traviata bring.FUT bad consequences
        'My singing the Traviata will not end well.'

(4)   [To oti fevyi i Niki] dhen ine provlima.
        The that leaves the Niki not is problem
        'That Niki is leaving is not a problem.'

    An immediate, very robust generalization that can be made about a number of mixed projections comes from Bresnan (1997, 4), also informing Borsley and Kornfilt (2000):

(5)   *Phrasal Coherence*: the mixed projection 'can be partitioned into two categorially uniform subtrees such that one is embedded as a constituent of the other' (after Malouf 2000).

According to Bresnan, Phrasal Coherence holds for mixed projections in a range of typologically unrelated languages: Hebrew, Arabic, Turkish, Kikuyu, Italian, Dutch, German, Dagaare (a Gur language of the Niger–Congo family) and others. What Phrasal Coherence essentially amounts to is that we never have alternating nominal and verbal constituents making up a mixed projection. In other words, the nominal and the verbal chunks in a mixed projection are distinct and occupy different 'sides' thereof; crucially, *they never intersperse*. Hence, in mixed projections there must always exist a cut-off point

---

[1] This decision is not made on purely methodological considerations regarding the status of adjectives. Mixed projections that combine adjectival and nominal characteristics are, well, adjectives (recall the discussion in Section 2.8 of Chapter 2); mixed projections combining adjectival and verbal characteristics will have to be set aside for future research, once there is a more concrete picture of the categorial status of adjectives.

where verbal/clausal characteristics end and nominal ones begin: verbal/ clausal and nominal characteristics and elements are located in different parts of the tree. See also Lapointe (1993), Borsley and Kornfilt (2000), Malouf (2000), Schoorlemmer (2001), Ackema and Neeleman (2004, 174). In order to visualize the state of affairs described by Phrasal Coherence, consider the following abstract phrase markers:

(6)   *A mixed projection abiding by Phrasal Coherence*

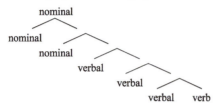

(7)   *A mixed projection* not *abiding by Phrasal Coherence*

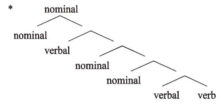

If Phrasal Coherence is a valid generalization and if mixed projections like the one portrayed in (7) are indeed impossible, then an important step has been made towards analysing mixed projections not as oddities or as exceptional constructions but as projections consisting of two phrasally coherent parts: two subtrees, each of which displays Categorial Uniformity.

Let us now take a closer look at two examples of mixed projections displaying Phrasal Coherence. First, in English Poss–*ing* gerunds the higher part of the projection may assign Genitive, which is a nominal characteristic (possibly the signature of a *Determiner*), whereas the lower part may assign Accusative, a verbal characteristic (the signature of *Voice*). It is also worth noting that the sequence of functional elements, the nominal above the verbal ones, resembles the hypothetical schema in (6), a matter to which we will return below. A second example of a mixed projection displaying Phrasal Coherence would be Japanese *verbal nouns*; see Tsujimura (1992, 477–9) and Manning (1993). In this case, the higher part of the projection may assign –*ga* Nominative, which would be a verbal characteristic (the signature of *Tense*), whereas the lower one may assign Genitive, a nominal characteristic (possibly the signature of *n*). The apparent sequence here is the reverse of what we have in the case of English POSS–*ing* gerunds, and (6), with verbal elements above the nominal ones (a matter to which we will return in Section 6.8.1).

If Phrasal Coherence is a first generalization about mixed projections, there is also a second generalization that can be surmised by surveying the literature on mixed projections: Borsley and Kornfilt (2000), Malouf (2000), Hudson (2003) more specifically: mixed projections externally behave as nominals.

(8)   Nominal External Behaviour: mixed projections externally behave as
        nominal constituents.

Externally, mixed projections generally display straightforward nominal behaviour; this behaviour is morphosyntactically manifested by the presence of a nominalizing element and case-marking, like in the Turkish example of a nominalized clause in (9), an article, as in Spanish nominalized infinitives in (10), or the licensing of a possessor in English POSS–*ing* gerunds in (11). Moreover, as is evident by looking at all the examples below, mixed projections can stand as run-of-the-mill arguments of verbs: for example, a direct object in the Turkish example in (9), a subject in the Spanish example in (10), and both in the English example in (11).

(9)   Hasan   [Ayşe-nin   gel-me-sin]-i   iştiyor.
        Hasan   Ayşe-GEN   come-NOM-3SG-ACC   wants
        'Hasan wants Ayse to come over.'

(10)   [El cantar yo La Traviata] traerá malas consecuencias.
        The sing.INF I La Traviata bring.FUT bad consequences
        'My singing the Traviata will have dire consequences.'

(11)   [Bob's insulting us all] annoyed them.
        Few took notice of [Bob's insulting us all].

Complementing this observation there is also a lack of indisputable evidence for bona fide mixed projections behaving externally as verbs or as clauses, while containing a 'real' nominal element, a lexical noun. The apparent exception of Japanese verbal nouns as adumbrated above will be discussed in Section 6.8.1, so, for the time being, we assume (8) as a working hypothesis which rests on a solid empirical basis.

So far we have hardly *explained* anything regarding the structure and the syntactic behaviour of mixed projections: all we have done is adopt Phrasal Coherence in (5) as a working hypothesis and acknowledge an empirical generalization on the nominal external behaviour of mixed projections. So, it is now that the truly tough question emerges – namely,

(12)   How can two categorially different subtrees, a nominal one and a verbal one, be combined to form a single projection?

Recall that we have captured the categorial uniformity of projections in terms of a biunique relation between functional heads and a lexical category, which is instantiated through categorial Agree between categorially deficient functional heads and (lexical) categorizers bearing interpretable categorial features. Consequently we have to answer (12) along the lines of where a *second* lexical head would have to be merged in a projection line in order for the functional part growing out of it to be supported. More precisely, consider the phrase marker in (6), repeated below for convenience and enriched with categorial features on every head, as predicted by Categorial Deficiency:

(13)   *Phrasal Coherence – but what about Categorial Deficiency?*

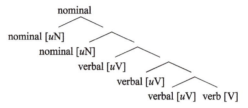

According to the account in Chapter 5, in the phrase marker above (which could be an abstract representation of POSS–*ing* gerunds and the like) the lower verbal functional part of the projection is licensed, in the broad sense, by the lexical verb, or more precisely by the feature [V] of *v*. But what about the two functional 'nominal' heads c-commanding the verbal functional structure? There is no head bearing an [N] feature for the [*u*N] feature on them to probe. Should the derivation in (13), then, not be ruled out on the same grounds on which functional structures without a categorizer/lexical head are banned, as we saw in the previous chapter?

6.4   Free-mixing mixed projections?

One way, a radical one, to explain how mixed projections are possible is to abandon any notion of categorial uniformity. So, (12) and the questions surrounding it would not pose a problem. This is the path Alexiadou (2001) takes, in the spirit of radical categorylessness (see Chapter 1). Recall that, like Borer (2003, 2005) and De Belder (2011), Alexiadou claims that there are *no* categorizers. Instead, the functional environment around a root actually defines the root's category. So, biuniqueness is superficial and, indeed, illusory as it is not Tense that 'goes with' a verb. Instead, a T category *makes* a root a verb: a root inside TP will surface as a verb (Alexiadou 2001, 19). Similarly, it is not the case that a Determiner 'goes with' a noun. Instead, a D category *makes* a root a noun: a root inside DP will surface as a noun (Alexiadou 2001, 19). This hypothesis is illustrated in the simplified trees below:

(14)

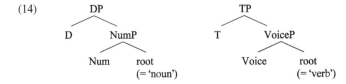

A consequence of the above is that, if there are no categorizing heads, there is no need for category-changing heads either, which would necessarily mediate between categorially uniform subtrees in a mixed projection. As a consequence, you can *freely* mix together any kind of functional heads – for example, D with Asp, T with Num, D with Voice, T with D. In this view, biuniqueness essentially does not exist, and Alexiadou's account describes the simplest state of affairs that would be conceptually possible. However, before we are lured by this option, the question, as ever, is whether it is the correct way of approaching the problem, empirically speaking.

In general, it seems that verbs behave as verbs and nouns as nouns even when there is very little functional structure above them. Precisely this point is convincingly elaborated upon in Baker (2003, 265–90) on the basis of inspecting cross-linguistic evidence on incorporation and compounding, with the conclusion summarized as follows: 'category-specific behaviour can arise even when there is no sign of any functional superstructure dominating the lexical head … [E]xactly where there is less functional structure, we find more categorial distinctiveness' (Baker 2003, 268). I believe this is the correct generalization, and it is tacitly incorporated in statements like Embick and Marantz's (2008) Categorization Assumption, which we discussed in length in Chapter 4. Let me then just complement Baker's observation by quickly looking at verbs and nouns with very little functional superstructure dominating them.

Beginning with verbs, they behave like verbs already at the *v*P level and certainly at the VoiceP level, as nexus constructions (Svenonius 1994) indicate – that is, structures like *Me drink alcohol? Never*, and the like. Constituents containing a root certainly do not have to wait for a full verbal/ clausal functional shell to be merged before they can display verbal behaviour in full as lexical verbs. Turning to nouns, there are of course Determiner-less constituents that are clearly and fully nominal. Illustrating this with Greek examples, consider kind readings of nouns in (15) and mass readings, as in (16), where there is no need for any Determiner:

(15)   Eyine   papia
        became   duck
        'S/he became a duck.'

(16)   Efaye   papia
        ate   duck
        'S/he ate duck.'

In (15), which would be felicitous in the context of a fairy tale or similar, *papia* ('duck') has a kind reading: the sentence is about something or someone switching kind into the kind 'duck'. In (16), *papia* ('duck') refers to duck meat. In both cases there is no determiner layer present but *papia* is unambiguously a noun. What is even more interesting is that even NumP, another functional projection which could be held accountable for categorizing roots, is also most possibly perfunctory in the examples above, as neither example involves individuation, to begin with; see Borer (2005, chap. 4, passim) for very extensive discussion on the function and the semantics of individuation and Number.

For the reasons reviewed above, the free-mixing version of how to capture mixed projections will not be pursued here. Now, a second way to understand how mixed projections are possible is to say that the two categorially uniform subparts of a mixed projection are linked by a category-changing head, a special type of categorizer. This is the path to be explored here, in a way that will bring together the insights in two distinct schools of thought on mixed projections. On the one hand, we will follow Jackendoff (1977), Pullum (1991), Lapointe (1993) and Bresnan (1997), who encode categorial duality into a head, our purported special categorizer; on the other hand, we will also incorporate elements from analyses positing a structure where an abstract *nominal* element selects a VP, as in Baker (1985), Abney (1987) and Yoon (1996a): again, our special categorizer.

6.5   SWITCHES as functional categorizers

The hypothesis proposed here aims to capture the existence and properties of mixed projections in the following fashion: mixed projections, unlike 'ordinary' categorially uniform ones, contain a 'mixed' category head between their two parts, which I will call a SWITCH for mnemonic purposes (Panagiotidis and Grohmann 2009).[2] This SWITCH head 'mediates' between the nominal and the verbal half, by virtue of its categorial feature makeup. More precisely, SWITCHES are categorizers, like *n* and *v*, hence they bear interpretable categorial features. What makes them special, and suitable as mediators between categorially different *functional* layers of structure, is that they also bear *uninterpretable* categorial features.

(17)   SWITCHES are categorizers that bear both interpretable [X] (i.e., 'categorizing') and uninterpretable [*u*X] (i.e., 'functional') categorial features.

Let us first consider how SWITCHES would work and then discuss their nature. I will exemplify on English POSS–*ing* gerunds.

Suppose, essentially following Reuland (1983) and Hazout (1994), that gerundive projections contain a head *Ger*. This Ger head takes a verbal complement but is selected by a Determiner or a Determiner-like element, initiating a switch of categorial identity within the projection line. More specifically, Ger takes a verbal complement, an AspP, as indicated by –*ing*.[3] I take this Ger head not to be an ad hoc category or, even, a gerund-specific element, but a functional categorizer as described in (17), a SWITCH. In keeping with our analysis in the previous chapter, and in line with what was claimed about the Categorial Deficiency of functional elements, we can now simply claim that a SWITCH bears a [*u*V] feature: SWITCH behaves as a verbal/clausal functional head that can participate in verbal/clausal projection lines by virtue of its uninterpretable categorial feature, which probes its complement for a [V] feature. Actually, van Hout and Roeper (1998) suggest that the verb head overtly climbs up to Ger, but this is probably wrong, when adverb placement is considered (Ad Neeleman, personal communication, February 2007).

Now, this Ger head (our SWITCH) appears, like nouns do, in the complement of the possessive Determiner head of the null variety, which assigns Genitive Case to SpecDP – as already claimed in Abney (1987), Borsley and Kornfilt (2000, 105) and elsewhere. This Ger head will then contain an [N] feature, given that Determiners bear a [*u*N] feature. Note that the intuition that

---

[2] Lapointe (1999) was the first to talk about 'category switchover points'. The term 'switch' is also used in Schoorlemmer (2001) to describe the point in the structure of nominalized infinitives where category changes.

[3] On why –*ing* itself cannot be the nominalizing morpheme, contra Abney (1987), Milsark (1988) and others, see Ackema and Neeleman (2004, 175–81). Johnson (1988) claims it to be a Tense affix but here we side with Siegel (1998) in considering it to be just an aspectual marker.

Ger contains a *nominal categorial feature* is already expressed in Reuland (1983, 113) and Hazout (1994), who actually claim Ger to be a noun.[4] However, this cannot be correct: Ger cannot be a noun and, more generally, no lexical noun can be responsible for the categorial shift within gerundive and other mixed projections; there are actually good empirical reasons why nouns as switching elements are impossible.

If a noun mediated between the nominal and the verbal/clausal part of a mixed projection, this 'noun' would necessarily be both a phrasal affix and a lexical noun – that is, a noun with an obligatory complement. This sounds like a very bizarre type of noun and this point has already been made in Borsley and Kornfilt (2000, 119), regarding Turkish nominalizations, which we will revisit in Section 6.6. Supposing, for the sake of argument, that affixal lexical nouns would be possible, the ones participating as Ger in the formation of gerundive projections would invariably select for a verbal complement which would, moreover, not be their argument. Furthermore, these nouns would have a morphological exponence of zero: in the discussion of category-changing elements in Ackema and Neeleman (2004, 175–81) it turns out that in head-initial languages the category-changing AFFIX *must* have a zero exponence, a conclusion also arrived at in Siegel (1998). Once more, this kind of morphophonological restriction on lexical nouns is unexpected. Finally, Borsley and Kornfilt (2000, 119) present an elaborate argument against Ger (and category-changing elements in general) as nouns: although this matter will not be discussed here, it is reasonable to assume that subjects of Poss–*ing* gerunds originate from within the verbal constituent. However, if they do, then the analysis of Poss–*ing* gerunds with Ger as a lexical noun would involve the extraction of a subject from the complement of a noun, Ger. This kind of extraction is impossible in English, as illustrated in the examples below, adapted from Borsley and Kornfilt (2000, 119).

(18)   John appeared _ to be drunk.

(19)   [John's appearing _ to be drunk] surprised us.

(20)   *[John's appearance _ to be drunk] surprised us.

So, Ger bears an [N] feature but is not a noun. Naturally, given the discussion in Chapter 4, the [N] feature on the Ger/SWITCH can be explained if the Ger head is a categorizer and, more specifically, a *nominalizer*, an *n* head.

---

[4] This is what Abney (1987) and van Hout and Roeper (1998) also seem to argue for.

However, nominalizers typically appear low: as repeatedly discussed, they head the lowest phases, taking as their complements either root projections (e.g., *dog* or *truth*) or *v*Ps (e.g., *destruction* in *the destruction of evidence*); see Chapter 3. At any rate, we would not expect a categorizer like *n* to take functional constituents as complements, as seems to be the case with Ger and its AspP complement. More precisely, we have so far not encountered categorizers taking complements that contain *any* functional structure: this suggests that SᴡɪᴛᴄHᴇꜱ are no ordinary categorizers (no ordinary nominalizers, in the case of Pᴏꜱꜱ–*ing* gerunds). We can therefore hypothesize that SᴡɪᴛᴄHᴇꜱ also contain an uninterpretable categorial [*u*V] feature, just like Asp and other verbal/clausal *functional* heads, and that this is how they can appear in the projection line of the verb: if this is true, then they take a verbal projection as their complement, an AspP, in line with how categorial Agree ensures categorial uniformity of the functional heads in a projection.

An illustration of the claims made so far in this section is given below in the form of a simplified tree for *Albert's eating herring* – see also Siegel (1998) and Moulton (2004).

(21)   *A simplified tree for* [Albert's eating herring].

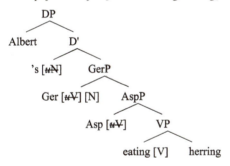

Thus, a nominal SᴡɪᴛᴄH, like 'Ger', contains a [*u*V] feature besides its [N] one. It is a *functional categorizer*.

The hypothesis of SᴡɪᴛᴄH as a functional categorizer should be quite straightforward by now; essentially, a SᴡɪᴛᴄH can be identified with the category-changing abstract phrasal ᴀꜰꜰɪx in Ackema and Neeleman (2004, 172–81). Such category-changing ᴀꜰꜰɪxᴇꜱ are postulated to attach on projections of various levels. More precisely, Ackema and Neeleman discuss nominalizing ᴀꜰꜰɪxᴇꜱ attaching on verbal projections of various sizes, a point to which we will return below. As regards its exponence, the category-changing ᴀꜰꜰɪx is phonologically null in head-initial languages and conversely so in head-final ones; this is a prediction made by a principle of Input

Correspondence (Ackema and Neeleman 2004, 140) that maps structures onto morphological forms, and is borne out in a number of languages (176–81).

Now, the above claims immediately beg the following questions:

a. whether it is possible for *two* categorial features to co-exist on a single head;
b. how come this co-existence does not induce a categorial clash;
c. what it *means* (LF-wise) for a syntactic head to be specified as [N] [*u*V].

First, as insistently claimed here, categorial features are not taxonomic-classificatory markers; they are LF-interpretable features. Rather than flags used purely to classify words and delineate constituents, categorial features are genuine instructions to be interpreted at the interfaces, as expected from formal features under Chomsky's (1995) *Full Interpretation*. A SWITCH like the so-called Ger head is a nominal categorizer by virtue of its interpretable, perspective-setting [N] feature. At the same time, Ger bears a [*u*V] feature, eliminable via categorial Agree: it can therefore be part of a verbal projection, behaving like a 'functional category'. Thus, the complement of an [N][*u*V] SWITCH element will be recategorized, in a way familiar from simplex categorizers (recall the denominal verb *tape*): the complement of SWITCH will be interpreted in the sortal perspective that [N] imposes. Additionally, the [*u*V] Probe on SWITCH will search for a [V] target. There is no categorial clash whatsoever, given that the [*u*V] feature of the SWITCH, along with the ones on Asp, Voice and so on, will be eliminated before Spell-Out; at the same time, this feature guarantees that a SWITCH acts like a functional element: given its [*u*V] feature it cannot take root material directly as its complement.

This state of affairs immediately derives Phrasal Coherence in (5). In order to illustrate this point, let us follow the derivational history of a mixed projection using abstract phrase markers like we did in (13).

(22)

$$\text{FH } [u\text{V}]$$
$$\text{FH } [u\text{V}]$$
$$v\,[\text{V}] \qquad \text{RootP}$$

First, a *v* (bearing [V]) is merged with the root material and a number of [*u*V] functional heads (FHs) recursively merge, giving a categorially uniform verbal/clausal subtree through successive applications of categorial Agree between the [*u*V] features and [V].

Then an [N][*u*V] head, the functional categorizer or SWITCH, is merged; its [*u*V] feature probes for a [V] and agrees with it.

(23)

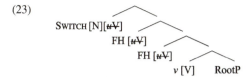

However, the next head to be merged must be [*u*N], not [*u*V], on the grounds of a version of minimality.[5] We cannot merge a [*u*V] functional head with a projection headed by a SWITCH because the SWITCH's interpretable [N] feature would intervene between a [*u*V] and the [V] on *v*, as illustrated below:

(24)   *

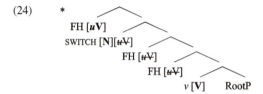

Consequently, the derivation will proceed as follows: the SWITCH head will participate in the lower verbal/clausal subtree and effectively 'begin' the nominal subtree dominating it, 'switching' the categorial identity of the derivation, it being a categorizer after all. The empirical result is that now Phrasal Coherence is readily captured, with the functional categorizer acting both as the SWITCHing element (by [N]) and as the 'glue' (by [*u*V]) between the two categorially distinct subtrees:

(25)

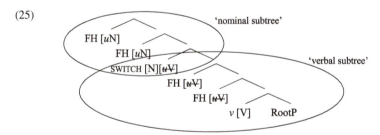

---

[5] Uninterpretable [*u*V] creating an intervention effect for a probing [*u*N], and vice versa, is independently necessary, as discussed in Chapter 5 in the context of deriving biuniqueness from categorial Agree. This of course suggests that [N] and [V] are in fact *values* of an attribute [perspective]. Thus, [N] must actually be [perspective:sortal] and [V] must be [perspective: temporal], exactly as discussed in Chapter 5. I will, however, continue using [N] and [V] as shorthand, for convenience.

Let us now briefly review how this proposal relates to the previous ones in the literature. A primary virtue of the account presented here is that it does not treat mixed projections as exceptional constructions resulting from weakened labelling conditions – for example, allowing a V-headed constituent project as an NP – or from the projection of categorially dual elements. Recall that this second option is impossible, already by a version of Baker's *Reference–Predication Constraint* (2003, 165): the same syntactic node cannot be both 'nominal' and 'verbal'. A SWITCH, being only nominal (as its [uV] will be eliminated before it gets a chance to be interpreted), respects that.

Second, our analysis only utilizes the two categorial features independently argued for and it invokes the concept of an uninterpretable feature as a Probe for Agree to derive both 'ordinary' (i.e., categorially homogeneous) and 'exceptional' (i.e., mixed) projections. Focusing on the SWITCH head, it is indeed a categorially dual head, as expressed by the intuition in Jackendoff (1977), Pullum (1991), Lapointe (1993) and Bresnan (1997) – making the best of the explanatory merits of the Agree system. Looking at the abstract phrase marker in (25) or, more concretely, at the one of a POSS–*ing* gerund in (21), we can observe that mixed projections are simply structures created when a functional nominalizer, the SWITCH, selects a verbal projection, continuing the line of reasoning of Baker (1985), Abney (1987) and Yoon (1996a). However, in our case this nominalizer's selection for a verbal projection comes not as an ad hoc stipulation but due to Categorial Deficiency, precisely because the nominalizer, SWITCH, is itself a *functional* element bearing a [uV] feature.[6]

Summarizing, we capture the duality of mixed projections as the result of the co-occurrence of an interpretable [N] and an uninterpretable [uV] feature on the same syntactic node: mixed projections are not special in any way that has to do with their phrase-structure status, and heads that are *interpreted* as both nominal and verbal are not necessary in order to explain mixed projections.

6.6   Morphologically overt SWITCHES

Having argued for the existence of functional categorizers, it would be interesting to review some instances of morphologically overt SWITCH heads so as to examine their properties. Ackema and Neeleman's (2004, 140)

---

[6] See Section 6.10 of this chapter on why we need functional categorizers in mixed projections, instead of ordinary ones such as *n* and *v*.

principle of Input Correspondence predicts that overtly realized SWITCH heads, their category-changing AFFIXES, will be found only in head-final languages. This is a prediction that is borne out, at least in the small sample of languages I have surveyed. Indeed, Korean, Turkish and Basque – all head-final languages – each have overt functional categorizers. For reasons of exposition clarified in footnote 19, I will only discuss Basque and Turkish SWITCH heads here.

Basque contains a nominalizing element inserted among functional morphemes which easily qualifies as a functional nominalizer according to Borsley and Kornfilt (2000, 111–12). We therefore have examples like the following, adapted from the same source:[7]

(26) [Jon-ek   bere   hitzak   hain   ozenki   es-te-a-n]   denok   harritu
      Jon-ERG his   words   so   loudly   say-FN-D-INESS   all   surprise
      ginen.
      AUX
      'We were all surprised at John saying his words so loudly.'

(27) [Zu-k   etxea   prezio   honetan   hain   errazki   sal-tze-a-re-kin]
      you-ERG house   price   that-in   so   easily   sell-FN-D-GEN-with
      ni-k   ez   dut   ezer   irabazten
      I-ERG   NEG   AUX   anything win
      'I don't get anything out of your selling the house so easily.'

The suffixal *te/tze* element, the functional nominalizer by hypothesis, nominalizes Tense Phrases. The constituent it heads is the complement of a Determiner *–a*, the same used with noun phrases, which in turn can be the complement of a Kase element, as in (26), or of a postposition like *with* in (27) – again, as happens with ordinary nominal constituents. The resulting picture is therefore pretty straightforward.

Turkish presents a slightly more intriguing situation when it comes to the morphological – or, rather, morphosyntactic – status of SWITCH heads. Turkish, although it does possess a subordinating Complementizer, *ki*, is famous for the fact that subordination in this language is done mainly via nominalizing the phrasal complement. In (9), repeated below for convenience, we saw an instance of a nominalized infinitive, known as 'action nominalization' in the literature on Turkish:[8]

---

[7] ERG = Ergative Case, FN = Functional Nominalizer, D = Determiner, INESS = Inessive Case.
[8] Kornfilt (1997) is a classic description of the language in English.

(28)   Hasan   [Ayşe-nin   gel-me-sin]-i   iştiyor.
       Hasan   Ayşe-GEN   come-FN-3SG-ACC   wants
       'Hasan wants Ayşe to come over.'

In the example above I provisionally gloss –*me* (whose underlying form is *mA*) as the functional nominalizer, but this is a matter that we will not investigate further. Suffice it to say for our purposes here that in 'action nominalizations', like (28), the overt subject of the nominalized clause is invariably in the genitive case; this corroborates an analysis thereof as nominalized infinitives.

The picture of nominalizations in Turkish becomes more stimulating (and intriguing) when one turns to a different type of nominalized clause, what Kornfilt (1997) and Borsley and Kornfilt (2000) term 'factive nominalizations'. The example below is from the latter:

(29)   Ben   [siz-in   tatil-e   çık-tığ-ınız-ı]   duy-du-m.
       I   you-GEN   vacation-DAT   go.out-FN.PAST-2PL-ACC   hear-PAST-1SG
       'I heard that you had gone on vacation.'

In both (28) and (29), what follows the purported nominalizing suffixes, –*me*– and –*tığ*– respectively, are purely nominal functional elements: nominal agreement and (accusative) Case. Concentrating on (29), the important element in examples like it is the underlying form of –*tığ*– (i.e., *dIk*) which Borsley and Kornfilt (2000) gloss as 'factive'. The interesting twist here is that the particular form also encodes past tense and that *dIk* is a form similar, although non-identical, to the verbal past morpheme *dI*. Moreover, this 'factive' element also comes in a future tense version, *AcAk*, which is identical to the verbal future tense suffix. Hence, the example below forms a minimal pair with (29):

(30)   Ben   [siz-in   tatil-e   çık-acağ-ınız-ı]   duy-du-m.
       I   you-GEN   vacation-DAT   go.out-FN.FUT-2PL-ACC   hear-PAST-1SG
       'I heard that you will go on vacation.'

Calling an element that forces a future interpretation 'factive' is something of a paradox. This is perhaps somehow reflected in Borsley and Kornfilt (2000, 108) taking both 'action' *mA* and the two versions of the 'factive' nominalizer, *dIk* and *AcAk*, to be the realization of a *nominal mood* (MN) category. This choice of term is quite telling because, I think, it reflects the inherent duality of nominalizing *dIk* and *AcAk*, which are called (inevitably perhaps) nominal but are also acknowledged as encoding 'mood', a verbal/clausal category which here should be identified with Tense. If *dIk* and *AcAk* are indeed dual heads, as the analysis goes, then their very duality reveals the kind of morphosyntactic interactions a SWITCH can establish with other heads of the verbal/clausal part of a mixed projection. Perhaps the [*u*V] feature on a SWITCH enables it also to encode Tense features, making it both a genuine member of the verbal/ clausal projection line – and one carrying a temporal specification, too – *and* a nominalizer at the same time. We could further speculate that this type of SWITCH encoding temporal features is made possible in Turkish because functional nominalizers, AFFIXES in Ackema and Neeleman (2004, 172–81), *must* be overt in head-final languages: it just happens that they additionally carry temporal features.

However, unpublished work by Tosun (1999) offers a more elegant account of how Turkish functional nominalizers of the 'factive' denomination end up with past and future Tense specifications. First, she addresses analyses according to which the 'factive' nominalizers, *dIk* and *AcAk*, are actually Tense morphemes followed by a version of the Complementizer *ki*. In the case of *dIk* this would entail analysing the form as *dI* (past) + *k* (the Complementizer): these forms would be the exponents of Tense + Complementizer sequences. However, evidence suggests that *independent* Tense/Aspect morphemes are not allowed inside subordinate nominalized clauses:[9]

(31)   gid-iyor-du-m   *in main clauses*
        go-IMPERF-PAST-1SG
        'I was going.'

(32)   git-tiğ-im   *in embedded clauses*
        go-FN.PAST-1SG

(33)   * gid-iyor-duğ-um   *in embedded clauses*
        go-IMPERF-FN.PAST-1SG

The above examples illuminate the following state of affairs: although two Tense/Aspect morphemes may co-exist in Turkish main clauses, as in (31), no such thing is possible in nominalized embedded ones (33), where an independent Tense head is not available. Actually, it is impossible to express aspectual information in 'factive' nominalizations, as the ungrammaticality of (33) demonstrates, and the correct form in (32) appears to encode Tense features only via the nominalizer, which is *dIk* in this example. Tosun (1999, 7) claims exactly this: that the 'factive' nominalizer – more precisely, a form like *dIk* (i.e., *-tığ-*) in our (32) – 'bears both tense and nominal features'. So, the above examples take the same direction as Borsley and Kornfilt (2000, 108) in that there is a single *head* encoding both nominal and temporal features.

Tosun (1999), however, argues against the existence of a single syntactic head by looking at the availability of object shift and scope ambiguity with

---

[9] I have adapted the glossing to reflect the working hypotheses here.

indefinites, 'Diesing effects' after Diesing (1992), in embedded nominalized clauses. Tosun finds out that object shift is possible, when not obligatory, and that Diesing effects available in *all* embedded nominalized clauses – that is, both 'action' nominalizations with *mA* and 'factive' ones with *dIk* and *AcAk* are available. According to Bobaljik (1995) and Bobaljik and Thráinsson (1998), the availability of object shift and Diesing effects entails the presence of *two* syntactic heads, each projecting a specifier. This in turns leads Tosun to offer a Fusion analysis (Halle and Marantz 1993) within the Distributed Morphology framework, according to which in nominalized embedded clauses there are indeed two heads: a Tense head and a Gerundive head (our functional nominalizer, the SWITCH), which provide the necessary specifiers that enable or sanction object shift and permit scope ambiguities regarding indefinites (the 'Diesing effects'). These heads are then fused together and subsequently either *AcAk*, a form identical to the verbal future morpheme, or *dIk*, a form non-identical to the verbal past morpheme *dI*, is inserted into this fused node.

The conclusion of this brief survey is that SWITCH heads may have diverse morphological realizations. They are typically realized as null morphemes in head-first languages. They may be realized as identifiable morphemes in head-last languages like Korean (the *–um* element) and Basque (the suffixal *te/tze* element). Finally, in Turkish they can fuse with Tense heads, as both belong to the group of verbal/clausal functional heads by virtue of their [uV] features.[10]

6.7　SWITCHES and their complements

We have now reached a point where the issue regarding the position of SWITCHES must be addressed. I claimed that these heads are functional categorizers, by virtue of their bearing an interpretable categorial feature. However, in Chapters 3 and 4 I have sided with Marantz's (2000) claim that categorizers are phase heads – a prediction I have understood to stem precisely from their bearing an interpretable categorial feature, which sets an interpretive perspective for the categorizer's complement and closes off root material. Consequently, all other things being equal, projections headed by a SWITCH

---

[10] In the spirit of van Riemsdijk (1998b) and Hegarty (2005), one could perhaps speculate that fusion is only possible between heads bearing identical uninterpretable categorial features – that is, if both heads are marked as [uN] or as [uV]. Unfortunately, in the context of this study I can only offer this as mere speculation.

should also be phases, as a SWITCH also bears an interpretable categorial feature. Having said that, if we turn to the literature on mixed projections and phasehood, to the best of my knowledge, there is nothing on whether subconstituents within mixed projections constitute phases, let alone whether functional categorizers constitute phase heads.[11] As a consequence of this, the discussion here will have a preliminary and exploratory character; we begin by phrasing the question from an empirical point of view, in three versions:

(34)   *Phases within mixed projections*
         a. What types and sizes of nominal and verbal/clausal constituents can be part of a mixed projection?
         b. Where can we place a SWITCH within a derivation?
         c. What are the possible types and sizes of SWITCH complements?

Let us now attempt to sketch an answer basing ourselves on theoretical assumptions compatible with the theory of categorial features developed here. If SWITCHES contain categorial features, features which I have claimed in Chapter 4 induce phasehood, then SWITCHES themselves must trigger a phase every time they are merged. This would in turn suggest that they can never be merged *mid-phase*: phases are by definition interpretive units readable by the interfaces and inserting a SWITCH in the midst of a phase, would induce something like an 'incomplete phase', a contradiction in terms. So, we can begin by proposing that SWITCHES can only be merged at the edge of phases. Granting that, we can examine whether functional categorizers are themselves heads inducing phases, phasal heads. We will now explore some evidence that might lend support to this idea.

6.7.1   Locating the SWITCH: the size of its complement

Dutch nominalized infinitives are a type of mixed projection that has been scrutinized and analysed in considerable detail, also with reference to the cut-off point between the nominal and the verbal/clausal subconstituent. Schoorlemmer (2001) has argued that there are two types of nominalized infinitives: 'expressive' infinitives, which contain a large verbal/clausal subconstituent, a TP, and 'plain' infinitives, which only project an AspP.[12]

---

[11] Most of the work on phases looks only at uniform verbal/clausal projections (CPs). The question of whether or not (categorially uniform) DPs are phases has been addressed to a lesser extent, with some representative discussion in Svenonius (2004) and Hicks (2009, chaps. 4 and 5).

[12] This statement on 'plain' nominalized infinitives is refined and revised below, in Section 6.9.2. Panagiotidis and Grohmann (2009) also address the matter; the discussion in this section revisits some of their arguments and observations.

This state of affairs is exemplified below, with the verbal/clausal subtree placed in brackets for convenience. The examples below are taken from Ackema and Neeleman (2004, 173):

(35)   Deze   zanger is vervolgd   voor dat [*stiekem* succesvolle liedjes
        this   singer is prosecuted for that   [sneakily successful   songs
        jatten].
        pinch.INF]

(36)   Deze   zanger is vervolgd   voor dat *stiekeme* [succesvolle liedjes
        this   singer is prosecuted for that sneaky   successful   songs
        jatten].
        pinch.INF]
        'This singer is prosecuted for sneakily pinching successful songs.'[13]

In (35) the verbal/clausal constituent ('expressive infinitive') is large enough to contain a projection hosting an adverb, *stiekem* ('sneakily'). The SWITCH is merged with this large verbal/clausal subtree and the superimposed nominal part of the mixed projection seems to consist solely of the demonstrative *dat*.

(37)   *A verbal/clausal subtree with an adverb*

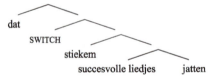

Turning to the nominalized 'plain' infinitive in (36) the cut-off point between the nominal and the verbal/clausal subtree of the mixed projection is lower: the verbal/clausal projection is too small to contain an adverb (it is nominalized below the position where adverbs attach) and this is why the adjective *stiekeme* ('sneaky') is merged, instead of an adverb. In this case, the superimposed nominal subtree is large enough for both the demonstrative *dat* and for a position below it to host the adjective:

---

[13] Schoorlemmer (2001) also explains away an apparent violation of Categorial Uniformity: in nominalized infinitives nominal and verbal properties look like they can be interspersed, with direct objects of the verb showing up as phrases headed by *van* ('of').

        (i) nominal ... verbal ... nominal

She shows that low *van* phrases may merge inside the verbal phrase if they can later be checked against a higher nominal functional structure, i.e. that dominating the verbal/clausal constituent.

(38)   *An adverb-less verbal/clausal subtree*

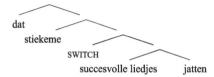

The validity of the structures outlined in (37) and (38) is corroborated by the fact that in Dutch an adjective modifying the nominalized infinitive may precede an adverb (Ackema and Neeleman 2004, 174):

(39)   Deze zanger is vervolgd   voor dat constante [*stiekem* succesvolle
         liedjes   jatten]
         this   singer is prosecuted for that constant [sneakily successful
         songs   pinch.INF]

The structure for the example above is given in the phrase marker below:

(40)   *Adjective plus a verbal/clausal subtree with an adverb*

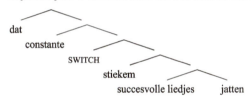

The reverse, an adverb preceding the modifying adjective, *is not* possible, however.

(41)   *... dat   *constant*   *stiekeme*   [succesvolle   liedjes   jatten]
              that   constantly   sneaky   successful   songs   pinch.INF
         'This singer is prosecuted for constantly sneakily pinching successful songs.'

Again, the structure for the ungrammatical adverb–adjective order is given in the phrase marker below:

(42)   *An impossible state of affairs: an adverb within the nominal subtree*

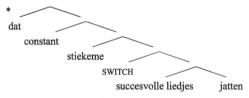

The impossibility of (42) is multiply interesting. First, it is yet another example against the crude version of an analysis where functional elements can mix for free and where there is no biuniqueness or categorial uniformity at play. Second, it both illustrates Phrasal Coherence and is compatible with a SWITCH analysis. Third, it also illustrates the impossibility of *flip-flopping*

(David Adger, personal communication, February 2007) – namely, a state of affairs where we start building a verbal/clausal tree, then we switch (using a SWITCH) to a nominal tree, only to switch back to a verbal/clausal one, and so on. As to *why* flip-flopping is in principle impossible, we will try to work out an answer in the following section.

Turning to Spanish, we observe a very similar set of possibilities: on the one hand, nominalized infinitives with just a VoiceP-internal accusative object in (43); on the other, nominalized infinitives containing a nominative TP-internal subject in (45) (examples adapted from Ackema and Neeleman 2004, 178):

(43)   El   [tocar   la   guitarra]   de   Maria . . .
        the   play.INF   the   guitar   of   Maria
        'Maria's playing the guitar . . .'

(44)   [$_{DP}$ El [[$_{SWITCHP}$ SWITCH [$_{VoiceP}$ tocar la guitarra]] de Maria]]

(45)   El   [cantar   yo   La   Traviata] . . .
        the   sing.INF   I   *La*   *Traviata*

(46)   [$_{DP}$ El [$_{SWITCHP}$ SWITCH [$_{TP}$ *pro* cantar yo La Traviata]]]]

In (44) a Voice Phrase includes the verb *tocar* ('play') and its object in accusative Case, which is assigned by the Voice head. It must be that the SWITCH takes that VoiceP as its complement, because the external argument *de Maria* is expressed as an adjunct on the resulting nominal constituent, in a manner reminiscent of that of 'possessive' subjects in English POSS-*ing* gerunds. In (46) the verbal/clausal constituent is large enough to include a Tense head, one that assigns nominative to a post-verbal subject *yo* ('I').[14]

A first conclusion is therefore that a SWITCH can appear in different positions even in the same language: the complement of a SWITCH head in (36) is smaller than the one in (35). Similarly, the complement of the SWITCH head in (43) seems to be roughly the size of a VoiceP, excluding the nominative-assigning structure, whereas in (45) the complement of the SWITCH seems to be the size of (at least) a TP. Interestingly, in many languages, including Modern Greek, a Determiner can appear in the syntactic nominalization of a full CP complement, a mixed projection:

---

[14] At first glance, the nominative in the context of an infinitive is unexpected. Even if it is not a complete TP that is nominalized here and even if the source of nominative is not T, it still remains the case that the verbal/clausal constituent in (45) is large enough to contain a postverbal subject. Yoon and Bonet-Farran (1991) discuss the Case-marking of Spanish infinitival subjects both in nominalized and in 'sentential' infinitives, arguing that Nominative is not a default Case, but indeed is the result of Case-marking.

(47)   Ksero   [to   [poso   sklira   agonizeste]]
       I.know the   how.much   hard   you.are.fighting
       'I know how hard you are fighting.'

(48)   [_DP_ to [_SWITCHP_ SWITCH [_CP_ poso sklira agonizeste]]]

The preliminary conclusion is that it is indeed the case that verbal/clausal constituents of various sizes can be the complement of SWITCH, even within the same grammar, as Dutch and Spanish examples demonstrate.

Although we will return to this topic below, we need to say a few more words about the nominalization of CP constituents before continuing: in their discussion of Spanish nominalized infinitives, Yoon and Bonet-Farran (1991, 364–5) follow Plann (1981) in claiming that whenever a full CP is nominalized, this is actually done via the mediation of an empty noun synonymous to *hecho* ('fact'). This would be quite plausible to the extent that such nominalizations would have a factive reading, which seems not always to be the case with nominalized infinitives in Spanish, anyway (Rosemeyer 2012). In the remainder of this subsection we will compare the two alternative accounts for the nominalization of full CPs, which are schematically illustrated in the phrasal markers below, with the empty noun (e_N) analysis to the left and the functional categorizer one to the right.

(49)   *Alternatives to* [_DP_ D CP]

Before proceeding, note that neither of the above accounts suffers from the paradoxical state of affairs of an analysis where D directly selects a CP. A [_DP_ D CP] constituent would either violate biuniqueness, as it has D (a [*u*N] head) select a CP, or would force us to concede that *all* Complementizers are nominal – see Roussou (1990, sec. 4.1), Davies and Dubinsky (1998, 2001) and Manzini (2010) for discussion of the (non-)nominal character of (all) Complementizers.

So, let us now turn to languages with bona fide nominalizations of complete CPs, such as Polish and Greek.[15] Roussou (1990) already discusses the implausibility of an account involving an empty noun, on the grounds that this

---

[15] Borsley and Kornfilt (2000, 116–17) discuss Kabardian as one more language where full CPs can be nominalized and be assigned Case.

noun cannot host an adjective or, indeed, *any* other element associated with nouns. Expanding on this observation by Roussou, nothing can intervene between the article *to* (the neuter gender and default form) and the CP in structures like the one in (47). Moreover, the role of e_N, the phonologically empty non-descriptive noun of Panagiotidis (2003b), is very well understood in languages like Greek: its lack of interpretation underlies a number of pronominal and elliptical structures, and their functions.[16] However, in the context of nominalized CPs e_N would have to mean 'fact', as in Plann (1981) and Yoon and Bonet-Farran (1991, 364–5), 'matter', 'question' and the like. This range of different interpretations for the empty noun e_N does not look feasible.

This last point takes us to the relevant Polish and Greek structures. In both languages, *all* subordinate CPs can be nominalized: declarative and interrogative, in either indicative or subjunctive; in Polish demonstratives *to*, *tego* and *tym* are used, whereas in Greek the default article *to* is used. Some data from the two languages clearly illustrate this:[17]

(50) [To, że Maria zmienia pracę] Jan oznajmił. *Polish*
      that COMP Maria is.changing job Jan announced
      'Jan announced that Mary is changing her job.'

      [To oti i Maria alazi dhulia] anakinose o Yanis. *Greek*
      the COMP the Maria is.changing job announced the John
      'John announced that Mary is changing her job.'

The nominalized declarative CPs have been fronted to show that they form a single constituent together with the Det-element introducing them. Note that the examples above are compatible with both of the alternatives in (49), as a 'fact' empty noun between the demonstrative or the article and the clause would be compatible with their interpretation – keeping in mind, of course, the objections on the distribution, interpretation and compatibility with adjectives that characterize true e_N in Greek. These objections become even more relevant in examples like the ones below:

(51) Jan rządał [(tego), żeby Maria zmieniła pracę]. *Polish*
      Jan demanded that COMP Maria changed job
      'Jan demanded that Maria change her job.'

      [To na fiyis] ine efkolo. *Greek*
      the IRREALIS leave.2SG is easy
      'For you to leave is easy.'

---

[16] In the spirit of Harley's (2005a) analysis, e_N would have to be identified with an *n* head not associated with any root material; see the discussion in Section 4.5 in Chapter 4.

[17] Polish examples and discussion from Borsley and Kornfilt (2000, 113–14).

(52)   Jan zastanawia się   nad   [tym, czy   kupić nowy samochód].   *Polish*
       Jan wondered   over   that   whether buy   new   car
       'Jan wondered whether to buy a new car.'

       Eksetazis   [to   an   tha   fiyi].   *Greek*
       examine.2SG   the   if   will   leave.3SG
       'You are considering whether s/he will go.'

(53)   Jan zastanawia się   nad   [tym, kiedy kupić nowy samochód].   *Polish*
       Jan wondered   over   that   when buy   new   car
       'Jan wondered when to buy a new car.'

       Epaneksetazo   [to   pote   tha   fiyi].
       re-examine.1SG   the   when   will   leave.3SG
       'I am re-examining when s/he will leave.'

       Epaneksetazo   [to   pion   tha   kalesis].
       re-examine.1SG   the   who   will   invite.2SG
       'I am re-examining who you will invite.'

In (51) we have nominalized subjunctive CPs – thus the purported empty noun would have to be interpreted not as 'fact' but as something else, although it is unclear as to what exactly. In (52) the demonstrative *tym* in Polish and the article *to* in Greek introduce nominalized subordinate yes/no questions and in (53) an embedded *wh*-question with *when* and – for Greek – with *who*.

It becomes obvious from the above that no noun can mediate between the D-element and the clause in nominalized CPs, even an abstract one meaning 'fact' and the like. At the same time, a SWITCH, a functional nominalizer, inserted very high so as to take a complete CP as its complement, is compatible with all the empirical facts presented and discussed in this section.

6.7.2   *Phases and* SWITCHES

The follow-up question is, if the complements of a SWITCH can be of *any* size, as Ackema and Neeleman (2004, 173) argue, whether a SWITCH head can take any verbal/clausal constituent as its complement. As already announced, here I will examine Lapointe's (1999) intuition that the subtrees participating in a mixed projection, the possible complements of a SWITCH head in our analysis, have to be of particular sizes. The strong version of its claim is crystallized in the statement below:

(54)   SWITCHES can be merged with phase heads, themselves inducing a phase.

Pausing for a moment, we must ask why we have to argue that complements of SWITCH must be the size of phases. The reasons will have to be of a theory-internal nature but, hopefully, should reflect some more generally received ideas about how syntactic structures are dealt with at the interfaces. Consider (21) and suppose that *Ger* (our SWITCH) indeed takes an AspP complement, as illustrated in the diagram. Is an Aspectual Phrase complete in any sense? Does it constitute a complete interpretive unit? The answer is most likely negative: Aspectual Phrases apparently denote time intervals in which events unfold, but these time intervals are neither anchored in time nor suitably ordered with respect to an instance and/or another time interval.

Why would this matter? It would if we expect that the two uniform subtrees in a mixed projection would be able to stand as complete interpretive units. In previous work, I have precisely argued for this – namely, that the complements of SWITCH must be complete interpretive units by themselves. In Panagiotidis and Grohmann (2009) a central claim is that complements of SWITCH must be the size of Prolific Domains (Grohmann 2003), whereas in unpublished work I take complements of SWITCH to be the size of a *phase*, claiming that 'SWITCHES will be merged with phases and induce themselves a phase', exactly as in (54) above.

This last claim brings us to an interesting dilemma. If SWITCH heads bear interpretable categorial features, interpretive perspective-setting features, then we expect them to be phasal heads, like 'ordinary' categorizers *n* and *v* (see Chapter 4): in other words, we expect them to *induce* a phase themselves. So, the claim that 'SWITCHES ... induce themselves a phase' is consistent with what we have seen so far on categorial features and phasehood. However, if a SWITCH head is phasal, its complement certainly need not be: for instance, the complement of a phasal head like a Complementizer is certainly not a phase. Being more precise about the phasehood of categorizers, both *n* and *v* and functional SWITCH, categorial features on them are sufficient to impose an interpretive perspective on material that cannot be otherwise interpreted – for example, root material – and to complete a phase with it. Thus, categorial features on both a categorizer (*n* and *v*) and a SWITCH could surely also make a phase out of *any* other material consisting of UG features, including functional structures. It therefore is not necessary for the complement of SWITCH, a phasal head, also to be a phase. *A fortiori*, if Richards (2007) is correct, it *cannot* be a phase: phase and non-phase heads must actually alternate.[18]

---

[18] Furthermore, if Richards (2007) is indeed correct, then denominal structures (e.g., the verb *tape* in Chapters 4 and 5) cannot have a [*v* [*n*P]] structure and, respectively, nominalizations cannot have an [*n* [*v*P]] structure: both *n* and *v* are phase heads. This would suggest that a projection must intervene between them, but this is an empirical matter that will not be explored here.

Given that there is no *theoretical* need for the complements of SWITCHES to come in particular sizes – that is, the size of a phase – I will restrict myself to closer scrutiny of what type of functional material these complements can contain and how this affects their syntactic behaviour. But before embarking on this, there is one matter that needs be addressed.

6.8   Are all mixed projections externally nominal?

Let us return to the generalization in (8), the 'second' generalization in the literature regarding mixed projections – the first being of course Phrasal Coherence in (5). According to (8), mixed projections display 'nominal external behaviour': they externally behave as nominal constituents. We saw that the nature and function of SWITCHES, functional categorizers, captures Phrasal Coherence. What about the curiosity that Nominal External Behaviour seems to be?

So far, all the mixed projections examined – for example, POSS–*ing* gerunds, nominalized infinitives and D+CP clauses – had the following general structure in terms of their categorial features (see the diagram in (25) as well):

(55)   *Mixed projections: nominal external behaviour*

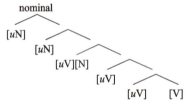

The higher part of (such) mixed projections – hence their 'external' behaviour – is nominal. According to the account developed here, this external nominal behaviour is a direct consequence of the SWITCH's feature specification, [*u*V][N], which effectively nominalizes its complement and shifts the categorial identity of the whole constituent to 'nominal' through its interpretable [N] feature. Apparently, a hypothetical SWITCH head with a [*u*N][V] specification would take 'nominal' functional phrases and verbalize them, rendering the mixed projection externally verbal. Such a mixed projection would behave as a verbal and/or clausal constituent, despite having a noun at its heart, as its lexical head. However, as Borsley and Kornfilt (2000) admit,

---

Some suggestions about what these intermediate projections could be may be extracted from Alexiadou's (2001) account on different types of nominalizations.

there are no unambiguous exceptions to (8) and the state of affairs in (55). Nevertheless, weaker challenges to Nominal External Behaviour exist and apparent exceptions to Nominal External Behaviour are actually attested, even if they are not examples of *verbal/clausal* external behaviour. Following the discussion in Panagiotidis (2010), I will present and discuss an example of a mixed projection that externally seems to behave as a *non*-nominal constituent: Japanese and Korean verbal nouns.

6.8.1   Verbal nouns

Verbal nouns (VNs) in Japanese and in Korean share some very remarkable properties: morphologically they are *nouns* (Yoon and Park 2004) and no special nominalizing morphology is attached to them, contrasting them, in the case of Korean at least, with nominalizations of complete TPs, suffixed by *–um* (Yoon and Park 2004). Furthermore, unlike what happens with the *–um* nominalizations in Korean, no adverbs are possible with verbal nouns, although adjectives are generally acceptable.[19]

Verbal nouns, however, display two prototypically verbal/clausal characteristics: (a) they assign verbal Case in both Japanese (Iida 1987) and Korean (Yoon and Park 2004), including *–ga* Nominative in Japanese; (b) they project full argument structures; see Tsujimura (1992, 477–9), Manning (1993) and Yoon and Park (2004), from where the following Korean example is adapted:

(56)   [Kim-paksa-ka   woncahayk-ul   yenkwu]-cwung-ey   cencayng-i
       Kim-dr-NOM   atom.nucleus-ACC   research-midst-LOC   war-NOM
       ilena-ss-ta.
       broke.out-PST-DECL
       'The war broke out while Dr Kim was researching the atom nucleus.'

In the example above, (functional material associated with) the VN *yenkwu* ('research') assigns not just accusative, like English POSS–*ing* gerunds, but also nominative, to a Theme *woncahayk-ul* ('atom nucleus') and an Agent *Kim-paksa-ka* ('Dr Kim') respectively.

---

[19] Yoon (1996b) discusses *–um* and points out that it can also be used as a lexical nominalizer, presumably an *n*, directly attached on verbs: for example, *cwuk* ('die') is nominalized as *cwuk-um* ('death' or 'dying'). Now, in (59) I argue that verbal nouns in Korean (and Japanese) also involve an *n* head, which is (crucially for the analysis here) phonologically null. If this is the case, then Korean *–um* can be the morphological exponence

(a)   either of a functional categorizer, a SWITCH, when it nominalizes TPs,
(b)   or of an *n*, when it nominalizes *v*Ps *in the absence* of a SWITCH further up the tree. In the structure in (62) there exist both a (low) nominalizer *n* and a (high) functional nominalizer, a SWITCH, so *n* surfaces as a null morpheme.

Now, unlike the other mixed projections reviewed in this chapter, VNs *cannot* be arguments but are typically embedded within modifying expressions with *a temporal interpretation*, as this Japanese example from Shibatani (1990, 247) illustrates:

(57) [Sensei-ga kaigai-o ryokoo]-no sai ...
      teacher-NOM abroad-ACC travel.VN-GEN occasion
      'On the occasion of the teacher's travelling abroad ...'

Alternatively, VNs can combine with a copula/light verb (the equivalent of *do*) to yield the Light Verb Construction (Yoon and Park 2004); in these cases they contribute the predicative content to the complex verbal predicate. Summarizing:

(58) Verbal nouns
      a. are morphologically simplex nouns that may be modified by adjectives;
      b. also contain a verbal/clausal layer that may license an Agent and assign accusative and nominative Case, but not adverbs;
      c. must contain a high nominal layer, which enables them to be complements of temporal adpositions and which makes them possible (incorporated?) arguments for light verbs.[20]

Let us put all those ingredients together and see what kind of structure emerges. Our rationale here will be that the diverse characteristics of verbal nouns must be the results of features structurally interacting with each other, in the spirit of the analysis in Ahn (1991), albeit with different results. Thus, we start with the fact that VNs display *nominal* morphology, precisely the way that English gerunds always contain a verbal morphological chunk. Under the fairly innocuous assumption that adjectives adjoin to noun phrases, we would get the following structure as the bottom of a VN tree:

(59) *A nominal subtree*

Apparently, the nominal chunk in (59) is verbalized immediately above the *n*P. Here a first crucial dilemma emerges, especially for our theory of categorial features, which enables grammars to possess both categorizers, *n* and *v*, *and* functional categorizers – that is, SWITCHES: which of the two links an *n*P like the one in (59) with the verbal/clausal functional material directly dominating it? In principle, both a *v* and a SWITCH specified as [V][*u*N] would be possible here

---

[20] This last point makes sense if one considers that in complex verbal predicates the non-light verb element is necessarily non-verbal – recall the discussions about Farsi and Jingulu in Chapter 2.

and both would do the same job.[21] If there is some economy metric according to which a *v* head, consisting of a single [V] feature, is more economical than a [*u*N][V] head, then we can perhaps argue that an ordinary categorizer, a *v*, will do here. The intuitive idea behind this assumed economy metric here is as simple as not inserting uninterpretable and unvalued features unless we have to. Already suggested in the discussion below (17) is that a lexical categorizer can categorize lexical material but not functional constituents and that a functional categorizer, a SWITCH, will not be used to convert purely lexical material (see also Section 6.10). Incidentally, a VN, which keeps its ability to take adjectives, is in this analysis nothing more than a transparent denominal verb, like *tape*. One of the ways it differs from *tape*, however, is that there is no morphological fusion of the material under *n* with the material under *v*, and the two heads remain separate with *v* being silent:

(60)   *A verbalized* nP

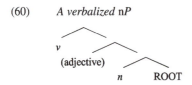

What immediately follows is a fully blown verbal clausal layer, possibly a full TP, if Nominative in Japanese and Korean is assigned by T, and given that nominative arguments are possible with VNs. A Voice head, assigning Accusative, is also required, in order to capture examples like (56) and (57) above, where accusative Case is assigned.

(61)   *A verbalized* nP *with its verbal/clausal projections*

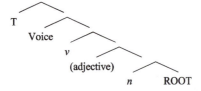

Finally, to complete the picture adumbrated in (58), we need to add a nominal layer on top of the extended verbal/clausal subtree. A SWITCH will

---

[21] Assuming of course that, for the sake of the argument, the unattested functional verbalizers, [V] [*u*N] SWITCH heads, exist. Borsley and Kornfilt (2000, 120) claim that 'there are no nominal properties that reflect a nominal functional category located below a verbal functional category', having stipulated that '[c]lausal constructions with nominal properties are a consequence of the association of a verb with one or more nominal functional categories instead of or in addition to the normal verbal functional categories, appearing above any verbal functional categories' (102). This is equivalent to saying that no functional verbalizers, [V][*u*N] SWITCH heads, exist.

be used here, as the transition will now be from (verbal/clausal) functional to (nominal) functional material.[22]

(62)   *VN: a mixed projection containing a transparently denominal verb*

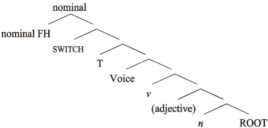

The provisional conclusion is that there is still no solid evidence for a [V][*u*N] SWITCH. So, it seems that either there is a mysterious asymmetry here or that we need to look harder. I am not going to pursue this apparent asymmetry any further here, with the exception of footnote 3 in the Appendix.

6.9   The properties of mixed projections

We have seen that mixed projections are possible because functional categorizers, SWITCH heads, exist. From this, we have also easily derived Categorial Uniformity and the dual categorial properties of mixed projections. Functional categorizers, bearing an interpretable categorial feature, are phasal heads, meaning that they induce a new interpretive unit. Empirically speaking, we saw that these verbal/clausal subconstituents that a SWITCH can turn into an interpretive unit can be

- Voice Phrases, as in Spanish nominalized infinitives in (44);
- Aspect Phrases, as in English POSS–*ing* gerunds in (21) and in Dutch 'plain' nominalized infinitives in (36);
- Tense Phrases, as in Spanish nominalized infinitives in (46), in Dutch 'expressive' nominalized infinitives in (37) and in Korean and Japanese verbal nouns in (62);
- Complementizer Phrases, as in Greek D+CP in (48) and Turkish nominalized clauses in (9).

What we now need to turn to, as promised earlier in the chapter, is a closer examination of how the kind of functional material contained in mixed projections affects their syntactic behaviour. The nominal subconstituent of mixed projections seems to be quite restricted: with exceptions like that of

---

[22] More discussion on VNs and mixed projections used exclusively as modifiers can be found in Panagiotidis (2010) and in references therein.

adjectivally modified Dutch infinitives in (36), it consists of just the SWITCH and a Determiner, possibly needed for the purposes of argumenthood. We will hence examine the functional structure of the verbal/clausal subtree of mixed projections and discuss how such scrutiny can explain some of their properties.

6.9.1   *Similarities: Nominalized Aspect Phrases in English and Dutch*
It has been argued that both English POSS–*ing* gerunds in (21) and Dutch 'plain' nominalized infinitives in (36) are nominalized AspPs. Indeed they share a number of common properties, which can be taken to follow from their lack of a Tense head and from the constitution of their verbal/clausal functional structure. One interesting similarity between English gerunds and Dutch 'plain' nominalized infinitives is their obligatory subjects, albeit never in the nominative.[23] These properties are easy to capture: Dutch and English are both non-null subject languages, therefore it is impossible for a null subject other than PRO to be generated inside a verbal/clausal (sub-)constituent. However, POSS–*ing* gerunds and 'plain' nominalized infinitives both contain an AspP subtree, complete with the full argument structure of the verb. Given that the Tense node, the licenser of PRO, is radically absent, the subjects must be overt. In POSS–*ing* gerunds subjects are licensed by the possessive Determiner c-commanding the AspP, whereas in Dutch they surface as *van*-phrases, thanks to the licensing properties of the nominal layer dominating the AspP (Schoorlemmer 2001, secs. 5 and 6) (see also footnote 13).

Concluding, the two mixed projections share the same properties despite the different morphology on the verb, infinitival in Dutch and aspectual in English. The similarity is due to the fact that in both structures, 'plain' nominalized infinitives in Dutch and POSS–*ing* gerunds in English, the same verbal subtree is nominalized, an Aspect Phrase.

6.9.2   *Differences: two types of Dutch 'plain' nominalized infinitives*
Zooming in on Dutch 'plain' nominalized infinitives, as we saw in Section 6.7.1 and in the previous subsection, Schoorlemmer (2001) identifies them as mixed projections in which the verbal/clausal subtree is the size of an Aspect Phrase. However, Schoorlemmer (2002) takes a closer look at 'plain' nominalized infinitives and finds out that they actually fall into two distinct classes. Each of these classes is characterized by a clustering of properties.

---

[23] See Siegel (1998) and Pires (2006, chap. 1) on why ACC–*ing* and PRO–*ing* gerunds are *not* mixed projections but bare TPs.

The first class is 'plain' nominalized infinitives with adverbial modification, which are different from the 'expressive' nominalized infinitives (Schoorlemmer 2001) reviewed in Section 6.7.1. 'Plain' nominalized infinitives in this first class have propositional readings and become severely degraded if an event reading is forced upon them by the context:[24]

(63)   *'Plain' nominalized infinitives with adverbs: propositions only*
?? Het gebeurde tijdens [het   snel   tenten opzetten van   Jan]   Dutch
It   happened during the   quickly tents pitch.INF of   Jan
'It happened during John's quickly pitching tents.'
[Het snel   tenten opzetten van Jan]   staat   buiten   kijf
the   quickly   tents pitch.INF of Jan   is   beyond dispute
'The quick pitching of tents by John is beyond dispute.'

Furthermore, adverbially modified 'plain' nominalized infinitives can support object shift and specific or definite direct objects. They can also appear in the 'perfect tense':

(64)   *'Plain' nominalized infinitives with adverbs: perfect aspect*
[Het   hardnekkig   scheidsrechters   belaagd   hebben]   . . .
the   persistently   referees   harassed   have.INF
'The persistently having harassed referees . . .'

This battery of properties – that is, adverbial modification, exclusively propositional readings, the possibility of specific objects, Object Shift and perfect aspect – is compatible with the analysis in Schoorlemmer (2001) of these nominalized infinitives as containing an AspP verbal/clausal subtree:

(65)   *'Plain' nominalized infinitives with an Aspect Phrase*

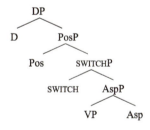

The Aspect node can be correlated with the licensing of adverbs, the obligatory propositional reading, the providing of a specifier for Object Shift and, of course, the possibility for perfect aspect.

---

[24] All examples in this subsection are from Schoorlemmer (2002). The phrase markers in (65) and (68) have been adapted in order to reflect this framework, which incorporates the SWITCH head hypothesis.

The above class of 'plain' nominalized infinitives contrasts with one that has very different properties, although it also constitutes a 'low' nominalization, with the SWITCH taking a 'small' verbal/clausal complement. Such 'plain' nominalized infinitives, when modified by an *adjective*, may have event readings. Compare the following with (63):

(66)   *'Plain' nominalized infinitives with adjectives: event reading possible*

| Het | gebeurde | tijdens | [het | snelle | tenten | opzetten | van | Jan] |
| It | happened | during | the | quick | tents | pitch.INF | of | Jan |

'It happened during John's quick pitching of tents.'

However, in adjectivally modified structures, no specific readings for the direct object and no perfect aspect is possible; compare the following with (64):

(67)   *'Plain' nominalized infinitives with adjectives: no perfect aspect*

| ??[Het | hardnekkige | scheidsrechters | belaagd | hebben] | ... |
| the | persistent | referees | harassed | have.INF |

'The persistent having harassed referees ...'

This battery of properties – that is, adjectival modification, the possibility of event readings, the ban on specific objects and Object Shift and the impossibility of perfect aspect – clearly defines this class of nominalized infinitives. Schoorlemmer (2002) claims, correctly I think, that these are all the result of a structure from which the Aspect head (and its specifier) are radically absent: there is no host for adverbs, there are no aspectual features to support 'perfect tense' and, of course, there is no proposition-creating Asp category. Additionally, the specifier that would host the shifted object and give rise to a specific reading thereof with the object taking scope over the rest of the verbal/clausal subtree, à la Diesing (1992), is not there, either. Schoorlemmer (2002) proposes the following structure:

(68)   *'Plain' nominalized infinitives without an Aspect Phrase*

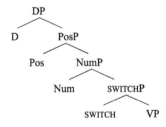

Besides the language-specific interest of the above analysis, I believe it serves as a case study of how we can follow a promising methodological blueprint: every time two types of mixed projections appear to differ along a battery of properties, the first attempt at explaining their differences should be to examine if this battery can be correlated with the *presence* versus the *absence* of a particular functional head inside the verbal/clausal subtree.[25] In the case of low nominalizations in Dutch examined here, this was achieved by correlating a battery of properties (event/proposition reading, adverbs vs adjectives, Object Shift, specificity and aspect) with the presence or absence of an Aspect head.

However, not all differences among mixed projections can be explained along the lines of the presence versus the absence of a category: sometimes structures containing the same verbal/clausal subconstituents can display very different behaviours.

6.9.3   Fine-grained differences: different features in nominalized Tense Phrases

Consider now mixed projections with a TP verbal/clausal constituent: Spanish nominalized infinitives with nominative postverbal subjects in (46), Dutch 'expressive' nominalized infinitives in (37) – see also Schoorlemmer (2001), and Korean and Japanese verbal nouns in (62). These are structures that behave in very different ways, as digested in (69).

(69)   *Comparing mixed projections: nominalized TPs*

	Overt subjects	In nominative	Adverbs
Spanish nominalized infinitives	yes	yes	yes
Dutch nominalized infinitives	no	no	yes
Korean/Japanese verbal nouns	yes	yes	no

Following the methodology of Alexiadou (2001), I am suggesting that the different properties of the above mixed projections can be reduced to the kind of functional heads that participate in their verbal/clausal subconstituent.

The most predictable behaviour is that exhibited by the Dutch expressive infinitives: these being infinitives, their TPs are headed by a defective Tense head that cannot assign nominative, hence cannot license overt subjects in SpecTP. The Spanish version of a nominalized Tense Phrase is morphologically an infinitive; however, its T head looks like it can assign nominative

---

[25] Of course, this is the line of reasoning followed in Section 6.7.1, where we teased apart TP 'expressive' nominalized infinitives and AspP 'plain' ones in Dutch.

Case and support non-null subjects, hence the two Tense heads have different *feature content*. Similar facts hold for Korean and Japanese verbal nouns: both overt subjects and nominative assignment are possible. What we have in Spanish and Korean/Japanese is a type of Tense head that is reminiscent of that in 'absolute' Greek gerunds (Panagiotidis 2010), with 'quasi-independent temporal reference'.[26] In any case, differences can be accounted for by the different feature makeup of the Tense head. Finally, the inability of adverbs to be licensed within the TP of verbal nouns must again be a result of the feature content or even the absence of the relevant functional head.

6.10   Why functional categorizers?

In Chapter 3 we looked into the category-changing function of *v* with regard to the derivation of denominal verbs like *tape*, with identical facts being true of *n*, of course. We saw there that a categorizer can take an already categorized constituent, an *n*P or a *v*P, and recategorize it.[27] As surveyed there, structures such as [*v* [*n*P]], which give us denominal verbs like *tape* and *dígest*, contrast with verbs such as *hammer* and *digést*, derived via direct root categorization – that is, [*v* RootP]. Moreover, I have argued in Chapter 4 that categorizers are lexical heads, the only lexical heads, as they are the only syntactic nodes capable of categorizing roots and root material and, therefore, support lexical content. The assumption so far has been that categorizers *n* and *v* can have only two kinds of complement:

a. root material, to which they assign an interpretive perspective in order to render it interpretable at LF and 'matchable' with a concept;
b. *n*Ps or *v*Ps, which they *transparently* convert.

The obvious question at this point is why a *second* type of categorizer must be posited in this chapter: the functional categorizer which we nicknamed SWITCH here. Can we not have an *n* categorizer mediate between the lower verbal/clausal and the higher nominal part of all the mixed projections surveyed, all of them displaying nominal external behaviour? Why can mixed projections not be simple cases of recategorization via a simple nominalizer *n*?

---

[26] 'Absolute' gerunds are the closest Modern Greek has to infinitives: their Tense head is not morphologically expressed, it can license temporal (not just aspectual) adverbs, sanction quasi-independent temporal reference, license periphrastic perfect tenses with an auxiliary, license a *pro* subject, and assign nominative to an overt subject (Panagiotidis 2010, 173).

[27] But recall footnote 18.

This is a question to which I have not been able to provide a final, rock-solid answer, so what follow are comments and intuitions of a more speculative nature, with some statements verging on the programmatic.

First of all, the difference between recategorizations and mixed projections can generally be described as follows: when a verb is nominalized or a noun is verbalized, it is lexical material (*n*P and *v*P) that participates as the lower subtree; it is purely lexical material that undergoes the conversion. On the other hand, in mixed projections, it is both functional *and* lexical material that participates as the lower subtree: in mixed projections we 'recategorize' a chunk of functional structure.

I think that we need to explicitly state a, so far elusive, principle to capture this situation: categorization of root and lexical material is the job of a lexical categorizer, whereas (re)categorization of functional material is the job of a functional head, a functional categorizer. In other words, we need to find a way, following on from general principles, that bans what looks like a counter-intuitive state of affairs: a lexical head interrupting a purely functional structure. Future research must derive the impossibility of the following structure, where the SWITCH in (25) has been replaced by a lexical nominalizer *n*:

(70)   *

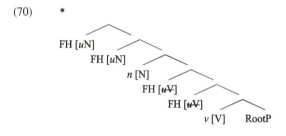

Let us now see if any insight can be offered to help ban the likes of (70). Generally, if *n* and *v* could freely take functional complements, then denominal verbs and deverbal nouns and mixed projections, on the other hand, should behave in exactly the same fashion; if this is indeed the case then we can perhaps do away with functional categorizers. A second point is this: *n* and *v* (or, more acrimoniously, the features [N] and [V]) appear to be necessary and universal; *all* languages have *n* and *v*. If the lexical categorizers *n* and *v* were responsible for mixed projections in addition to (re)categorizations, then functional categorizers would be unnecessary. However, I am not confident that *all* languages have mixed projections – but this is truly a matter of empirical enquiry. Finally, arguing that the element which makes mixed projections is a functional element with a particular feature structure – that is, [X][*u*Y] and, possibly, only [N][*u*V] – enables us to better frame the problem of the apparent absence of a functional verbalizer, of a [V][*u*N] SWITCH.

6.11   Conclusion

This chapter brings together two approaches to mixed projections, one arguing them to be categorially dual constituents and one conceiving of them as projections of a nominalizing head. I claim that they are indeed categorially dual constituents as a result of their containing a functional categorizer: in the same way that a lexical categorizer recategorizes lexical constituents, a functional categorizer recategorizes functional ones.

Evidence for the existence of functional categorizers was presented from head-final languages: Basque and Turkish. The existence of functional categorizers in natural language grammars was shown to be consistent with the theory of categorial features presented and advanced here: it results from the possibility of a categorial feature [N] to co-exist with an uninterpretable categorial feature [*u*V] as parts of the same feature bundle, of the same head. This nominalizing verbal/clausal functional head is understood to be a phasal head and can take verbal/clausal constituents of a variety of sizes. Moreover, as expected, verbal/clausal constituents of the same size – say, Aspect Phrases – may contain elements with different feature content. This derives the different behaviour of different mixed projections, as expected from a formal approach: different constituents and different features entail distinct grammatical behaviours and distinct batteries of grammatical properties.

The puzzle of what looks like the exclusive nominal external behaviour of mixed projections has been recast as the result of only nominalizing SWITCH, an [N][*u*V] head, existing. This merely rephrases the problem, one that future research will resolve either by deriving empirical evidence that verbalizing SWITCH heads – that is, [V][*u*N] elements – are possible or by deriving their impossibility on independent principles.

7 A summary and the bigger picture

7.1   A summary

The theory in this monograph attempts to explain why nouns are different from verbs and why they are most probably universal. In order to achieve this goal, it builds upon a series of empirical discoveries, theoretical advances and methodological principles of more than 50 years of work in generative grammar: empirical discoveries like those regarding the nature of long-distance dependencies, currently captured as the operations Agree and (internal) Merge, aka 'Move'; theoretical advances such as analysing the properties of lexical items on the basis of their formal features – this being a theory of categorial features, after all; and methodological principles like the functional–lexical distinction.

At the same time, research in this monograph has deliberately striven to synthesize insights, concepts and findings from a variety of frameworks and approaches to grammatical structure and to language in general. Investigating mixed projections, I turned to both LFG and HPSG in order to gain an understanding of how these structures are organized and whether they are exceptional or the consequence of principles applying everywhere else – Categorial Deficiency, in our case. Far more importantly, in order to gain an understanding of what kind of interpretive content each of the word classes 'noun' and 'verb' could have, I turned to functionalist and typological approaches, like Baker (2003) did. Crucially, Langacker (1987) and Anderson (1997) also proved major influences, in their combining notional approaches to lexical categories with a firm conviction that their interpretation is one of perspective, conceptualization or 'grammaticalization' of concepts – as opposed to a viewpoint according to which lexical categories form large pigeonholes into which different concepts are sorted.

Finally, this theory of categorial features attempts to deconstruct word class categories. Beginning with a criticism of weak lexicalism, I embrace syntactic decomposition of categories, in the version developed within the Distributed

Morphology framework, so as to capture four desiderata: first, the syntactic relevance of categorial features, which is well-hidden on occasion and hard to discern in lexicalist approaches; second, a clear and precise formulation of the actual interpretation of categorial features at the interface between the Language Faculty in the Narrow sense (FLN) and the Conceptual–Intentional/ SEM systems; third, the impossibility of uncategorized roots participating in syntax, the Categorization Assumption (Embick and Marantz 2008, 6), which can also be understood as the reason why there are no free-standing category-less *words*; finally, the role of categorial features in making lexical word classes, creating functional heads, and sanctioning the existence of mixed projections. This last desideratum is interweaved with the problem of 'idio-maticity' of words, the fact that morphological structure does not necessarily entail transparent compositional interpretations – something we explained as the result of categorial features interacting with semantically defective roots.

The theory proposes two unary categorial features: [N], which sets a sortal interpretive perspective, and [V], which sets a temporal/sub-eventive interpret-ive perspective. There is evidence that [N] and [V] are possibly different values – that is, [sortal] and [temporal] – of a [perspective] feature. The discussion about whether one of the two features (or values) is unmarked remained inconclusive in the absence of solid evidence to support such claims.

Categorial features 'make' categorizers, which are the only lexical heads in grammar, in that they can support 'descriptive content' by taking root material as their complements. The process of categorization is both about setting the perspective of the categorizers' complement, whether this be root material or an already categorized constituent, and about completing an interpretive unit, a (First) Phase. Categorizers, lexical heads, are the only necessary elements within a projection: roots are actually not, as the existence of semi-lexical heads – that is, *n* and *v* without a complement – demonstrates.

The existence of uninterpretable categorial features endows grammar with functional heads, each of them flagged by one of these features. Functional heads are thus members of nominal and verbal/clausal supercategories respect-ively: therefore they enable the association in local configurations of outlying nominal and verbal/clausal features with other constituents such as arguments and modifiers.

The interaction – that is, the Agree relations – between categorial features is also crucial: uninterpretable categorial features probe for interpretable categor-ial feature Goals, thus deriving two very important aspects of structure-building: first, categorial Agree indirectly constrains Merge, moulding syntactic structures to the effect that, for instance, lexical material only appears at the bottom of trees; second, categorial Agree relations play a significant role in deciding the head of the constituent after each application of Merge.

The theory developed in this monograph goes beyond answering the questions which it was designed to capture: how categorial features define lexical categories, what nouns and verbs are and how they differ from each other, the nature of functional heads, and the need for roots to be categorized. Its reliance on LF-interpretable categorial features enables this theory to make a precise hypothesis on the Janus-like element that lies at the heart of a mixed projection. This functional categorizer, a verbal functional head and a nominalizer at the same time, as far as attested cases go, gives the mixed projection its 'mixed' – that is, its categorially dual – character. It is neither a noun nor a hybrid head interpreted simultaneously as nominal and verbal, but a category-changing element that also belongs to the functional entourage of a verb. This in turn fits in nicely with the categorial uniformity of mixed projections, their being made up of two categorially consistent subtrees, a nominal one and a verbal/clausal one: at the point of categorial switch, the functional categorizer is found, gluing together two distinct constituents.

Summing up, a feature-based analysis of word classes enables us to go beyond lexical word classes as primitives: lexical categories are neither primitives nor are they necessarily organized in word classes – as Farsi illustrates pretty uncontroversially. At the same time, the fundamental grammatical and interpretive role of categorial features (licensing root material, supplying fundamental interpretive perspectives, making a phase) ensures that they will be found in *every* syntactic projection, creating the only indispensable element in it: the lexical head.

7.2   Loose ends

There is a number of loose ends stemming from the theory presented and argued for in this monograph. Three of these are reviewed below, and they concern broader matters as opposed to more empirical ones, or matters of execution (e.g., the true domain of 'lexical meaning', the behaviour of roots as if they are 'lexically categorized' or abiding by particular phonological restrictions in some languages etc.).

An immediate issue is the interaction between Agree and Merge. Suppose that, as in Section 5.9.4 of Chapter 5, Agree has a role in deciding the label of a projection. It follows from the analysis developed therein that every time Merge assembles an SO (syntactic object) from two [uX] ('functional') LIs (lexical items), it will not be possible to decide the label and the object should somehow be discarded *before it even reaches the LF-interface to be evaluated.* Agree may block the application of Merge. Is this possible? Does it reveal something about the relation between Agree, Merge and labelling? And if indeed it does, what decides the label when XP and YP merge, where no [*u*X] (uninterpretable categorial) features are at play?

A second matter concerns the uninterpretability of categorial features that make functional heads. Is there a way to recast uninterpretable categorial features as unvalued without losing empirical coverage – for example, with respect to biuniqueness? Speaking of the correct description of (categorial) features, one has to wonder why [sortal] and [temporal] are the only (?) values that the [perspective] attribute can take, giving us [N] and [V]. Are other values inconceivable? Possibly not. How can we then justify the prominence (to say the least) of sortality and temporality? Apparently, this will have to be done with reference to what matters as fundamental perspective for the Conceptual–Intentional systems, with FLN perhaps responding to some 'virtual conceptual necessity'. Having said that, at this point we may wonder whether we are better off replacing [sortal] with something like 'perceived as extending uninter-rupted in some spatial domain', as in Langacker (1987) and Uriagereka (1999). The abstractly spatial as nominal versus the abstractly temporal as verbal definitely looks like an elegant pair, but I can present no systematic arguments, let alone arguments of an empirical nature, to justify the superiority of a [spatial] interpretation for [N] over the much–better-understood [sortal] one that I am vouching for.

A third big question is that of adjectives. I think we have seen adequate evidence for three generalizations: (i) adjectives are not the unmarked lexical category and they are possibly not universal; (ii) if they are a lexical category, they are most likely not of the same ilk as nouns and verbs; and (iii) Degree is not an 'adjectival functional head': adjectives possess no functional category biuniquely associated with them. What are they, then? I hope to scrutinize the categorial status of adjectives in future research.

7.3   Extensions and consequences

A familiar pattern emerges when one considers the concepts, assumptions, hypotheses and proposals of this theory: natural objects, like FLN (the Language in the Narrow sense), reveal their workings under two conditions: once they are examined through the lens of a precisely articulated theory and once they are viewed at the right level and with the necessary amount of abstraction. To rehearse a rather trivial example from Chapter 2, the noun–verb distinction is not discernible if we are not mindful of misleading surface patterns, if we do not separate lexical nouns and verbs from their functional entourage and before we have some clearly spelled-out theoretical and methodological principles. Gazing at surface patterns is very often fascinating but hardly ever revealing.

Moving on, it is firmly hoped within the generative tradition that a theory of Universal Grammar can be formulated on the basis of empirical evidence coming from a single language. However, looking, for instance, at verbs being not word classes but syntactic categories in Farsi, Jingulu and the like, one can hardly overlook the necessity of cross-linguistic evidence in our successfully detecting the range, parametric or other, of linguistic phenomena: the limits of variation, in other words. Similar conclusions can be drawn once we look at mixed projections beyond Poss-*ing* gerunds: a limited empirical base was one of the reasons for the impasse that work on mixed projections reached in the 1970s and the 1980s – another one being the difficulties of having categorially dual endocentric projections: a theoretical difficulty. An issue related to the necessity of cross-linguistic evidence is the constant need to steer clear of the Scylla of eurocentrism and the Charybdis of exoticization: a reasonable way to go is to recognize the recurrent patterns, categories and distinctions in natural language looming just below the surface (or even deeper), while keeping in mind that such patterns, categories and distinctions are not necessarily the ones prominent in Germanic, Romance, Japanese and Semitic. To wit, Verb Second, pronominal clitics, Topic prominence and triconsonantal roots all reveal something crucial about Universal Grammar, something as crucial as classifiers, anticausatives, applicatives, incorporation and so on. And all have to be treated at the right level of abstraction.

Another question is that of the lexical–functional distinction. It is my conviction that understanding functional heads as satellites, or 'the entourage', of lexical categories is on the right track, as suggested already in work from the nineties reviewed in Chapter 5. On top of that, Categorial Deficiency captures the defective character of functional categories, a character that becomes manifest once one takes a look at the acquisition of first and second language, language breakdown and language change – remember the overview in Chapter 5 and, in more detail, in Muysken (2008). Unless there is a solid and generalized FLN-internal factor that contributes to the 'vulnerability' or the 'late/no acquisition' of functional categories, such behaviours will remain curiosities and the pervasive pattern suggesting that functional elements 'lack' something will go unexplained. I think that conceiving functional heads as categorially deficient, despite their otherwise crucial feature content, provides a sound basis for capturing their behaviour in language acquisition, diachrony and language disorders.

The treatment of mixed projections in this monograph captures, as mentioned before, fundamental properties such as their categorial uniformity, while upholding biuniqueness. The key to capturing both their ubiquitous presence and their categorial duality lies not in positing special conditions and conventions but in holding fast to the conviction that surface complexity is reducible to structural simplicity and to having the right theory (one of categorial features, in our case) in which to describe functional categorizers. The moral in this case is pretty obvious: sometimes one has to wait.

8   *Appendix: notes on Baker (2003)*

8.1   Introduction

There is a non-negligible point of criticism that can potentially be raised against the theory of word class categories presented and discussed in this book, one that views nouns and verbs as by-products of two fundamental LF-interpretable features that set interpretive perspectives. The point would be roughly as follows: Baker (2003) has already developed in detail a theory of lexical categories based on two unary categorial features; moreover, Baker's theory is based on a wealth of empirical data. Why is a theory like the one presented here, one that builds on assumptions, arguments and discoveries by Baker, necessary at all? Why do we need yet another generative theory of word class categories?

First of all, Baker's (2003) book exclusively discusses lexical categories: nouns, verbs, and adjectives. Here, departing from categorial features as makers of the word classes 'noun' and 'verb', we see that their uninterpretable versions are necessary elements in the creation of functional heads and, consequently, in the assembling of supercategories (Extended Projections); we also argue that Agree relations among categorial features both affect structure-building and play a central role in defining the label of a projection after the application of Merge. We finally make good on our understanding of the workings of categorial features so as to derive the (ultimately unexceptional) nature of mixed projections. To be fair, some of the issues mentioned are insightfully touched upon in Baker (2003, 2008), but not in the systematic fashion we scrutinize them and account for them here.

A second point is that Baker's theory, while recognizing the importance of categories and their unary features being LF-intepretable, does not place an emphasis on features themselves but on nouns, verbs and adjectives as *virtually primitive lexical categories*. This is, of course, to be expected since, in his system, [N] features exclusively appear on lexical nouns (and, possibly, Determiners) and [V] features on lexical verbs (and, possibly, a functional predicator *Pred*). Categorial features are not particularly active in his theory:

they merely create the above categories, nouns with their referential indices and verbs with their specifiers; they then quietly wait to be interpreted at LF.

A third matter, of which this Appendix will be dedicated to providing an overview, is the fact that a number of arguments and theses in Baker's (2003) theory of lexical categories (and his understanding of categorial features) are the object of extensive controversy. Some of those arguments and theses are quite central to his theory; others are primarily of methodological concern or matters of interpreting empirical data. The purpose of this Appendix is to discuss those controversial points in Baker's (2003) account that merit a rethink; it will also remind the reader of how the theory presented here addresses these points, hopefully in a satisfactory fashion.

8.2   Are nouns referential?

Baker (2003, 95) opens his discussion of nouns with the following claim, 'the leading idea' of his account:

(1)   a. Semantic version: nouns and only nouns have *criteria of identity*, whereby they can serve as standards of sameness.
        b. Syntactic version: X is a noun if and only if X is a lexical category and X bears a *referential index*, expressed as an ordered pair of integers.

Nouns bearing a referential index has as its consequence a *Noun Licensing Condition* (Baker 2003, 96 et seq.): nouns can only be licensed as arguments or as members of chains.[1] Baker (2003, 98) explicitly states that 'nouns ... (and their projections) constitute the canonical argument phrases' and that 'nouns are always inherently argumental as a matter of Universal Grammar' (116) – that is, even in the languages in which Chierchia (1998) argues that Determiner Phrases are argumental instead.

The functioning of nouns as predicates is a problem for Baker's analysis. In examples like the ones below, but not exclusively, *hero* is not referential: it does not serve as an argument and it is not a member of a chain:

(2)   a. Alex is/became a hero.
        b. They made/consider Alex a hero.
        c. Alex, a hero, has always been close to us.

Baker (2003, 34–9; 2003, chap. 3 passim) sets out to explain away these and more complex examples by taking predicate nominals to be always embedded within a predicate-making functional projection: Bowers' (1993) *Pred*.

---

[1] Functional projections like CP and DP may also bear referential indices (Baker 2003, 139).

This *Pred* head acts as the predicator while its specifier hosts the subject of predication. According to this recasting of nominal predicates, these actually have the following structure:

(3)   *Baker's predicative noun configuration*

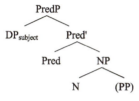

The general practice of making nouns (and adjectives) predicative by embedding them within a functional PredP is itself not without problems, as we will see below.

A general issue here is with Baker's thesis that 'nouns are always inherently argumental as a matter of Universal Grammar' (2003, 116), a thesis which is both empirically very difficult to justify and generally runs against the consensus in the literature. Even if nouns denote sortal concepts – a hypothesis that seems to be accurate and that has not been seriously contested – this does not automatically make nouns referential and/or argumental. Indeed, the majority view among scholars is that nouns are *not* referential. On the contrary, referentiality is understood as something that Determiners 'do'; DPs are referential, NPs are (usually) not: Higginbotham (1985), Stowell (1991), Longobardi (1994), Chierchia (1998), Borer (2005, chaps. 3–6), Acquaviva (2009a).[2] I will not say more on this debate here; suffice it to say that it is at least problematic to suggest that the two 'versions' of (1), semantic and syntactic, are directly related or, *a fortiori*, that they are different realizations of the same principle. Nouns are indeed sortal *predicates* – but they are inherently predicative, just like verbs and, probably, adjectives as well.

8.3   Syntactic predication, semantic predication and specifiers

There is a far more serious issue regarding the foundations of Baker's theory: namely, the interpretation of the [V] feature. Baker (2003, 23) posits that

(4)   X is a verb if and only if X is a lexical category and X has a specifier.

---

[2] Again, Chierchia (1998) provides the more or less standard account on what happens with argumenthood in Determiner-less languages. Also to be consulted: Cheng and Sybesma (1999), Massam, Gorrie and Kellner (2006), Willim (2000), Bošković (2008).

This is far from a purely mechanistic syntax-internal characteristic; on the contrary the projection of specifiers is viewed as the distinctive characteristic of verbs, which in turn are understood as the one truly predicative category: 'only verbs are true predicates, with the power to license a specifier, which they typically theta-mark' (Baker 2003, 20). In short, throughout the second chapter of the book (i) verbs are understood as predicates, to the exclusion of nouns and adjectives, and (ii) specifiers are understood as subjects (of verbs). Nouns and adjectives can function as predicates only when they are embedded inside the complement of Pred, a functional category which is the equivalent of V; see also (3).

There are three very important problems here. The first is that syntactic predication mechanisms and semantic predication do not correspond to each other on a one-to-one basis: in his treatment of verbs-as-lexical-predicates, one may criticize Baker for blurring 'syntactic' predication – that is, the syntactic mechanisms matching a predicate and a subject – with semantic predication itself. The whole issue has been extensively discussed in Rothstein (1983, 1999) and elsewhere, and I will not make any more detailed comments here.

Second, turning to syntax proper and its mechanisms, it is empirically very odd to make a claim that nouns and adjectives do not project specifiers. Baker argues against *all* nominal and adjectival specifiers and recasts them as specifiers of PredP which embeds nouns and adjectives in their predicative uses. Again, without getting into the heart of the matter, arguing convincingly against all specifiers of lexical heads would by itself fill a monograph-sized piece of research.

A third and even more peculiar claim that Baker makes is that specifiers are essentially identified with subjects of predication. He also notes (2003, 25) that functional projections acquire specifiers via movement – that is, they do not have base-generated specifiers – although he reserves doubts about measure phrases as the specifiers of Degree Phrases and possessors as the specifiers of Determiner Phrases. In brief, the hypothesis can be summarized as follows: verbs and Pred heads are the only categories that project specifiers (by virtue of their [V] feature), which are identified with subjects of predication. The other two lexical categories, nouns and adjectives, do not project specifiers, and functional projections acquire specifiers via movement: moved/internally merged specifiers (like SpecTP) apparently do not function as subjects. The claim is too big and complex to evaluate, and one suspects it is flawed and largely misguided.

8.4   Are adjectives the unmarked lexical category? Are they roots?

Baker (2003, 190–2) claims that there is 'nothing special' about adjectives: adjectives are exactly the lexical category which is not marked for any categorial features. This entails that a non-categorized root, one not bearing an [N] feature (forcing a 'referential index' for Baker) or a [V] feature (resulting in the 'projection of a specifier'), must surface as an adjective. Accordingly, adjectives are the lexical categories that lack *any* particular properties – that is, that lack categorial features: they are neither predicates (like verbs) nor referential (like nouns). A very prominent consequence of this take on adjectives, should it be true, is that adjectives would be essentially *uncategorized* – in stark contradiction to the Categorization Assumption. On top of that, as remarked in Chapter 2, if category-less roots surface as adjectives, expressing 'pure properties', then all languages should possess an adjective category. This is of course a claim Baker (2003, 238–63) dedicates extensive discussion to, despite ample typological evidence to the contrary: again, see Chapter 2. Furthermore, adjectives, as a default category virtually indistinguishable from uncategorized roots, should at least sometimes surface as morphologically simple elements, with each root available in a language having at least one adjective derived from it. However, recall that adjectives in most languages involve more rather than fewer functional layers – for example, they display concord with the noun inside a DP, just like *functional* elements like quantifiers, demonstratives, possessives and articles. Second, very few adjectives in Romance, Germanic and Greek are underived, leading us to the implication that Adjective is definitely not the unmarked category, let alone one co-extensive with roots. Third, if adjectives are not marked by *any* categorial feature whatsoever, how are adjective-making derivational affixes marked? Fourth, not all roots in a language derive an adjective, contrary to what should be expected for an unmarked (uncategorized) word class.

Finally, adjectives are taken not to project full phrase structure; thus they can take no complements when used as attributive adjectives (Baker 2003, 195–6): 'attributive adjectives cannot take complements, and cannot appear with a fully fledged degree system, they can be a little more than just a head . . . Apparently, it is possible for one head to adjoin to another to make a new head within an attributive modifier, but that is all' (196 footnote 5). Under a version of the generalized X' schema, the above sounds very odd – namely, banning a whole lexical category from taking complements on the grounds of its being *unmarked*. Effectively, this is a ban on Adjective Phrases, at least as attributive modifiers; cross-linguistically speaking, this constitutes a claim that looks largely misguided – for example, in the face of circumstantial data from Greek.

(5)   Enas [poli perifanos ya tin kori   tu] pateras.
        A   very proud   for the daughter his father
        'A father very proud of his daughter.'

More detailed discussion of the above and other points regarding the purported unmarkedness and the 'elsewhere' lexical category status of adjectives may be found in Chapter 2.

8.5   Pred and other functional categories

One of the merits of Baker's theory is that he sets out to give interpretive content to the features [N] and [V], rather than simply view them as convenient labels that create taxonomies. As repeated several times, this is a desirable move and – hopefully – a momentous one in our understanding of lexical categories. Given the pervasive, fundamental and universal character of the noun–verb distinction, he expectedly chooses fundamental interpretations for his categorial features [N] and [V]. This is a conceptually desirable, if not necessary, move: it would be eminently odd if categorial features encoded peripheral or parochial interpretations, after all.

Taking [N] to stand for 'has a referential index' and [V] for 'projects a specifier' has some conceptual side-effects. Beginning with [V] as forcing the projection of a specifier, the conclusion is that all predicative categories, both lexical and functional, must be marked for [V]; all referential categories must similarly bear an [N] feature. This observation is of course already incorporated in the last pages of Baker (2003, 324–5) and the resulting state of affairs is tabulated in (6), slightly revised from the table in Baker (2003, 325):

(6)   Baker's system: a typology[3]

	Lexical	Functional/ transparent	Functional/opaque
specifier	Verb	Aspect, Tense	Pred
referential index	Noun	Det, Num, Case	functional nominalizers
neither	Adjective	Degree	Adposition

[3] The typology in (6) suggests that *Pred* (Bowers 1993) could be perhaps the 'verbalizing' equivalent of 'category-shifting functional heads' ('functional nominalizers'), to which SWITCH (Chapter 6) belongs. This is an exciting topic for future research.

There are several things to be said about the above table, which effectively summarizes some key consequences of Baker's account. First, adjectives and degree elements ending up lumped together with adpositions is truly counterintuitive, although it is a claim consistent with the discussion throughout Baker's monograph. Second, and crucially, *there is no way to capture the lexical–functional distinction* using categorial features only; the lexical–functional distinction is tacitly assumed to constitute a kind of an unexplained primitive. Because of this blind spot, some basic questions remain unanswered: how do we distinguish a verb from a *Pred* head? How do we distinguish a noun from a Determiner? And so on. Third, a further distinction between *opaque* (category-shifting) categories and *transparent* categories that are members of the supercategory/Extended Projection to which the lexical head belongs is made. Unfortunately, this difference between opaque and transparent categories remains unexplained, though one account is offered in Chapter 6 of this monograph: *opaque* categories must be SWITCH heads.

My purpose is of course neither to engage in nit-picking nor to vindicate the theory presented here over its predecessor and a valuable source of intuition, discoveries and methodological solutions. On the contrary, I wish to show that, when proposing a theory of lexical categories or, in our case, of categorial features, we need to look at the consequences for elements beyond lexical categories.

8.6   Two details: co-ordination and syntactic categorization

In the final section of this Appendix I will quickly look into two more specific points in Baker's analysis. The first is with regard to co-ordination data and their interpretation as support for the non-predicative nature of bare nouns and adjectives. The second concerns Baker's lexicalist commitments blurring into an account of categories that needs to call upon syntactic categorization.

Baker (2003, 37–9) presents potent empirical evidence in support of predicate nouns and adjectives in reality being nouns and adjectives embedded within projections of Pred. This evidence comes from co-ordination facts like the following:

(7)   a. *Eating poisoned food made Chris [$_A$ sick] and [$_V$ die].
         b. *A hard blow to the head made Chris [$_V$ fall] and [$_N$ an invalid].
         c. I consider John [$_A$ crazy] and [$_N$ a fool].

The above sentences exemplify co-ordination options between different categories. Causatives and secondary predication are deliberately selected as the environments in which to illustrate such options, so as make sure that the co-ordinated constituents contain as little functional structure as possible. The idea, of course, is to apply the constituency test already known from syntax textbooks – that is, that only identical categories may be co-ordinated. In the first two examples in (7) we have the expected mismatch between the verb and the other category – adjective in (7)a. and noun in (7)b. – inducing ungrammaticality. The important one is (7)c., where we have a well-formed case of co-ordination with an adjectival and a nominal conjunct. Baker takes this to suggest that both nouns and adjectives are embedded within Pred projections, thus making the two conjuncts categorially identical in (7)c. Of course, PredPs are still categorially distinct from VPs; that is why (7)a. and (7)b. are ungrammatical.

The argument is not trouble-free, however. First of all, both V and *Pred* bear a [V] categorial feature, so apparently they are distinct because the former is lexical and the latter functional. Having said that, Baker (2003, 201, 210) argues that there are two varieties of *Pred*: $Pred_A$, taking adjectival complements, and $Pred_N$, taking nominal complements. Apparently, these are categorially identical for co-ordination purposes in (7). Finally, and more generally, in recent years the growing consensus has been that co-ordination facts involve identical *semantic* categories, rather than *syntactic* projections; this resolves a host of paradoxical situations where, for instance, co-ordination of a PP and an adverb is licit.[4]

(8)   The package arrived [safely] and [on time].

Without getting into too much detail here, if VPs are – roughly speaking – *events* and predicate nouns and adjectives in isolation are *predicates*, then the examples in (7) can be accounted for without appealing to PredPs.

Let us now turn to the final issue, that regarding theoretical commitments. In Chapter 5 of his book, Baker mainly discusses whether grammatical category is inherent or syntactically assigned, as supported here. He argues extensively against the syntactic categorization hypothesis, while he acknowledges that his theory runs in parallel with it (Baker 2003, 267). In the pages that follow (268–75), he offers a solid, coherent and very convincing critique against radical categorylessness. He first calls upon evidence from Incorporation to support the finding that distinct categorial behaviour in syntax exists even in the absence of 'any functional superstructure dominating the

---

[4] Ellipsis and gapping are notorious for introducing much noise when co-ordinated, and are set aside.

functional head' (268), suggesting that lexical category is inherent, as opposed to assigned by a categorizer. Thus, it is not the case that anything can incorporate into anything, as one might expect from bare acategorial roots; actually, the reverse seems to hold. So, although Greenlandic, Mayali and Nahuatl allow APs to partly incorporate into verbal roots, they do not permit incorporation of bare *adjectival* 'roots'; similarly in Quechua, Chichewa and Japanese, causatives take full AP and NP small clause complements but can only tolerate bare *verbal* roots to incorporate into them. Finally, incorporation into nouns is 'universally impossible' (272). Baker then argues that syntactic categorization has a more limited explanatory power than an account where every element in syntax bears category. The reason is that if lexical elements are category-less roots, the impossibility of combining some roots with Num, and some roots with T – biuniqueness, in other words – becomes a mystery (see Chapter 5). Finally, Baker anticipates Embick and Marantz's (2008) Categorization Assumption: acategorial roots do not appear anywhere in syntax; they must be embedded within a categorizing structure (Baker 2003, 269). Certain morphological processes are rather permissive to category, seemingly manipulating category-less roots, in stark contrast with comparable syntactic processes. So, root compounding can have pretty much anything category-wise as a first member: *draw-bridge* (V), *dog-house, sky-high* (N), *dark-room, red-hot* (A), *cranberry, huckleberry* (X). Syntactic processes like attributive modification, on the other hand, can only be of the adjective–noun type (271–2).[5]

However, his account is more syntactic decompositional than the above criticism suggests. As almost admitted in a footnote in Baker (2003: 269), it is virtually impossible to distinguish between acategorial roots and categorially featureless adjectives or degree elements or 'heavy' adpositions like *above, behind* and so on; consider also (6). This renders moot the distinction between a category-less root and an adjective, with things becoming quite serious when adjectives are derived – for example, *heart-y, clue-less, industri-al, meteor-ic* and so on – as already mentioned several times.

Second, Baker (2003, 79–83) proposes that we syntactically decompose verbs into a V head and *an adjective* (essentially a category-less root).[6] His discussion of the semantics of V is uncomfortably close to accounts of

---

[5] Interestingly, all these points of criticism have been addressed by recent research on syntactic decomposition and categorization, including this book. De Belder (2011) and De Belder and Van Koppen (2012) contain some exciting work on compounding.

[6] There is no escape from a complex structure for verbs – see also Chapter 4.

standard syntactic decomposition for verbs, such as Folli and Harley (2005) or even Ramchand (2008). In other words, how is *verb* = V + A different from *verb* = *v* + ROOT, especially if adjectives are not marked for categorial features? Generalizing somewhat, and bringing nouns into the discussion, how is Baker's structure for predicative nouns in (3), repeated below for convenience as (9), different from the one in (10)?

(9)   *Baker's predicative noun configuration*

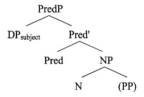

(10)   *Predicative nouns à la syntactic decomposition*

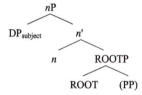

The question is anything but facetious. For Baker's view to have explanatory weight as a hypothesis which is in contrast with syntactic decomposition, it must first be shown that the *Pred* and the N nodes in (9) are indeed distinct. This is very difficult to ascertain within Baker's framework because according to it nouns by definition *do not project specifiers*. Consequently, predicative N will always be *strictly* adjacent to *Pred* and, if *Pred* is phonologically null and/or morphologically non-distinct from the N head, then it is extremely difficult to establish the existence of both. Even if this is successfully done, it is also very hard to show that both the *Pred* and the N nodes in (9) are categorially marked.

So, it turns out that the differences between (9) and (10) are indeed very narrow.

References

Abney, Steven P. 1987. *The English Noun Phrase in Its Sentential Aspect*. PhD thesis, MIT, Cambridge, Mass.

Ackema, Peter, and Ad Neeleman. 2004. *Beyond Morphology: Interface Conditions on Word Formation*. Oxford Studies in Theoretical Linguistics 6. Oxford University Press.

Acquaviva, Paolo. 2009a. 'The Roots of Nominality, the Nominality of Roots'. http://ling.auf.net/lingbuzz/000824

2009b. 'Roots and Lexicality in Distributed Morphology'. In *York Papers in Linguistics*, edited by Alexandra Galani, Daniel Redinger and Norman Yeo, 2:1–21. University of York. http://ling.auf.net/lingbuzz/000654

Acquaviva, Paolo, and Phoevos Panagiotidis. 2012. 'Lexical Decomposition Meets Conceptual Atomism'. *Lingue E Linguaggio* XI (2): 105–20.

Adger, David. 2003. *Core Syntax: A Minimalist Approach*. Core Linguistics. Oxford University Press.

2006. 'Remarks on Minimalist Feature Theory and Move'. *Journal of Linguistics* 42: 663–73.

2010. 'A Minimalist Theory of Feature Structures'. In *Features, Perspectives on a Key Notion in Linguistics*, edited by Anna Kibort and Greville G. Corbett, 185–218. Oxford University Press.

Ahn, Hee-Don. 1991. *Clausal Architecture in Korean and English*. PhD thesis, University of Wisconsin, Madison.

Alexiadou, Artemis. 2001. *Functional Structure in Nominals: Nominalization and Ergativity*. Amsterdam: John Benjamins Publishing Company.

Alexiadou, Artemis, and Gereon Müller. 2007. 'Class Features as Probes'. In *Inflectional Identity*, edited by Asaf Bachrach and Andrew Nevins, 101–55. Oxford University Press.

Amritavalli, R., and K. A. Jayaseelan. 2004. 'The Genesis of Syntactic Categories and Parametric Variation'. In *Generative Grammar in a Broader Perspective: Proceedings of the 4th Asian GLOW*, edited by James Hye Suk Yoon, 19–41. Seoul: Hankook Publishing Company.

Anagnostopoulou, Elena, and Yota Samioti. 2009. 'Domains for Idioms'. Paper presented at the Roots Workshop, June, University of Stuttgart.

Anderson, John M. 1997. *A Notional Theory of Syntactic Categories*. Cambridge Studies in Linguistics 82. Cambridge University Press.

Arad, Maya. 2003. 'Locality Constraints on the Interpretation of Roots: The Case of Hebrew Denominal Verbs'. *Natural Language and Linguistic Theory* 21: 737–78.

2005. *Roots and Patterns: Hebrew Morpho-Syntax*. Dordrecht: Springer Verlag.

Aronoff, Mark. 1994. *Morphology by Itself: Stems and Inflectional Classes*. Linguistic Inquiry Monographs 22. Cambridge, Mass: MIT Press.

2007. 'In the Beginning Was the Word'. *Language* 83: 803–30.

Aronoff, Mark, and Frank Anshen. 1998. 'Morphology and the Lexicon: Lexicalization and Productivity'. In *The Handbook of Morphology*, edited by Andrew Spencer and Arnold M. Zwicky, 237–47. Blackwell Handbooks in Linguistics. Oxford: Blackwell.

Baker, Mark C. 1985. 'The Mirror Principle and Morphosyntactic Explanation'. *Linguistic Inquiry* 16: 373–415.

1988. *Incorporation: A Theory of Grammatical Function Changing*. University of Chicago Press.

2003. *Lexical Categories: Verbs, Nouns, and Adjectives*. Cambridge Studies in Linguistics 102. Cambridge University Press.

2008. *The Syntax of Agreement and Concord*. Cambridge Studies in Linguistics 115. Cambridge University Press.

Barner, David, and Alan Bale. 2002. 'No Nouns, No Verbs: Psycholinguistic Arguments in Favor of Lexical Underspecification'. *Lingua* 112: 771–91.

Basilico, David. 2008. 'Particle Verbs and Benefactive Double Objects in English: High and Low Attachments'. *Natural Language and Linguistic Theory* 26: 731–73.

Beard, Robert. 1995. *Lexeme-Morpheme Base Morphology: A General Theory of Inflection and Word Formation*. SUNY Series in Linguistics. Albany: State University of New York.

Bloom, Paul. 2000. *How Children Learn the Meanings of Words*. Cambridge, Mass.: MIT Press.

Bobaljik, Jonathan. 1995. *Morphosyntax: The Syntax of Verbal Inflection*. PhD thesis, MIT, Cambridge, Mass.

Bobaljik, Jonathan, and Höskuldur Thráinsson. 1998. 'Two Heads Aren't Always Better than One'. *Syntax* 1: 37–71.

Borer, Hagit. 2003. 'Exo-Skeletal vs. Endo-Skeletal Explanations: Syntactic Projections and the Lexicon'. In *The Nature of Explanation in Linguistic Theory*, edited by John Moore and Maria Polinsky, 31–67. Stanford, Calif.: CSLI Publications.

2005. *In Name Only*. Oxford Linguistics 1. Oxford University Press.

2009. 'Roots and Categories'. Paper presented at the 19th Colloquium on Generative Grammar, April, University of the Basque Country, Vitoria-Gasteiz, Spain.

Borsley, Robert, and Jaklin Kornfilt. 2000. 'Mixed Extended Projections'. In *The Nature and Function of Syntactic Categories*, edited by Robert Borsley, 101–31. New York: Academic Press.

Bošković, Željko. 2008. 'What Will You Have, DP or NP?'. In *Proceedings of NELS* 37, 101–14.

Botwinik-Rotem, Irina, and Arhonto Terzi. 2008. 'Greek and Hebrew Locative Prepositional Phrases: A Unified Case-Driven Account'. *Lingua* 118: 399–424.

Bowers, John. 1993. 'The Syntax of Predication'. *Linguistic Inquiry* 24: 591–656.

Bresnan, Joan. 1997. 'Mixed Categories as Head Sharing Constructions'. In *Proceedings of the LFG97 Conference*, edited by Miriam Butt and Tracy Holloway-King, 1–17. Stanford, Calif.: CSLI Publications.

Brody, Michael. 1995. *Lexico-Logical Form: A Radically Minimalist Theory*. Linguistic Inquiry Monographs 27. Cambridge, Mass.: MIT Press.

Caramazza, Alfonso, and Argye E. Hillis. 1991. 'Lexical Organization of Nouns and Verbs in the Brain'. *Nature* 349 (6312): 788–90. doi:10.1038/349788a0.

Chametzky, Robert. 2000. *Phrase Structure: From GB to Minimalism*. Generative Syntax 4. Oxford: Blackwell.

2003. 'Phrase Structure'. In *Minimalist Syntax*, edited by Randal Hendrick, 192–225. Oxford: Blackwell.

Cheng, Lisa Lai-Shen, and Rint Sybesma. 1999. 'Bare and Not-so-Bare Nouns and the Structure of NP'. *Linguistic Inquiry* 30: 509–42.

Chierchia, Gennaro. 1998. 'Reference to Kinds across Languages.' *Natural Language Semantics* 6: 339–405.

Chomsky, Noam. 1957. *Syntactic Structures*. 's-Gravenhage: Mouton & Company.

1965. *Aspects of the Theory of Syntax*. Cambridge, Mass.: MIT Press.

1970. 'Remarks on Nominalization'. In *Readings in English Transformational Grammar*, edited by Roderick Jacobs and Peter Rosenbaum, 184–221. Waltham, Mass.: Ginn & Company.

1986. *Knowledge of Language: Its Nature, Origin, and Use*. Convergence. New York: Praeger.

1995. *The Minimalist Program*. Current Studies in Linguistics 28. Cambridge, Mass.: MIT Press.

2000. 'Minimalist Inquiries: The Framework'. In *Step by Step: Essays on Minimalist Syntax in Honor of Howard Lasnik*, edited by Roger Martin, David Michaels and Juan Uriagereka, 89–155. Cambridge, Mass.: MIT Press.

2001. 'Derivation by Phase'. In *Ken Hale: A Life in Language*, edited by Michael Kenstowicz, 1–52. Cambridge, Mass.: MIT Press.

2004. 'Beyond Explanatory Adequacy'. In *Structures and Beyond*, edited by Adriana Belletti, 104–31. Oxford University Press.

2008. 'On Phases'. In *Foundational Issues in Linguistic Theory: Essays in Honor of Jean-Roger Vergnaud*, edited by Robert Freidin, Carlos Peregrin and Maria Luisa Zubizarreta, 133–66. Cambridge, Mass.: MIT Press.

Cinque, Guglielmo. 1999. *Adverbs and Functional Heads*. Oxford University Press.

Clahsen, Harald, Susanne Bartke and Sandra Göllner. 1997. 'Formal Features in Impaired Grammars: A Comparison of English and German Children'. *Journal of Neurolinguistics* 10 (2–3): 151–71.

Clark, Eve V., and Herbert H. Clark. 1977. 'When Nouns Surface as Verbs'. *Language* 55: 767–811.

Collins, Chris. 1997. *Local Economy*. Linguistic Inquiry Monographs 29. Cambridge, Mass.: MIT Press.

Corbett, Greville G. 1991. *Gender*. Cambridge Textbooks in Linguistics. Cambridge University Press.

Cormack, Annabel, and Neil V. Smith. 1996. 'Checking Theory: Features, Functional Heads, and Checking-Parameters'. *UCL Working Papers in Linguistics* 8: 1–40.

Corver, Norbert. 1997. 'The Internal Syntax of the Dutch Extended Adjectival Projection'. *Natural Language and Linguistic Theory* 15: 289–368.

2005. *Copular -Ly*. Unpublished ms. University of Utrecht.

Corver, Norbert, and Henk C. van Riemsdijk, eds. 2001. *Semi-Lexical Categories: The Function of Content Words and the Content of Function Words*. Studies in Generative Grammar 59. Berlin: Mouton de Gruyter.

Croft, William. 1991. *Syntactic Categories and Grammatical Relations: The Cognitive Organization of Information*. University of Chicago Press.

2001. *Radical Construction Grammar: Syntactic Theory in Typological Perspective*. Oxford University Press.

Davies, William D., and Stanley Dubinsky. 1998. 'Sentential Subjects as Complex NPs: New Reasons for an Old Account of Subjacency'. In *CLS 34–1: Papers from the Main Session*, edited by M. Catherine Gruber, Derrick Higgins, Kenneth S. Olson and Tamara Wysocki, 34: 83–94. Chicago Linguistic Society.

2001. 'Functional Architecture and the Distribution of Subject Properties'. In *Objects and Other Subjects: Grammatical Functions, Functional Categories, and Configurationality*, edited by William D. Davies and Stanley Dubinsky, 247–79. Dordrecht: Kluwer.

Davis, Henry. 1999. *On Nouns and Nominalizations in Salish*. Unpublished ms. University of British Columbia, Vancouver.

De Belder, Marijke. 2011. *Roots and Affixes: Eliminating Lexical Categories from Syntax*. Utrecht: LOT.

De Belder, Marijke, and Marjo Van Koppen. 2012. 'One Module, Different Levels of Merge: ANN Compounds in Dutch'. Paper presented at the Brussels Conference on Generative Linguistics 7, 17–18 December.

Déchaine, Rose-Marie. 1993. *Predicates across Categories*. PhD thesis, University of Massachusetts, Amherst.

Déchaine, Rose-Marie, and Martina Wiltschko. 2002. 'Decomposing Pronouns. Linguistic Inquiry'. *Linguistic Inquiry* 33: 409–22.

Den Dikken, Marcel. 2006. *Relators and Linkers: The Syntax of Predication, Predicate Inversion, and Copulas*. Linguistic Inquiry Monographs 47. Cambridge, Mass.: MIT Press.

Diesing, Molly. 1992. *Indefinites*. Cambridge, Mass.: MIT Press.

Dixon, Robert M. W. 1982. *Where Have All the Adjectives Gone? And Other Essays in Semantics and Syntax*. Berlin: Walter de Gruyter.

Don, Jan. 2004. 'Categories in the Lexicon'. *Linguistics* 42: 931–56.

Donati, Caterina. 2006. *Labels and Merge*. Paper presented at the Interphases Conference, May, University of Cyprus, Nicosia.

Doron, Edit. 2003. 'Agency and Voice: The Semantics of the Semitic Templates'. *Natural Language Semantics* 11: 1–67.

Drachman, Gaberell. 2005. 'A Note on "Shared" Allomorphs'. *Journal of Greek Linguistics* 6: 5–37.

Dubinsky, Stanley, and Sylvester Ron Simango. 1996. 'Passive and Stative in Chichewa: Evidence for Modular Distinctions in Grammar'. *Language* 72: 749–81.

Embick, David. 2000. 'Features, Syntax, and Categories in the Latin Perfect'. *Linguistic Inquiry* 31: 185–230.

Embick, David, and Alec Marantz. 2008. 'Architecture and Blocking. Linguistic Inquiry'. *Linguistic Inquiry* 39: 1–53.

Embick, David, and Rolf Noyer. 2001. 'Movement Operations after Syntax'. *Linguistic Inquiry* 32: 555–95.

Emonds, Joseph E. 1985. *A Unified Theory of Syntactic Categories*. Studies in Generative Grammar 19. Dordrecht: Foris Publications.

Evans, Nicholas, and Stephen C. Levinson. 2009. 'The Myth of Language Universals: Language Diversity and Its Importance for Cognitive Science'. *Brain and Behavioral Sciences* 32: 429–92.

Everett, Daniel. 2005. 'Cultural Constraints on Grammar and Cognition in Pirahã: Another Look at the Design Features of Human Language'. *Current Anthropology* 46: 621–34.

Family, Neiloufar. 2008. 'Explorations of Semantic Space. The Case of Light Verb Constructions in Persian'. Paper presented at the Conference on Complex Predicates in Iranian Languages, 5 July, Université Sorbonne Nouvelle-Paris III, France. http://iranianlinguistics.org/complexpredicates/presentations/family-2008.pdf

Felix, Sascha. 1990. 'The Structure of Functional Categories'. *Linguistische Berichte* 125: 46–71.

Folli, Rafaella, and Heidi Harley. 2005. 'Consuming Results in Italian and English: Flavours of v'. In *Aspectual Inquiries*, edited by Paula Kempchinsky and Roumyana Slabakova, 1–25. Dordrecht: Springer Verlag.

Folli, Rafaella, Heidi Harley and Simin Karimi. 2003. 'Determinants of Event Type in Persian Complex Predicates'. In *Cambridge Occasional Papers in Linguistics*, edited by Luisa Astruc and Marc Richards, 1:100–20. University of Cambridge.

Fox, Danny. 2000. *Economy and Semantic Interpretation*. Cambridge, Mass.: MIT Press.

Francis, Elaine J., and Etsuyo Yuasa. 2008. 'A Multi-Modular Approach to Gradual Change in Grammaticalisation'. *Journal of Linguistics* 44: 45–86.

Friedmann, Naama. 2006. 'Speech Production in Broca's Agrammatic Aphasia: Syntactic Tree Pruning'. In *Broca's Region*, edited by Yosef Grodzinsky and Katrin Amunts, 63–82. Oxford University Press.

Fu, Jingqi, Tom Roeper and Hagit Borer. 2001. 'The VP within Process Nominals: Evidence from Adverbs and the VP Anaphor "Do-So"'. *Natural Language and Linguistic Theory* 19: 549–82.

Fyndanis, Valantis. 2009. *Functional Categories in Greek Agrammatism*. PhD thesis, Aristotle University of Thessaloniki.

Galani, Alexandra. 2005. *The Morphosyntax of Verbs in Modern Greek*. PhD thesis, University of York.

Gil, David. n.d. *What Is Riau Indonesian?*. Unpublished ms. Max Planck Institute for Evolutionary Anthropology, Leipzig. http://sastra.um.ac.id/wp-content/uploads/2010/01/PU-David-Gil-Riau-Indonesian-.-.-..pdf

    1994. 'The Structure of Riau Indonesian'. *Nordic Journal of Linguistics* 17: 179–200.

    2000. 'Syntactic Categories, Cross-Linguistic Variation and Universal Grammar'. In *Approaches to the Typology of Word Classes (Empirical Approaches to Language*

Typology), edited by Petra M. Vogel and Bernard Comrie, 173–216. Berlin: Mouton de Gruyter.

2005. 'Word Order without Syntactic Categories: How Riau Indonesian Does It'. In *Verb First: On the Syntax of Verb-Initial Languages*, edited by Andrew Carnie, Heidi Harley and Sheila Dooley, 243–63. Amsterdam: John Benjamins Publishing Company.

2013. 'Riau Indonesian: A Language without Nouns and Verbs'. In *Flexible Word Classes: Typological Studies of Underspecified Parts of Speech*, edited by Jan Rijkhoff and Eva van Lier. Oxford University Press.

Givón, Talmy. 1984. *Syntax: A Functional-Typological Introduction*. Amsterdam: John Benjamins Publishing Company.

Grimshaw, Jane B. 1990. *Argument Structure*. Cambridge, Mass.: MIT Press.

1991. *Extended Projection*. Unpublished ms. Brandeis University.

2003. *Words and Structure*. CSLI Lecture Notes 151. Stanford, Calif.: CSLI Publications.

Grohmann, Kleanthes K. 2003. *Prolific Domains: On the Anti-Locality of Movement Dependencies*. Linguistik Aktuell = Linguistics Today 66. Amsterdam: John Benjamins Publishing Company.

Guilfoyle, Ethne, and Máire Noonan. 1992. 'Functional Categories and Language Acquisition'. *Canadian Journal of Linguistics* 37: 241–72.

Haegeman, Liliane M. V. 2006. *Thinking Syntactically: A Guide to Argumentation and Analysis*. Blackwell Textbooks in Linguistics 20. Oxford: Blackwell.

Haider, Hubert. 2001. 'Heads and Selection'. In *Semi-Lexical Categories*, edited by Norbert Corver and Henk van Riemsdijk, 67–96. Berlin: Mouton de Gruyter.

Hale, Kenneth L., and Samuel Jay Keyser. 1993. 'On Argument Structure and the Lexical Expression of Syntactic Relations'. In *The View from Building 20: Essays in Honor of Sylvain Bromberger*, edited by Kenneth L. Hale and Samuel Jay Keyser, 53–109. Cambridge, Mass.: MIT Press.

2002. *Prolegomenon to a Theory of Argument Structure*. Linguistic Inquiry Monographs 39. Cambridge, Mass.: MIT Press.

Halle, Morris, and Alec Marantz. 1993. 'Distributed Morphology and the Pieces of Inflection'. In *The View from Building 20: Essays in Honor of Sylvain Bromberger*, edited by Kenneth L. Hale and Samuel Jay Keyser, 111–76. Cambridge, Mass.: MIT Press.

Harley, Heidi. 2005a. 'Bare Phrase Structure, a-Categorial Roots, One-Replacement and Unaccusativity'. In *Harvard Working Papers on Linguistics*, edited by Slava Gorbachov and Andrew Nevins, 9: 1–19. Cambridge, Mass.: Harvard University Press.

2005b. 'How Do Verbs Get Their Names? Denominal Verbs, Manner Incorporation and the Ontology of Verb Roots in English'. In *The Syntax of Aspect: Deriving Thematic and Aspectual Interpretation*, edited by Nomi Erteschik-Shir and Tova Rapoport, 42–64. Oxford University Press.

2007. 'The Bipartite Structure of Verbs Cross-Linguistically, or Why Mary Can't Exhibit John Her Paintings'. Paper presented at the ABRALIN Congres 2007, March, UFMG, Belo Horizonte, Brasil.

2009. 'The Morphology of Nominalizations and the Syntax of *v*P'. In *Quantification, Definiteness, and Nominalization*, edited by Anastasia Giannakidou and Monika Rathert, 320–42. Oxford University Press.

2012a. *On the Identity of Roots*. Unpublished ms. University of Arizona. http://ling. auf.net/lingBuzz/001527

2012b. *External Arguments and the Mirror Principle: On the Distinctness of Voice and v*. Unpublished ms. University of Arizona.

Harley, Heidi, and Rolf Noyer. 1998. 'Licensing in the Non-Lexicalist Lexicon: Nominalizations, Vocabulary Items and the Encyclopaedia'. *MIT Working Papers in Linguistics* 32: 119–37.

1999. 'State-of-the-Article: Distributed Morphology'. *GLOT International* 4 (4): 3–9.

2000. 'Formal versus Encyclopedic Properties of Vocabulary: Evidence from Nominalisations'. In *The Lexicon-Encyclopedia Interface*, 1st edn, edited by Bert Peeters, 349–74. Current Research in the Semantics/pragmatics Interface 5. Amsterdam: Elsevier.

Haspelmath, Martin. 2001. 'Word Classes and Parts of Speech'. *International Encyclopedia of the Social & Behavioral Sciences*. Amsterdam: Elsevier.

Haugen, Jason. 2009. 'Hyponymous Objects and Late Insertion'. *Lingua* 119: 242–62.

Hawkins, Roger, and Cecilia Yuet-hung Chan. 1997. 'The Partial Availability of UG in Second Language Acquisition: The "Failed Functional Features Hypothesis"'. *Second Language Research* 13 (3): 187–226.

Hawkins, Roger, and Hajime Hattori. 2006. 'Interpretation of English Multiple Wh-Questions by Japanese Speakers: A Missing Uninterpretable Feature Account'. *Second Language Research* 22 (3): 269–301.

Hazout, Ilan. 1994. 'Nominalizers in Theta Theory'. *The Linguistic Review* 11: 5–48.

Hegarty, Michael. 2005. *A Feature-Based Syntax of Functional Categories: The Structure, Acquisition, and Specific Impairment of Functional Systems*. Studies in Generative Grammar 79. Berlin: Mouton de Gruyter.

Hicks, Glyn. 2009. *The Derivation of Anaphoric Relations*. Linguistik Aktuell/Linguistics Today 139. Amsterdam: John Benjamins Publishing Company.

Higginbotham, James. 1985. 'On Semantics'. *Linguistic Inquiry* 16: 547–94.

Himmelmann, Nikolaus P. 2008. 'Lexical Categories and Voice in Tagalog'. In *Voice and Grammatical Relations in Austronesian Languages*, edited by Peter Austin and Simon Musgrave, 247–93. Stanford, Calif.: CSLI Publications.

Hinzen, Wolfram. 2006. *Mind Design and Minimal Syntax*. Oxford University Press.

Hudson, Richard. 2003. 'Gerunds without Phrase Structure'. *Natural Language and Linguistic Theory* 21: 579–615.

Iida, Masayo. 1987. 'Case-Assignment by Nominals in Japanese'. In *Working Papers in Grammatical Theory and Discourse Structure: Interactions of Morphology, Syntax, and Discourse*, edited by Masayo Iida, Stephen Wechsler and Draga Zec, 93–138. CSLI Lecture Notes 11. Stanford, Calif.: CSLI Publications.

Iwasaki, Yasufumi. 1999. *Three Subcategories of Nouns in Japanese*. PhD thesis, University of Illinois, Urbana-Champaign.

Jackendoff, Ray. 1977. *X Syntax: A Study of Phrase Structure*. Cambridge, Mass.: MIT Press.

Jelinek, Eloise. 1995. 'Quantification in Straits Salish'. In *Quantification in Natural Languages*, edited by Emmon Bach, Eloise Jelinek, Angelika Kratzer and Barbara Partee, 487–540. Dordrecht: Kluwer.

1996. 'Definiteness and Second Position Clitics in Straits Salish'. In *Approaching Second: Second Position Clitics and Related Phenomena*, edited by Aaron Halpern and Arnold M. Zwicky, 271–97. CSLI Lecture Notes 61. Stanford, Calif.: CSLI Publications.

Johnson, Kyle. 1988. 'Clausal Gerunds, the ECP, and Government'. *Linguistic Inquiry* 19: 583–609.

Jouitteau, Mélanie. 2005. 'Nominal Properties of *v*Ps in Breton, a Hypothesis for the Typology of VSO Languages'. In *Verb First: On the Syntax of Verb Initial Languages*, edited by Andrew Carnie, Heidi Harley and Sheila Ann Dooley, 265–80. Amsterdam: John Benjamins Publishing Company.

Karimi-Doostan, Gholamhosein. 2008a. 'Classless Words in Persian'. Paper presented at the Conference on Complex Predicates in Iranian Languages, 5 July, Université Sorbonne Nouvelle-Paris III, France. http://www.iranianlinguistics.org/papers/Abstract_Doostan.pdf

2008b. 'Separability of Light Verb Constructions in Persian'. Paper presented at the Conference on Complex Predicates in Iranian Languages, 5 July, Université Sorbonne Nouvelle-Paris III, France.

Kayne, Richard S. 1994. *The Antisymmetry of Syntax*. Linguistic Inquiry Monographs 25. Cambridge, Mass.: MIT Press.

2005. *Movement and Silence*. Oxford University Press.

2009. 'Antisymmetry and the Lexicon'. In *Linguistic Variation Yearbook 2008*, edited by Jeroen van Craenenbroeck, 1–32. Amsterdam: John Benjamins Publishing Company.

Kiparsky, Paul. 1982. 'Word Formation and the Lexicon'. In *Proceedings of the Mid-America Linguistics Conference*, edited by Fred Ingeman, 3–29. Lawrence: University of Kansas.

Kornfilt, Jaklin. 1997. *Turkish*. London: Routledge.

Kratzer, Angelika. 1996. 'Severing the External Argument from Its Verb'. In *Phrase Structure and the Lexicon*, edited by Johan Rooryck and Laurie Zaring, 109–37. Dordrecht: Kluwer.

Langacker, Ronald W. 1987. *Foundations of Cognitive Grammar*. Stanford University Press.

2000. *Grammar and Conceptualization*. Cognitive Linguistics Research 14. Berlin: Mouton de Gruyter.

Lapointe, Steve. 1993. 'Dual Lexical Categories and the Syntax of Mixed Category Phrases'. In *ESCOL '93*, edited by Andreas Kathol and Michael Bernstein, 199–210. Columbus, Ohio: Ohio State University.

1999. 'Dual Lexical Categories vs. Phrasal Conversion in the Analysis of Gerund Phrases'. In *University of Massachusetts Occasional Papers in Linguistics 24: Papers from the 25th Anniversary*, edited by Paul DeLacy and Anita Nowak, 157–89. Amherst, Mass.: GLSA Publications.

Larson, Richard K. 1998. 'Events and Modification in Nominals'. In *Proceedings of Semantics and Linguistic Theory (SALT) VIII*, edited by D. Strolovitch and

A. Lawson, 145–68. Ithaca, N.Y.: CLC Publications, Department of Linguistics, Cornell University.

Larson, Richard K., and Hiroko Yamakido. 2008. 'Ezafe and the Deep Position of Nominal Modifiers'. In *Adjectives and Adverbs. Syntax, Semantics, and Discourse*, edited by Louise McNally and Christopher Kennedy, 43–70. Oxford University Press.

Lecarme, Jacqueline. 2004. 'Tense in Nominals'. In *The Syntax of Time*, edited by Jacqueline Guéron and Jacqueline Lecarme, 441–76. Cambridge, Mass.: MIT Press.

Levin, Beth. 1993. *English Verb Classes and Alternations: A Preliminary Investigation*. University of Chicago Press.

Levin, Beth, and Malka Rappaport Hovav. 2005. *Argument Realization*. Research Surveys in Linguistics. Cambridge University Press.

Levinson, Lisa. 2007. *The Roots of Verbs*. PhD thesis, New York University.

Li, Yafei. 1990. *Conditions on X_o Movement*. MIT Working Papers in Linguistics. Cambridge, Mass.: MIT Press.

Lieber, Rochelle, and Sergio Scalise. 2007. 'The Lexical Integrity Hypothesis in a New Theoretical Universe'. In *On-Line Proceedings of the Fifth Mediterranean Morphology Meeting (MMM5) Fréjus 15–18 September 2005*, edited by Geert Booij, Luca Ducceschi, Bernard Fradin, Emiliano Guevara, Angela Ralli and Sergio Scalise, 1–24. Bologna: Università degli Studi di Bologna. http://mmm.lingue. unibo.it/proc-mmm5.php

Longobardi, Giuseppe. 1994. 'Reference and Proper Names: A Theory of N-Movement in Syntax and Logical Form'. *Linguistic Inquiry* 25: 609–65.

Lowenstamm, Jean. 2008. 'On N, √, and Types of Nouns'. In *Sounds of Silence: Empty Elements in Syntax and Phonology*, edited by Jutta M. Hartmann, Veronika Hegedüs and Henk van Riemsdijk, 107–44. North Holland Linguistic Series, Linguistic Variations. Amsterdam: Elsevier.

Maling, Joan. 1983. 'Transitive Adjectives: A Case of Categorial Reanalysis'. In *Linguistic Categories: Auxiliaries and Related Puzzles*, edited by Frank Heny and Barry Richards, 1:253–89. Dordrecht: Reidel.

Malouf, Robert. 2000. 'Verbal Gerunds as Mixed Categories in Head-Driven Phrase Structure Grammar'. In *The Nature and Function of Syntactic Categories*, edited by Robert Borsley, 133–66. New York: Academic Press.

Manning, Christopher D. 1993. 'Analyzing the Verbal Noun: Internal and External Constraints'. In *Japanese/Korean Linguistics 3*, edited by Soonja Choi, 236–53. Stanford, Calif.: Stanford Linguistics Association.

Manzini, M. Rita. 2010. 'The Structure and Interpretation of (Romance) Complementizers'. In *The Complementizer Phase: Subjects and Operators*, edited by Phoevos Panagiotidis, 167–99. Oxford University Press.

Marantz, Alec. 1991. 'Case and Licensing'. In *Proceedings of ESCOL 1991*, 234–53. Columbus, Ohio: Ohio State University.

1997. 'No Escape from Syntax: Don't Try Morphological Analysis in the Privacy of Your Own Lexicon'. *U. Penn Working Papers in Linguistics* 4: 201–25.

2000. *Words*. Unpublished ms. New York University.

2005. *Rederived Generalizations*. Unpublished ms. MIT.

2006. *Phases and Words*. Unpublished ms. MIT. https://files.nyu.edu/ma988/public/ Phase_in_Words_Final.pdf

Massam, Diane, Colin Gorrie and Alexandra Kellner. 2006. 'Determiners in Niuean: Everywhere and Nowhere'. *Proceedings of the 2006 Annual Conference of the Canadian Linguistic Association*: 1–16.

Matthewson, Lisa. 2001. 'Quantification and the Nature of Crosslinguistic Variation'. *Natural Language Semantics* 9: 145–89.

Matushansky, Ora. 2006. 'Head Movement in Linguistic Theory'. *Linguistic Inquiry* 37: 69–109.

McGinnis, Martha. 2002. 'On the Systematic Aspect of Idioms'. *Linguistic Inquiry* 33 (4): 665–72.

Milsark, Gary. 1988. 'Singl-Ing'. *Linguistic Inquiry* 19: 611–34.

Miyagawa, Shigeru. 1987. 'Lexical Categories in Japanese'. *Lingua* 73: 29–51.

Moulton, Keir. 2004. 'External Arguments and Gerunds'. *Toronto Working Papers in Linguistics* 22: 121–36.

Muysken, Pieter. 2008. *Functional Categories*. Cambridge University Press.

Neeleman, Ad, Hans van de Koot and Jenny Doetjes. 2004. 'Degree Expressions'. *The Linguistic Review* 21: 1–66.

Nevins, Andrew, David Pesetsky and Cilene Rodrigues. 2009. 'Pirahã Exceptionality: A Reassessment'. *Language* 85: 355–404.

Newmeyer, Frederick J. 1998. *Language Form and Language Function*. Language, Speech, and Communication. Cambridge, Mass.: MIT Press.

2004. 'On Split-CPs, Uninterpretable Features, and the "Perfectness" of Language'. *ZAS Papers in Linguistics* 35: 399–422.

Nordlinger, Rachel, and Louisa Sadler. 2004. 'Nominal Tense in Cross-Linguistic Perspective'. *Language* 80: 776–806.

Nunberg, Geoffrey, Ivan Sag and Thomas Wasow. 1994. 'Idioms'. *Language* 70: 491–538.

Oga, Kyoko. 2001. 'Two Types of "of" and Theta-Role Assignment by Nouns'. In *Newcastle and Durham Working Papers in Linguistics*, edited by Mamiko Akita and Kyoko Oga, 6: 95–108. University of Durham, Department of English and Linguistics.

Ouhalla, Jamal. 1991. *Functional Categories and Parametric Variation*. Theoretical Linguistics. London: Routledge.

Panagiotidis, Phoevos. 2000. 'The Categorial Features of Functional Heads'. Unpublished ms. University of Essex.

2002. *Pronouns, Clitics and Empty Nouns: 'Pronominality' and Licensing in Syntax*. Amsterdam: John Benjamins Publishing Company.

2003a. 'One, Empty Nouns and Theta Assignment'. *Linguistic Inquiry* 34: 281–92.

2003b. 'Empty Nouns'. *Natural Language and Linguistic Theory* 21: 381–432.

2004. 'Categorial Deficiency, Head Movement and Phrase Structure'. Paper presented at the Lisbon Workshop on Alternative Views on the Functional Domain, 8–9 July, Universidade Nova de Lisboa.

2005. 'Against Category-Less Roots in Syntax and Word Learning: Objections to Barner and Bale (2002)'. *Lingua* 115: 1181–94.

2008. 'Diachronic Stability and Feature Interpretability'. In *The Limits of Syntactic Variation*, edited by Theresa Biberauer, 441–56. Amsterdam: John Benjamins Publishing Company.

2010. 'Non-Argumental Mixed Projections'. *Syntax* 13: 165–82.

2011. 'Categorial Features and Categorizers'. *The Linguistic Review* 28: 325–46.

Panagiotidis, Phoevos, and Kleanthes K. Grohmann. 2009. 'Mixed Projections: Categorial Switches and Prolific Domains'. *Linguistic Analysis* 35: 141–61.

Panagiotidis, Phoevos, Anthi Revithiadou and Vassilios Spyropoulos. 2013. 'Verbalizers Leave Marks: Evidence from Greek'. Submitted for publication. University of Cyprus, Aristotle University of Thessaloniki and University of Athens.

Pensalfini, Robert. 1997. *Jingulu Grammar, Dictionary, and Texts*. PhD thesis, MIT, Cambridge, Mass.

Pesetsky, David. 1995. *Zero Syntax: Experiencers and Cascades*. Cambridge, Mass.: MIT Press.

Pesetsky, David, and Ester Torrego. 2004. 'Tense, Case and the Nature of Syntactic Categories'. In *The Syntax of Time*, edited by Jacqueline Guéron and Jacqueline Lecarme, 495–537. Cambridge, Mass.: MIT Press.

2005. 'Subcategorization Phenomena and Case-Theory Effects: Some Possible Explanations'. Lecture delivered at the LAGB Annual Meeting, 3 September, Fitzwilliam College, University of Cambridge.

Pires, Acrisio. 2006. *The Minimalist Syntax of Defective Domains: Gerunds and Infinitives*. Linguistik Aktuell = Linguistics Today 98. Amsterdam: John Benjamins Publishing Company.

Plann, Susan. 1981. 'The Two El + Infinitive Constructions in Spanish'. *Linguistic Analysis* 7: 203–40.

Prasada, Sandeep. 2008. *Aspects of a Fully Psychological Theory of Sortal Representation*. Unpublished ms. Hunter College, CUNY, New York.

Preminger, Omer. 2010. 'Nested Interrogatives and the Locus of Wh'. In *The Complementizer Phase: Subjects and Operators*, 200–35. Oxford University Press.

Pullum, Geoffrey. 1991. 'English Nominal Gerund Phrases as Noun Phrases with Verb Phrase Heads'. *Linguistics* 29: 763–99.

Pylkkänen, Liina. 2008. *Introducing Arguments*. Cambridge, Mass.: MIT Press. http://site.ebrary.com/id/10229589

Radford, Andrew. 1990. *Syntactic Theory and the Acquisition of English Syntax: The Nature of Early Child Grammars of English*. Oxford: Blackwell.

1996. 'Towards a Structure-Building Model of Acquisition'. In *Generative Perspectives on Language Acquisition*, edited by Harald Clahsen, 43–89. Amsterdam: John Benjamins Publishing Company.

Ramchand, Gillian. 2008. *Verb Meaning and the Lexicon: A First-Phase Syntax*. Cambridge Studies in Linguistics 116. Cambridge University Press.

Rappaport Hovav, Malka, and Beth Levin. 1998. 'Building Verb Meanings'. In *The Projection of Arguments: Lexical and Compositional Factors*, edited by Miriam Butt and Wilhelm Geuder, 97–134. Stanford, Calif.: CSLI Publications.

Rauh, Gisa. 2010. *Syntactic Categories: Their Identification and Description in Linguistic Theories*. Oxford Surveys in Syntax & Morphology 7. Oxford University Press.

Reuland, Eric. 1983. 'Governing "–ing"'. *Linguistic Inquiry* 14: 101–36.

Richards, Marc. 2004. *Object Shift and Scrambling in North and West Germanic: A Case Study in Symmetrical Syntax.* PhD thesis, University of Cambridge.

2007. 'On Feature Inheritance: An Argument from the Phase Impenetrability Condition'. *Linguistic Inquiry* 38: 563–72.

Richards, Marc, and Theresa Biberauer. 2005. 'Explaining Expl'. In *The Function of Function Words and Functional Categories*, edited by Marcel Den Dikken and Christina Tortora, 115–54. Amsterdam: John Benjamins Publishing Company.

Rizzi, Luigi. 1997. 'The Fine Structure of the Left Periphery'. In *Elements of Grammar: A Handbook of Generative Syntax*, edited by Liliane M. V. Haegeman, 281–337. Dordrecht: Kluwer.

Robins, Robert Henry. 1964. *General Linguistics: An Introductory Survey.* Indiana University Studies in the History and Theory of Linguistics. Indiana University Press.

Rosemeyer, Malte. 2012. 'On the Interplay between Transitivity, Factivity and Informativity: Spanish Nominal and Verbal Infinitives'. In *Aspectualidad – Transitividad – Referencialidad*, edited by Valeriano Bellosta von Colbe and Marco García García. Studia Romanica et Linguistica. Frankfurt am Main: Peter Lang.

Ross, John. 1973. 'Nouniness'. In *Three Dimensions of Linguistic Theory*, edited by Osamu Fujimura, 137–258. Tokyo: TEC Co.

Rothstein, Susan. 1983. *The Syntactic Forms of Predication.* PhD thesis, MIT, Cambridge, Mass.

1999. 'Fine-Grained Structure in the Eventuality Domain: The Semantics of Predicate Adjective Phrases and "be"'. *Natural Language Semantics* 7: 347–420.

Roussou, Anna. 1990. *Nominalization in the Syntax of Modern Greek.* MA dissertation, University College London.

Schachter, Paul. 1985. 'Parts-of-Speech Systems'. In *Language Typology and Syntactic Description*, edited by Timothy Shopen, 1: 3–61. Cambridge University Press.

Schoorlemmer, Maaike. 2001. 'Dutch Nominalised Infinitives as Non-Identical Twins'. UiL OTS Working Paper uil-ots-01005-CL/TL. Utrecht University.

2002. 'Adjectives and Adverbs in Dutch Nominalised Infinitives'. Paper presented at the TIN Dag Workshop, 26 January, Utrecht.

Schütze, Carson. 2001. 'Semantically Empty Lexical Heads as Last Resorts'. In *Semi-Lexical Categories*, edited by Norbert Corver and Henk van Riemsdijk, 127–87. Berlin: Mouton de Gruyter.

Shibatani, Masayoshi. 1990. *The Languages of Japan.* Cambridge Language Surveys. Cambridge University Press.

Siddiqi, Daniel. 2006. *Minimize Exponence: Economy Effects on a Model of the Morphosyntactic Component of the Grammar.* PhD thesis, University of Arizona.

Siegel, Laura. 1998. 'Gerundive Nominals and the Role of Aspect'. In *Proceedings of ESCOL '97*, edited by Jennifer Austin and Aaron Lawson. Ithaca, New York: Cornell Linguistics Club Publications. http://www.ling.upenn.edu/~lsiegel/escolrev.pdf

Simons, Peter. 1987. *Parts: A Study in Ontology.* Oxford: Clarendon Press.

Starke, Michal. 2009. 'Nanosyntax – A Short Primer to a New Approach to Language'. In *Norlyd*, edited by Peter Svenonius, Gillian Ramchand, Michal Starke and Knut Tarald Taraldsen, 36.1:1–6. Tromsø: CASTL. http://ling.auf.net/lingbuzz/001183

2011. *Towards Elegant Parameters: Language Variation Reduces to the Size of Lexically Stored Trees*. Unpublished ms. Barcelona. http://ling.auf.net/lingbuzz/001183.

Stiebels, Barbara. 1999. 'Noun–Verb Symmetries in Nahuatl Nominlizations'. *Natural Language and Linguistic Theory* 17: 783–836.

Stowell, Tim. 1981. *Origins of Phrase Structure*. PhD thesis, MIT, Cambridge, Mass.

1991. 'Determiners in NP and DP'. In *Views on Phrase Structure*, edited by Katherine Leffel and Denis Bouchard, 37–56. Dordrecht: Kluwer.

2007. 'The Syntactic Expression of Tense'. *Lingua* 117: 437–63.

Svenonius, Peter. 1994. *Dependent Nexus: Small Clauses in English and the Scandinavian Languages*. PhD thesis, University of California at Santa Cruz.

2004. 'On the Edge'. In *Peripheries: Syntactic Edges and Their Effects*, edited by David Adger, Cécile De Cat and George Tsoulas, 261–87. Dordrecht: Kluwer.

2005. *Idioms and Domain Boundaries*. Unpublished ms. CASTL, University of Tromsø.

2007. 'Adpositions, Particles, and the Arguments They Introduce'. In *Argument Structure*, edited by Eric Reuland, Tanmoy Bhattacharya and Giorgos Spathas, 63–103. Amsterdam: John Benjamins Publishing Company.

2008. 'Projections of P'. In *Syntax and Semantics of Spatial P*, edited by Anna Asbury, Jakub Dotlacil, Berit Gehrke and Rick Nouwen, 63–84. Amsterdam: John Benjamins Publishing Company.

Terzi, Arhonto. 2010. 'Locative Prepositions and Place'. In *Mapping Spatial PPs*, edited by G. Cinque and L. Rizzi, 196–224. The Cartography of Syntactic Structures. Oxford University Press.

Thráinsson, Höskuldur. 1996. 'On the (non-) Universality of Functional Categories'. In *Minimal Ideas: Syntactic Studies in the Minimalist Framework*, edited by Werner Abraham, Samuel D. Epstein, Höskuldur Thráinsson and Jan-Wouter Zwart, 253–82. Amsterdam: John Benjamins Publishing Company.

Tonhauser, Judith. 2005. 'Towards an Understanding of the Meaning of Nominal Tense'. In *Proceedings of Sinn und Bedeutung 9*, edited by Emar Maier, C. Bary and J. Huitnink, 475–88. Nijmegen Centre of Semantics.

2007. 'Nominal Tense? The Meaning of Guarani Nominal Temporal Markers'. *Language* 83: 831–69.

Tosun, Gülsat. 1999. *Fused Functional Heads and Turkish Facts*. Unpublished ms. Harvard University.

Traugott, Elizabeth. 2007. 'The Concepts of Constructional Mismatch and Type-Shifting from the Perspective of Grammaticalisation'. *Cognitive Linguistics* 18 (4): 523–57.

Tremblay, Mireille. 1996. 'Lexical and Non-Lexical Prepositions in French'. In *Configurations: Essays on Structure and Interpretation*, edited by Anna-Maria Di Sciullo, 79–98. Sommerville, Mass.: Cascadilla Press.

Trommelen, Mieke. 1989. 'Lettergreepstruktuur en Woordkategorie'. *De Nieuwe Taalgids* 82: 64–77.

Tsimpli, Ianthi Maria. 2003. 'Clitics and Determiners in L2 Greek'. In *Proceedings of the 6th Generative Approaches to Second Language Acquisition Conference (GASLA 2002)*, edited by Juana M. Liceras, 331–9. Sommerville, Mass.: Cascadilla Press.

Tsimpli, Ianthi Maria, and Maria Dimitrakopoulou. 2007. 'The Interpretability Hypothesis: Evidence from Wh-Interrogatives in Second Language Acquisition'. *Second Language Research* 23: 215–42.

Tsimpli, Ianthi Maria, and Maria Mastropavlou. 2007. 'Feature Interpretability in L2 Acquisition and SLI: Greek Clitics and Determiners'. In *The Role of Formal Features in Second Language Acquisition*, edited by Juana M. Liceras, Helmut Zobl and Helen Goodluck, 143–83. London: Routledge.

Tsimpli, Ianthi Maria, Antonella Sorace, Caroline Heycock and Francesca Filiaci. 2004. 'First Language Attrition and Syntactic Subjects: A Study of Greek and Italian Near-Native Speakers of English'. *International Journal of Bilingualism* 8: 257–77.

Tsimpli, Ianthi Maria, and Stavroula Stavrakaki. 1999. 'The Effects of a Morphosyntactic Deficit in the Determiner System: The Case of a Greek SLI Child'. *Lingua* 108: 31–85.

Tsujimura, Natsuko. 1992. 'Licensing Nominal Clauses: The Case of Deverbal Nouns in Japanese'. *Natural Language and Linguistic Theory* 10: 477–522.

Uriagereka, Juan. 1999. 'Warps: Some Thoughts on Categorization'. *Theoretical Linguistics* 25: 31–73.

Vainikka, Anne. 1994. 'Case in the Development of English Syntax'. *Language Acquisition* 3: 257–325.

Valgina, N. S., D. E. Rosental and M. I. Fomina. 2002. Современный Русский Язык Учебник [*Modern Russian Language Textbook*]. Московский государственный университет печати [Moscow State University Press].

Van Hout, Angelique, and Tom Roeper. 1998. 'Events and Aspectual Structure in Derivational Morphology'. *MIT Working Papers in Linguistics* 32: 175–220.

Van Riemsdijk, Henk. 1998a. 'Categorial Feature Magnetism: The Endocentricity and Distribution of Projections'. *Journal of Comparative Germanic Linguistics* 2: 1–48.

1998b. 'Head Movement and Adjacency'. *Natural Language and Linguistic Theory* 16: 633–79.

Volpe, Mark. 2009. 'Root and Deverbal Nominalizations: Lexical Flexibility in Japanese'. Unpublished ms. http://ling.auf.net/lingBuzz/000789

Wasow, Thomas. 1977. 'Transformations and the Lexicon'. In *Formal Syntax*, edited by Peter Culicover, Thomas Wasow and Joan Bresnan, 324–60. New York: Academic Press.

Willim, Ewa. 2000. 'On the Grammar of Polish Nominals'. In *Step by Step: Essays on Minimalist Syntax in Honor of Howard Lasnik*, edited by Roger Martin, David Michaels and Juan Uriagereka, 319–46. Cambridge, Mass.: MIT Press.

Yoder, Brendon. 2010. 'Syntactic Underspecification in Riau Indonesian'. In *Work Papers of the Summer Institute of Linguistics, University of North Dakota Session*, edited by Joan Baart, 50: 1–15. Grand Forks, N. Dak.: SIL International.

Yoon, James Hye Suk. 1996a. 'Nominal Gerund Phrases in English as Phrasal Zero Derivations'. *Linguistics* 34: 329–56.

1996b. 'A Syntactic Account of Category-Changing Phrasal Morphology: Nominal-izations in English and Korean'. In *Morphosyntax in Generative Grammar: Proceedings of the 1996 Seoul International Conference on Generative Grammar*, edited by Hee-Don Ahn, Myung-Yoon Kang, Young-Suck Kim and Sookhee Lee, 357–68. Seoul: Hankook Publishing Company.

Yoon, James Hye Suk, and Neus Bonet-Farran. 1991. 'The Ambivalent Nature of Spanish Infinitives'. In *New Analyses in Romance Linguistics: Selected Papers from the Linguistic Symposium on Romance Languages XVIII*, edited by Dieter Wanner and Douglas A. Kibbee, 353–70. Amsterdam: John Benjamins Publishing Company.

Yoon, James Hye Suk, and Chongwon Park. 2004. *Process Nominals and Morpho-logical Complexity*. Unpublished ms. University of Illinois, Urbana-Champaign.

Index

For EU product safety concerns, contact us at Calle de José Abascal, 56–1°, 28003 Madrid, Spain or eugpsr@cambridge.org.

www.ingramcontent.com/pod-product-compliance
Ingram Content Group UK Ltd.
Pitfield, Milton Keynes, MK11 3LW, UK
UKHW020327140625
459647UK00018B/2053